East Asia's De Facto Economic Integration

Other books by IDE-JETRO

INDUSTRIAL CLUSTERS IN ASIA
Akifumi Kuchiki and Masatsugu Tsuji (*editors*)

SPATIAL STRUCTURE AND REGIONAL DEVELOPMENT IN CHINA
Nobuhiro Okamoto and Takeo Ihara (*editors*)

GENDER AND DEVELOPMENT
The Japanese Experience in Comparative Perspective
Mayumi Murayama (*editor*)

RECOVERING FINANCIAL SYSTEMS
China and Asian Transition Economies
Mariko Watanabe (*editor*)

East Asia's De Facto Economic Integration

Edited by Daisuke Hiratsuka

palgrave macmillan

IDE-JETRO

First published 2006 by
PALGRAVE MACMILLAN
Houndmills, Basingstoke, Hampshire RG21 6XS and
175 Fifth Avenue, New York, N.Y. 10010
Companies and representatives throughout the world

PALGRAVE MACMILLAN is the global academic imprint of the Palgrave Macmillan division of St. Martin's Press, LLC and of Palgrave Macmillan Ltd. Macmillan® is a registered trademark in the United States, United Kingdom and other countries. Palgrave is a registered trademark in the European Union and other countries.

ISBN 13: 978–0–230–00782–6 hardback
ISBN 10: 0–230–00782–1 hardback

This book is printed on paper suitable for recycling and made from fully managed and sustained forest sources.

A catalogue record for this book is available from the British Library.

Library of Congress Cataloging-in-Publication Data

East Asia's de facto economic integration / edited by Daisuke Hiratsuka.
p. cm.
Includes bibliographical references and index.

ISBN 0–230–00782–1 (cloth)
1. East Asia–Commerce. 2. East Asia–Economic integration. I. Hiratsuka, Daisuke

HF3820.5.Z5.E376 2006
333.1′5–dc22

2006044785

10 9 8 7 6 5 4 3 2
15 14 13 12 11 10 09 08 07

Printed and bound in Great Britain by
Antony Rowe Ltd, Chippenham and Eastbourne

Contents

List of Figures

List of Tables

Foreword

Looking at the night pictures of the earth, we can see three brilliantly lit regions: North America, Europe and East Asia. Generally, we can imagine that those lights are shining from offices and residences where populations have concentrated. But the story may be different for East Asia. The lights of East Asia might indicate the agglomeration of factories. When we visited some factories operating in Southeast Asia, I heard that the factories operate twenty-four hours a day. The coast line of East Asia has become one of the major manufacturing belts in the world, providing goods at reasonable prices.

The main engine of recent rapid changes in the worldwide economic and political system has been brought about by the reduction of transportation costs for goods, services, money, people and information through the IT revolution. The significance of national boundaries has decreased, while the importance of regions and cities has increased. Nation-states have now become too small for economic activities. Major reorganization of socio-economic systems beyond and within national economies has advanced at various geographical scales. In other words, globalization and localization are progressing, which necessitates new institutional super-national systems and/or sub-national systems.

From the point of view of spatial economics, which is my own area, agglomeration forces and dispersion forces work interchangeably. In order to reduce transportation costs, agglomeration forces work very strongly, and then, due to the increases in wages, dispersion forces emerge later. This repeated process forms the fractal and hierarchical core–periphery structure. However, gradual shifts in the environments of transportation, production technologies, population and so on will lead to destabilization of the core–periphery structure, which will dynamically change over time.

In 2004 the Institute of Developing Economies (IDE) initiated a three-year project, entitled "Studies in East Asian Economic Integration." Its aim is to understand the prospects and tasks of regional integration in East Asia. We have organized several study teams; this book is one of the outcomes of the project. It discusses the production networks which have developed in East Asia, and their role in the regionalization of East Asian economies and helps us to understand what is likely to happen in

East Asia in the future. I thank all the contributors for their support and cooperation in the project.

Masahisa Fujita
President
Institute of Developing Economies, JETRO

Acknowledgements

Since 2004, the Institute of Developing Economies (IDE), JETRO, has conducted a research project entitled "Challenges for East Asia." On January 21, 2004, as part of the project, we held an international workshop called "De Facto Economic Integration" at our Institute in Chiba, Japan. The workshop found that production fragmentation (sharing across borders) has advanced in East Asia. Consequently, regionalization has progressed in East Asia, and intra-industry trade and intra-regional trade have expanded. After the workshop, our IDE study team conducted the field studies in East Asia to see how production processes have been split, and how multinational corporations and suppliers have considered transportation costs in purchasing components and parts. This volume contains the revised version of papers presented at the workshop incorporating the field studies.

I am deeply indebted to the following: Fukunari Kimura (Keio University) for his great contribution to our studies including the introductory chapter, and Michel Fouquin (the Centre d'Etudes Prospectives et d'Informations Internationales; CEPII) and the CEPII for their extra efforts in our joint studies between CEPII and IDE. Their efforts made these studies successful. I am also indebted to Kiichiro Fukasaku (OECD Development Center), Françoise Nicola (Institute Française de Relations Internationales), Alain Henriot (Chambre de Commerce et d'Industrie de Paris), and Tsuyoshi Nakai (JETRO, Paris) for their comments at the preparatory meeting at the CEPII in Paris on October 15, 2004, and to Nobuaki Hamaguchi (Kobe University), Kazuhiko Yokota (International Center for Study of East Asian Studies of Development, Kitakyushu), and Hikari Ishido (Chiba University) for their comments at the IDE 2004 workshop. I would also like to thank Masahisa Fujita (Kyoto University and President of IDE) for giving us a special keynote speech at the IDE meeting and for some useful comments.

My special thanks go to Toh Kin Woon (Penang State Executive Councillor) and Invest Penang for arrangement of interviews in Penang, Malaysia, and Hajime Akaoka (Soode Johor), Masamitsu Horike (Hitachi Global Storage Technologies, Thailand), Canon Hi-Tech Thailand, Dell Computers in Penang, ENG Teknologi, Fujitsu Thailand, Kobay Technology, LKT Industrial Berhad, Sanmina-SCI Malaysia, Pentamaster Corporation, Toyota Motor Asia Pacific, Toyota Thailand, Venture

Corporation in Singapore, Toshiba Asia Pacific for interviews. The interviews made us understand what had really been happening in East Asia.

Daisuke Hiratsuka
Project Coordinator of Challenges for East Asia
Director of Regional Integration Studies Group, IDE

Contributors

Pierre Ecochard	Economist, CEPII
Lionel Fontagné	Director, CEPII
Michel Fouquin	Deputy Director, Centre d'Etudes Prospectives et d'Informations Internationales (CEPII)
Michael Freudenberg	Senior Market Analyst, International Trade Center (ITC)
Guillaume Gaulier	Economist, CEPII
Daisuke Hiratsuka	Director General, Development Studies Center, Institute of Developing Economies (IDE)
Fukunari Kimura	Professor, Faculty of Economics, Keio University
Ikuo Kuroiwa	Senior Research Fellow, IDE
Françoise Lemoine	Senior Economist, CEPII
Thierry Paulmier	Associate Expert, ITC
Deniz Ünal-Kesenci	Economist, CEPII
Soledad Zignago	Economist, CEPII

Introduction: East Asia's De Facto Economic Integration

Michel Fouquin, Daisuke Hiratsuka and Fukunari Kimura

1 Introduction

It is often claimed that de facto economic integration has proceeded in East Asia. The claim is partially true and partially false. In fact, few rigorous studies have been conducted on how far integration has been realized or what sort of integration has been accomplished. We intuitively know that de facto economic integration in East Asia has not reached the level of the European Union (EU) at this point in time. Furthermore, the trajectory currently followed by East Asia seems to be different to the path which Europe once followed. The nature and characteristics of de facto economic integration are crucially important not only for academic interest but also for policy discussion on the currently promoted de jure economic integration in East Asia. This book is devoted to a deeper understanding of the on-going de facto economic integration in East Asia.

The aggregated level of statistics clearly presents the recent advancement of de facto economic integration in East Asia. Figure 0.1 shows the share of intra-regional trade (exports and imports) within several economic areas. The share of intra-East Asia trade, where East Asia is defined as ASEAN 10, China, Japan, Hong Kong, the Republic of Korea and Taiwan, rose remarkably from 34.9 percent in 1980 to 52.4 percent in 2003. Surprisingly, this figure is higher than that of NAFTA (44.6 percent) though a bit lower than that of the European Union (58.7 percent). East Asia has no doubt achieved a high level of de facto economic integration in terms of international trade transactions within the region. The integration process has not been seriously interrupted even by the Asian currency crisis in the late 1990s.

Figure 0.1: Intra-regional trade (%)

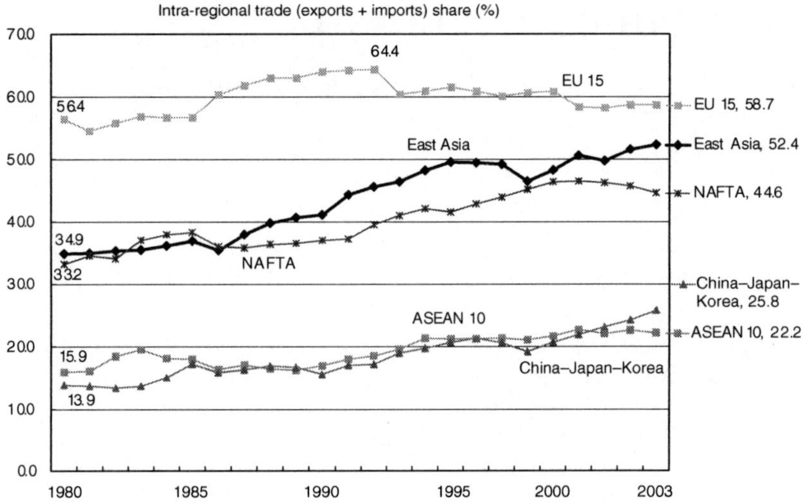

Note: East Asia is ASEAN 10 excluding Myanmar, China, Hong Kong, Japan, Korea and Taiwan.
Source: Direction of Trade, 2004, CD-ROM. Council for Economic Planning and Development, Republic of China, Taiwan Statistical Data Book, 2004 for Taiwan. COMTRADE for NAFTA and EU 15.

However, economic integration in East Asia does not seem to develop in an even manner. The share of intra-regional trade of the ASEAN 10 and China–Japan–Korea in 2003 remains at only 22.2 percent and 25.8 percent respectively, against that of East Asia (52.4), which suggests that economic activity needs a large space in which to expand, and East Asia has enhanced its regionalization in trade, as the spatial economists argue (Fujita 2004). Moreover, Figure 0.2 shows the trade shares of East Asia by partner countries/regions where we can see that China and the ASEAN 5 (Indonesia, Malaysia, the Philippines, Singapore and Thailand) increased their shares in East Asian trade. This suggests that countries at relatively low income levels have played a significant role in the expansion of the intra-regional trade in East Asia. What we observe in East Asia is an explosive increase in trade in intermediate goods, particularly in machinery industries, based on production-process-wise international division of labor among countries at different income levels and development stages. To analyze the mechanism of vertical production/distribution networks, we must introduce new analytical tools in inter-

Figure 0.2: Trade share of East Asia with partner country

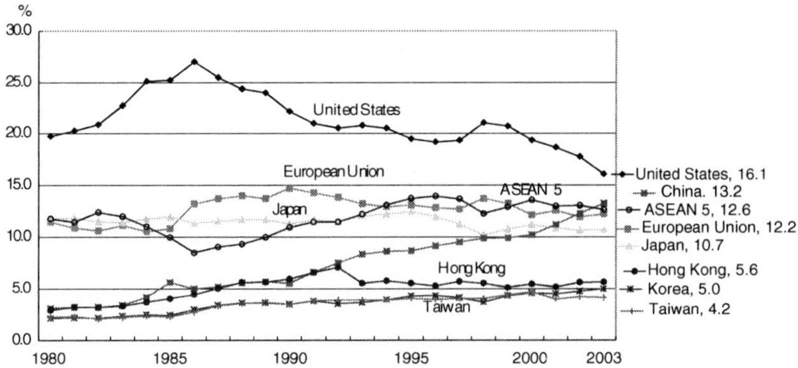

Note: East Asia consists of ASEAN 10, China Japan, Hong Kong, South Korea and Taiwan.
Source: United Nations COMTRADE for EU 15 and NAFTA, Direction of Trade, 2004, CD-ROM, and Council for Economic Planning and Development, Republic of China, Taiwan Statistical Data Book, 2004 for Taiwan.

national trade theory, namely, the fragmentation theory and the agglomeration theory.

The environment of international trade policies in East Asia is also our concern. The development of vertical production networks in East Asia has certainly been supported by a trade liberalization effort. In particular, unilateral removal of tariffs on semiconductor-related parts and components by East Asian countries under the APEC initiative in the latter half of the 1990s seems to be crucial. Extensive application of the duty drawback system to imported parts and components in order to produce exported goods also works effectively. However, it is also true that the trade regime of East Asia is still far from one of free trade. East Asian countries are still imposing substantial trade barriers.

Table 0.1 summarizes simple average tariff rates in 2004 imposed by East Asian countries. Simple average applied tariff rates for all products are 7.2 percent in Indonesia, 7.1 percent in Japan, 11.9 percent in the Republic of Korea, 8.6 percent in Malaysia, 7.1 percent in the Philippines, 12.0 percent in Thailand, and 18.5 percent in Vietnam. These figures are much higher than those of Australia (4.3 percent), Canada (3.9 percent), New Zealand (3.4 percent), and the United States (5.1 percent) (see Table 0.1). Notably, East Asian countries tend to impose high tariffs on the imports of agricultural products, textiles and clothing, and other light industrial products in addition to transport equipment.

Table 0.1: Simple average applied tariff rates by products (2004, %)

	All goods	Agriculture excluding fish	Fish and fish products	Petroleum oils	Wood, pulp, paper and furniture	Textiles and clothing	Leather, rubber, footwear and travel	Metals	Chemical & photographic supplies	Transport equipment	Non-electric machinery	Electric machinery	Mineral products, precious stones & metals	Manufactured articles, n.e.s
Vietnam	18.5	27.7	27.7	16.8	15.7	37.3	18.7	9.4	7.2	13.9	7.2	13.3	13.6	14.1
Thailand	12.0	25.8	8.4	2.6	11.4	17.0	16.0	9.0	4.6	20.3	4.8	9.3	5.6	13.3
Korea	11.9	46.2	16.8	5.8	2.6	9.8	8.9	4.7	6.0	6.0	5.5	5.9	6.2	
China	11.3	16.8	12.2	6.3	7.0	15.2	13.6	7.4	7.4	15.9	8.6	9.9	9.4	12.3
Malaysia	8.6	3.0	1.9	0.5	2.7	12.4	12.9	17.4	5.3	36.9	6.0	8.7	9.6	7.4
Indonesia	7.2	8.6	5.0	5.0	4.1	10.5	6.6	8.1	5.5	17.0	2.3	6.1	4.6	7.7
Japan	7.1	20.9	6.0	3.6	1.6	6.7	17.3	0.8	2.5	0.1	0.0	0.2	0.9	1.3
Philippines	7.1	7.9	8.4	2.9	6.4	11.4	6.6	5.4	4.9	17.0	2.5	4.5	5.1	4.8
United States	5.1	9.8	2.0	2.5	1.1	9.6	7.0	2.1	3.8	2.6	1.3	2.0	3.7	3.2
Australia	4.3	1.4	0.0	0.0	3.8	12.8	6.9	3.4	1.9	5.3	3.4	3.2	1.7	2.0
Canada	3.9	4.0	1.4	3.1	1.6	9.0	5.6	1.9	2.9	5.2	1.7	2.4	2.0	3.1
New Zealand	3.4	2.1	0.6	1.3	1.3	7.8	6.2	3.0	1.5	5.3	3.7	3.6	1.7	3.0
Singapore	0.0	0.0	0.0	0.0	0.0	0.0	0.0	0.0	0.0	0.0	0.0	0.0	0.0	

Source: Tariff Summary Report 2004, APEC Electronic Individual Action Plan, http://www.apec-iap.org/

As for non-tariff barriers, although reliable and comparable information is not available, we are sure that governments tend to protect domestic industries with non-tariff barriers. In fact, significant barriers will be found especially for agriculture, light industry, and food and beverages.

Furthermore, substantial barriers in service trade still remain in East Asia. Table 0.2 lists the number of service sectors in each country and region with commitments under the GATS concession table. Developed countries have largely committed to liberalization for more than 100 of the total 155 service sectors, but many East Asian countries have made concessions in less than half the sectors. For example, the number of service sectors with significant liberalization under the GATS commitments is 75 for Thailand and Malaysia, 51 for the Philippines and only 47 for Indonesia. These figures reflect the fact that these countries are still protecting their domestic service industries.

The development of vertical production networks as well as remaining trade barriers certainly affects the nature of on-going de jure economic integration in East Asia. ASEAN has played a leading role in de jure integration since the 1990s. In 1992, ASEAN agreed to establish the ASEAN

Table 0.2: Number of GATS service sectors with commiments

Countries/regions	*Number of GATS service sectors with commiments*	*Countries/regions*	*Number of GATS service sectors with commiments*
Taiwan	123	Turkey	75
Switzerland	117	Hong Kong	69
EU	115	Singapore	67
Norway	112	Argentina	65
Japan	110	Venezuela	64
United States	110	Israel	62
Canada	105	Brazil	60
Australia	104	Columbia	58
Cambodia	95	Philippines	51
Republic of Korea	95	Indonesia	47
China	94	Pakistan	47
South Africa	91	Egypt	45
New Zealand	90	Chile	40
Thailand	75	India	37
Malaysia	75	Macao	25
Mexico	75	Brunei	23

Source: WTO statistics database (http://statwto.org/CountryProfile/WSDBC CountryPFView aspx?Language=E&Country=).

Free Trade Area (AFTA) through a Common Effective Preferential Tariff (CEPT) scheme, in order to attract foreign direct investment (FDI) from abroad through improvement of trade and investment environment in ASEAN. Quantitative restrictions and other non-tariff barriers were also to be eliminated. By the beginning of 2003, the ASEAN 6, that is, the original six member states (Brunei, Indonesia, Malaysia, the Philippines, Singapore and Thailand) accomplished AFTA's tariff level of 0–5 percent for 98.4 percent of products out of a total of 44,060. Vietnam is expected to achieve the AFTA compliance in 2006, Laos and Myanmar in 2008, and Cambodia in 2010. ASEAN will eliminate all imported duties by 2010 for the six original members and by 2015 for the new members (ASEAN Secretariat 2004).[1]

ASEAN has also played the role of partner to FTAs that have recently proliferated in East Asia (see Figure 0.3). In November 2002, ASEAN

Figure 0.3: The East Asian community

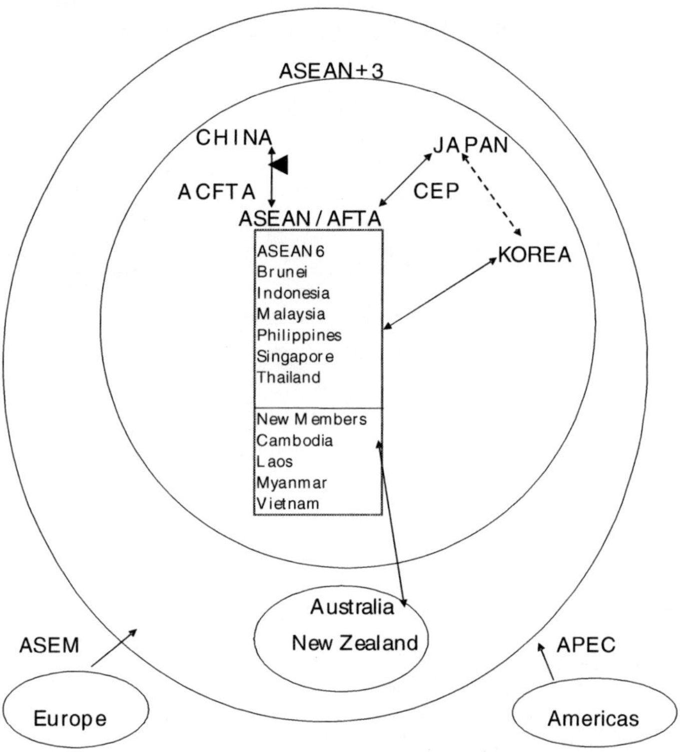

Source: Authors' own.

and China signed the framework agreement on Comprehensive Economic Cooperation that will establish the ASEAN–China Free Trade Area (ACFTA) within ten years, and in November 2004 both parties agreed to establish the ACFTA, to cover more than 90 percent of tariff lines at HS 6-digit level,[2] by 2010 for the original ASEAN six member states and China, and by 2015 for the newer ASEAN member states. The ACFTA was enforced in July 2005, and started the tariff reduction program. ASEAN has also extended its FTAs to Japan. The Japan–Singapore FTA was enforced in November 2002, and in October 2003 ASEAN and Japan signed the framework for a Comprehensive Economic Partnership (CEP) between ASEAN and Japan. Japan–Philippines, Japan–Malaysia and Japan–Thailand FTAs reached basic agreements in November 2004, May 2005 and July 2005, respectively. Official negotiations on the Japan–Indonesia and ASEAN–Japan FTA also started in mid-2005.

Also, in November 2004, ASEAN and the Republic of Korea agreed the overall framework to establish free trade areas. The negotiations commenced in 2005 and are to be completed within two years.

Obviously, the East Asia markets are progressing towards de jure economic integration. However, the economic effects of growing FTAs have not been thoroughly analyzed yet. The designing of FTAs considering the status of de facto economic integration has not been properly conducted. For fully-fledged integration, we must deepen our understanding on the nature and characteristics of de facto economic integration in East Asia as well as the existing impediments to a seamless business environment.

2 Summary of individual chapters

In examining the above research subjects and questions, the book covers various aspects of East Asia's economic integration. It falls into three main parts. The first four chapters explore the nature and characteristics of de facto economic integration in East Asia, by analyzing international trade patterns with special emphasis on extensive fragmentation of production activities and intra-industry trade. Chapters 5 and 6 concentrate on detailed analysis on the triangular trade pattern with China and international networking in the hard disk drive industry. Finally, Chapters 7 and 8 discuss the policy issues to be challenged for de jure economic integration in East Asia.

2.1 Fragmentation and intra-industry trade

Chapter 1, "The Development of Fragmentation in East Asia and its Implications for FTA," by Fukunari Kimura, proposes an analytical framework to examine de facto economic integration in East Asia. Kimura defines the complete integrated economy in pure economics in which all goods and productive factors are perfectly mobile and factor prices are converged. The current situation of East Asia's economic integration is far from the complete integrated economy. Kimura, however, claims that East Asia is following an unprecedented path of de facto economic integration. To explain such a phenomenon, Kimura introduces the fragmentation theory. Fragmentation (first defined by Deardorff 2001) is the splitting of a production process into two or more steps that can be undertaken in different locations but that lead to the final product. Kimura proposes the concept of two-dimensional fragmentation that consists of geographic fragmentation (domestic or cross-border fragmentation) and uncontrollability or disintegration of firms (intra-firm or inter-firm fragmentation). East Asia has an advantage in the first type of fragmentation because of its large diversity in income and development stages. In addition, service link costs for connecting fragmented production blocks are reduced to overcome the handicap of distance, by policy efforts (improvement of infrastructure and tax incentives), participation of foreign capital in logistic services, the development of talents for procurement, and so on. With lowered service link costs, multinational corporations (MNCs) have explored different location advantages by locating their operations across the region. The diversity of location advantages and low service link costs have developed region-wide production/distribution networks in East Asia, which have not been observed in any other regions such as the EU and NAFTA.

Chapters 2 and 3 are empirical studies on intra-industry trade, which support the fragmentation argument introduced in Chapter 1. The chapters employ quite different approaches: Chapter 2 analyzes international trade, and Chapter 3 gives an analysis of the production side based on the international input–output table.

Chapter 2, "Intra-Industry Trade and Economic Integration," by Pierre Ecochard, Lionel Fontagné, Guillaume Gaulier and Soledad Zignago, uses international trade data at an HS 6-digit level, and compares the pattern of intra-industry trade (IIT) among the EU, NAFTA, East Asia and Mercosur. The study classifies finely disaggregated trade flows into three types: one-way trade (exports and imports are widely unbalanced); vertical differentiated IIT (both exports and imports are active though unit prices of exports and imports differ widely); and horizontal differentiated IIT (both exports and imports are active, and unit prices of exports and imports are similar). The study finds that one-way trade still dominates in East Asia but vertical differentiated IIT is rapidly increasing. This observation suggests that different manufacturing processes are operating in different countries and active back-and-forth transactions of parts and components are developing in East Asia. Meanwhile, the EU has a large share of horizontal differentiated IIT, which implies that the EU has developed horizontal trade because of a preference for over product variety.

The study also investigates the determinants of the share of vertical and horizontal IIT. It finds that, first, countries with similar factor endowments tend to trade similar products, but countries with different factor endowments are likely to trade vertically differentiated products. Second, geographical distance has a strong negative relationship with the vertical differentiated IIT. These results suggest that fragmentation would develop in the region where there is close geographical proximity but a large diversity in terms of income and industrial development among countries. Third, high tariffs impede IIT of horizontally differentiated products. This result would imply that high tariffs in East Asia were an obstacle for horizontal IIT, and the reduction of tariffs and the bilateral and plurilateral FTAs would promote horizontal IIT.

Chapter 3, "Production Networks and Spatial Linkages in East Asia," by Ikuo Kuroiwa, conducts an empirical study of the production networks in East Asia, based on the international input–output table. The international input–output table is a powerful tool in analyzing inter- and intra-industry production linkages across countries. Kuroiwa finds that intra-industry trade in intermediate goods increased remarkably in East Asia. He also finds that the intra-industry spatial linkages, i.e. backward and forward cross-border production linkages within the same industry, were weak in East Asia in 1975, but became remarkably strong after 1990, particularly in the electric machinery industry. Further, it is demonstrated that the production networks of the electric machinery industry expanded rapidly with Japan, East Asia and the US respectively located in the upstream, midstream and downstream of roundabout production. These findings confirm the development of fragmentation in East Asia, with Japan and the US deeply involved. The MNCs' operation in East Asia which has formed the production/distribution networks expands the intra-industry spatial linkages as well as intra-industry trade, and catalyzes the catching up in manufacturing by latecomers in the region.

Chapter 4, "Catching Up of Manufacturing Cum De Facto Economic Integration in East Asia," by Daisuke Hiratsuka, examines the background of development of the intra-industry trade, from the point of view of the catching up in manufacturing activity, assuming the flying geese development pattern. The ASEAN 4 (Malaysia, Thailand, Indonesia and the Philippines) and China, which are latecomers to industrialization, and the Asian NIEs (South Korea, Taiwan, Hong Kong and Singapore), which were second runners after Japan, have transformed from net importers of various products to net exporters. In some industries, the frontrunner Japan has moved to the position of a net importer, while in certain industries the latecomers have leapfrogged even the Asian NIEs. The catching up with the forerunners by the latecomers has diffused from industry to industry in a very short period in the 1990s. The performances in the catching up in machinery industry vary according to country. For instance, the ASEAN 4 and China are very competitive in light machinery assembling, while the Asian NIEs and Thailand are very competitive in its parts. The study shows evidence that the fragmentation in East Asia has advanced in the light machinery industry.

2.2 Case studies by country and industry

In East Asia's production/distribution networks, what role does each country have? Chapter 5, "China's Specialization in East Asian Production Sharing," by Guillaume Gaulier, Françoise Lemoine and Deniz Ünal-Kesenci, discusses this issue, focusing on China. The study claims that vertical production/distribution networks in East Asia have formed a "triangular trade" pattern, where the MNCs use China as an export base for the final assembly, in order to export finished goods to the US and Europe. China's position in the international production/distribution networks is a final assembly point while firms operating in other East Asian countries/regions as well as their head facilities in home countries export parts and components to China. This triangular trade pattern raised the position of China in East Asia's intra-regional trade and the vertical intra-industry trade.

Chapter 6, "Vertical Intra-Regional Production Networks in East Asia: a Case Study of Hard Disc Drive Industry," by Daisuke Hiratsuka, is an empirical study, at industry and firm levels, of the development of fragmentation and international production/distribution networks in East Asia. Hiratsuka argues that the fragmentation has advanced especially in home and digital appliances, and the electronics industries in East Asia. When the core firms, namely assemblers, advance to East Asia, suppliers follow them, in order to reduce transportation costs including communication costs with the core firms. Hence, due to the core firm and supplier effect, the advancement of the core firms has formed industrial clusters in the host country, and the subsequent formation of industrial clusters has transformed East Asia into a manufacturing belt where industrial clusters are systematically linked as a result of low transportation costs. The firm level study confirmed that the assemblers of hard disc drives (HDD) have operated as core firms to catalyze the suppliers to form the HDD industrial clusters. Hiratsuka finds that the HDD clusters developed in East Asia have almost the same lineups, and that the assembler of HDD procures the same components and parts from the multiple suppliers located in different countries so as to spread production risk, and from both intra-firm and inter-firm networks in order to respond to rapid increases in demand and to remain competitive. The study implies that multiple equilibriums are possible under low transportation costs, and that the East Asian countries can develop together under the East Asia-wide FTA if transportation costs are kept low.

2.3 Policy issues to be challenged and the perspective of integration

Chapter 7, "A Comparison of De Jure Economic Integration in East Asia: Is East Asia Discriminating Against Itself?," by Michael Freudenberg and Thierry Paulmier, finds that East Asian countries apply high tariffs for protected sectors, namely, agriculture, food and beverage, and light industry including textile and apparel. The chapter also shows that in every sector East Asian countries apply higher effective tariffs on products manufactured within the region than on imports from the EU and NAFTA, which means that East Asia is essentially discriminating against itself. Another interesting finding is that three types of applied tariff patterns exist in East Asia. Japan, South Korea, Malaysia, Brunei, Cambodia and the Philippines apply high tariffs for the sectors in which they suffer from comparative disadvantage; these countries practice defensive protectionism. Thailand, China and Vietnam, on the other hand, apply high tariffs mainly in sectors in which they enjoy a comparative advantage; this is offensive protectionism. Myanmar, Laos, Taiwan and Indonesia, meanwhile, apply high tariffs in both sectors in which they have a comparative advantage and a disadvantage.

Chapter 8, "Regionalization in East Asia: Simulations Using a CGE Model MIRAGE," by Michel Fouquin presents a scenario of regional liberalization in East Asia using the CEPII's Computable General Equilibrium model called MIRAGE. The computed results show that East Asia will produce a large trade creation effect, but the effect does not seem to occur in an even manner. Japan and Korea will be the main benefactors in the machinery industry, while China and other East Asian countries will gain in labor-intensive industries. In other words, specialization will advance along the lines of integration. This result shows that some East Asian countries might prefer to continue the traditional dual-track policy that mixes export-oriented policies with import-substituting policies without strong political will.

3 Conclusion and policy implication

Now we can answer the questions raised before about the nature of economic integration in East Asia, and understand where East Asia stands in the process of fully-fledged economic integration.

First, East Asia has achieved economic integration only in terms of trade in intermediate goods, but has not yet accomplished integration in trade in consumption goods and services, and in terms of mobility. This is quite different from the EU and NAFTA where trade in goods and services, except agricultural products, is liberalized.

Second, because of the large diversity in income and industrial stage, or heterogeneity between countries, cross-border fragmentation (splitting of a production process into several steps in different locations for a final product) has developed in East Asia more than in any other region such as the EU and NAFTA. East Asia has evolved the vertical regional production/distribution networks, where industrial clusters developed in different countries are systematically linked. This view is confirmed by the intra-industry spatial linkages (backward and forward cross-border linkage within the same industry) which are observed especially in the machinery industry. The advancement of cross-border fragmentation has led an expansion of intra-regional trade through vertical intra-industry trade (international trade within the same products or industry). Indeed, we can confirm, by the regression result, that the large differences in factor endowments increase the vertical intra-industry trade.

Third, as confirmed by the regression results, geographical proximity increases vertical intra-industry trade. This implies that because of geographical proximity, East Asia will develop further integration in the form of vertical production/distribution networks.

Fourth, reduction of service link costs has promoted vertical intra-industry trade. In this regard, policy efforts, as well as much human talent, have contributed to overcoming the handicap of being remotely situated between segmented production blocks and markets.

Fifth, high trade barriers such as high tariffs have impeded horizontal intra-industry trade. This implies that East Asia will increase horizontal intra-industry trade if trade barriers are reduced. In this regard, to some extent, the AFTA, the ASEAN-China FTA, and the ASEAN-Japan FTA will contribute to horizontal intra-industry trade, as long as they succeed in reducing tariffs in consumer goods sufficiently.

Sixth, against the background of within-border and cross-border fragmentation, catching up by the Asian NIEs (Hong Kong, South Korea, Singapore and Taiwan) with Japan, as well as by the latecomers of the ASEAN 4 (Indonesia, Malaysia, the Philippines and Thailand) and China with the earlier starters of Japan and the Asian NIEs, has advanced.

Seventh, we see that de jure integration will result in a large trade creation effect. But the effect will be different by industry and by country, which will push forward specialization in industry between countries.

Lastly, we observe, from a case study of hard disc drives, that with lower transportation costs, the multiple suppliers located in different countries can grow together in diversification of risk.

What messages are derived from our studies regarding further integration? First, East Asia will enhance the de facto economic integration with respect to trade, based on fragmentation, and this will lead to further expansion of intra-regional trade through vertical intra-industry trade, due to a large diversification in income per capita. Second, considering the evolution of fragmentation across countries in the region, East Asia requires a seamless business world. To put it differently, it is hoped that East Asia will reduce trade barriers in goods and services, simplify custom clearance, harmonize the rules of origin employed in various FTAs, and enhance each fragmented production block and connecting services. Third, the reduction of tariffs on finished goods will encourage horizontal trade like that of the EU. In this regard, de jure integration, namely, bilateral and plurilateral FTAs, benefit the participant countries, and the East Asian-wide FTA benefits the whole of East Asia. But, it is unlikely that a completely free trade area even in certain manufactured products, as well as in services, will be realized in East Asia. Automobile manufacture is one industry that is likely to be excluded from the list of tariff concessions. Indeed, the Japan and Thailand FTA concluded that Thailand would exclude automobiles from the concession list.[3] Thailand will take the same stance in negotiations with South Korea. South Korea and China will follow the strategy in negotiations with Japan. In other words, East Asia will have to await the fully-fledged integration in trade until the large diversity of incomes and industrial stages converge between countries.

Notes

1. Besides liberalization of trade in goods, ASEAN has endeavored to take the next step to create a community. In October 2003, the ASEAN leaders agreed to achieve a dynamic, cohesive, resilient and integrated ASEAN Community by 2020, by creating the ASEAN Security Community, ASEAN Economic Community, and ASEAN Socio-cultural Community. The ASEAN Economic Community is the realization of a single market and production base, to create a stable, prosperous and highly competitive ASEAN economic region by the year 2020 in which there is a free flow of goods, services and investment, as well as freer flows of capital, equitable economic development and reduced poverty and socio-economic disparities. The realization of a fully integrated economic community requires implementation of both liberalization and cooperation measures. These will involve rules for facilitating business, the presence of skilled labor and human resources development, capacity building, recognition of educational qualifications, closer consultation on macroeconomic and financial policies, trade financing measures, enhanced infrastructure and communications connectivity, development of electronic transactions through e-ASEAN, integrating industries across the region to promote regional sourcing, and the enhancement private sector involvement (ASEAN Secretariat 2003).
2. The ACFTA agreed the modality for tariff reduction for tariff lines placed by each party. Each party can place 400 tariff lines at the HS 6-digit level (about 5000 lines) and 10 percent of the total import value, based on 2001 trade statistics for the ASEAN 6 and China; 500 tariff lines at the HS 6-digit level for Cambodia, Laos and Myanmar; and 500 tariff lines at the HS 6-digit level and the ceiling of import value determined not later than the end of 2004. Details are given in ASEAN Secretariat (2004).
3. Strictly speaking, Thailand will reduce the tariff on more than 3000cc automobiles, from 80 percent to 60 percent by 2010.

References

ASEAN Secretariat (2002) "Southeast Asia: a Free Trade Area", http://www.aseansec.org/viewpdf. asp?file=/pdf/afta.pdf (April 5, 2005).

ASEAN Secretariat (2003) Declaration ASEAN Concord II (Bali Concord II), http://www.aseansec.org/15159.htm (April 5, 2005).

ASEAN Secretariat (2004) Annex 2, Modality for Tariff Reduction and Elimination for Tariff Lines Placed in the Sensitive Track, *Agreement on Trade in Goods of the Framework Agreement on Comprehensive Economic Co-operation between the Association of Southeast Asian Nations and the People's Republic of China* (http://www. aseansec.org/4979.htm).

Deardorff, Alan V. (2001) "Fragmentation in Simple Trade Model," *North American Journal of Economics and Finance*, 13: 121–37.

Fujita Masahisa (2004) "Future of East Asian Regional Economies," International Symposium on *Globalization and Regional Integration from the Viewpoint of Spatial Economics*, December 2, organized by the Institute of

Developing Economies, IDE JETRO (http://www.ide.go.jp/Japanese/Inter/Sympo/pdf/ fujita_hand.pdf., January 12, 2005).

Ministry of Foreign Affairs of Japan (MOFA) (2004) Joint Press Statement, A Japan–Philippines Economic Partnership Agreement, http://www.mofa.go.jp/region/asia-paci/philippine/joint0411.html (April 8, 2005).

1
The Development of Fragmentation in East Asia and its Implications for FTAs

Fukunari Kimura

1 De facto integration in East Asia

Has East Asia recently experienced de facto integration? The answer is yes and no. The "yes" factors and the "no" factors in fact interact with each other, and this interaction is an essential element in the formation of international production and distribution networks in this region. To discuss policy issues, such as the designing of de jure integration, it is crucially important to understand in what sense the East Asian economy has integrated.

"The integrated economy" in pure economic theory is defined as an economy realizing an identical equilibrium to the theoretical (or fictitious) one in which all goods, productive factors and other economic elements, such as technology, are perfectly mobile so that prices of all goods and factors are equalized across markets or geographical areas. In other words, the economy replicates the equilibrium such that the economy does not have any spatial dimension (i.e. the economy is dimension zero without congestion). Theoretically, such an equilibrium can be reached even if not all goods, factors and other economic elements are perfectly mobile; for example, an equilibrium where the factor price equalization theorem holds in the standard Heckscher-Ohlin model can replicate the integrated economy equilibrium even if productive factors are immobile across national borders.

The actual economy, of course, never literally replicates the integrated economy equilibrium. However, using such a pure benchmark, we can evaluate the degree of economic integration by assessing the closeness to this theoretical equilibrium. There are at least two ways to measure the degree of economic integration. One is to check the mobility of goods, productive factors and other elements, and the other is to assess the degree of equalization in prices of goods and productive factors.

The European economy, particularly of the core member countries, is regarded as a well-integrated economy but is not yet fully integrated in certain senses. Actually, even the United "States" of America is not perfectly integrated in the pure theoretical sense. A core–periphery model in the economic geography literature typically describes these economies so that tradable goods (in particular, horizontally differentiated manufactured goods with increasing returns technology) and physical/human/knowledge capital can move across nations/regions with low transport costs while unskilled labor or consumers barely move, which results in the formation of agglomeration in the balance of market access effect, the cost-of-living effect, and the market crowding effect.[1] A key feature is that production conditions are roughly the same everywhere and almost everything is mobile across nations/regions. Only mild differences in transport costs across goods/factors generate market-oriented industrial location.

What has happened in East Asia? The East Asian economy has definitely become increasingly integrated recently but so far has moved in a direction widely divergent from the European case. It is true that intra-regional trade ratios have drastically increased and intra-industry trade instead of inter-industry/one-way trade has expanded in share. However, factor prices, particularly wages, are still far from equalized due to the international immobility of labor. Production processes are extensively fragmented beyond national borders, but such forces do not immediately equalize factor prices in the region. Rather, service link costs connecting remotely located production blocks have become low enough to take advantage of differences in wages and other location advantages. Production technologies as well as managerial ability for vertical production/distribution networks are transplanted to developing countries through foreign direct investment (FDI) and other channels of technology transfer. Furthermore, the agglomeration of industrial activities becomes one of the important elements of location advantages in FDI; benefits from agglomeration are generated not only by economies of scale in service links but also by facilitating arm's-length (inter-firm) transactions. The forces of fragmentation and agglomeration have generated production-condition-oriented industrial location and have constructed sophisticated international production/distribution networks in East Asia.

It is true that policy integration in East Asia is far behind the region's de facto economic integration and East Asia can learn much from the experiences of other regions which have formally integrated. However, we should not naively apply the whole institutional design of existing integration models, such as the EU model, the NAFTA model, or the Latin American model, to East Asian integration. We must first analyze the nature of de facto integration in the region very carefully. Economic preconditions as well as the policy background for de facto integration have to be examined. Then important policy issues should be pinpointed so that some of them can be incorporated when designing East Asian de jure integration.

The next section presents an analytical framework for explaining the mechanics of fragmentation and production/distribution networks in East Asia, and section 3 provides some empirical evidence. Section 4 examines the policy background of the development of production/distribution networks and discusses the implications of institutionalizing economic integration. Section 5 concludes the chapter.

2 The mechanics of fragmentation in East Asia

The most salient phenomenon in the recent international trade in East Asia is the formation of international production/distribution networks. Networks are found in various industries, but most important, both qualitatively and quantitatively, are those in machinery industries including general machinery, electric machinery, transport equipment and precision machinery. Machinery industries involve a large number of multilayered vertical production/distribution processes, and East Asian firms including Japanese firms have a competitive edge in exploring modulation techniques and constructing vertical value chains. International production/distribution networks in East Asia are distinctive and are the most developed in the world at this point in time in (i) their significance in each economy, (ii) their extensiveness in covering a number of countries in the region, and (iii) the sophistication in their structure consisting of both intra-firm and arm's-length transactions.[2]

The literature on fragmentation theory and its empirical applications has grown since a seminal work by Jones and Kierzkowski (1990) and has proved its applicability in analyzing the mechanics of cross-border production sharing at the production process level.[3] International production/distribution networks in East Asia, however, have developed beyond the original idea of fragmentation, and some expansion of the analytical framework is needed. Kimura and Ando (2005) propose the concept of two-dimensional fragmentation, particularly to analyze the mechanics of networks in East Asia.

Figure 1.1 displays various types of fragmentation in a two-dimensional space. The horizontal axis denotes geographical distance. From the original position, located at the origin, a production block can be detached and placed at a geographical distance. The dotted line in the middle is a national border, separating cross-border fragmentation from domestic fragmentation. On the other hand, the vertical axis represents the (un)controllability or disintegration of a firm. A fragmented production process may be conducted by either intra-firm establishments or unrelated firms. The dotted line is the boundary of a firm, separating arm's-length (inter-firm) fragmentation or outsourcing from intra-firm fragmentation.

When does fragmentation make sense? First, there must be substantial production cost reduction in a fragmented production block (see Table 1.1). Geographical distance may provide opportunities to explore different production conditions. In particular, cross-border fragmentation enables firms to enjoy diversified location advantages including workers' wages, economic infrastructure, policy environment and other advantages. The uncontrollability axis yields chances to utilize the strengths of business partners. Instead of doing everything

Figure 1.1: Two dimensions of fragmentation

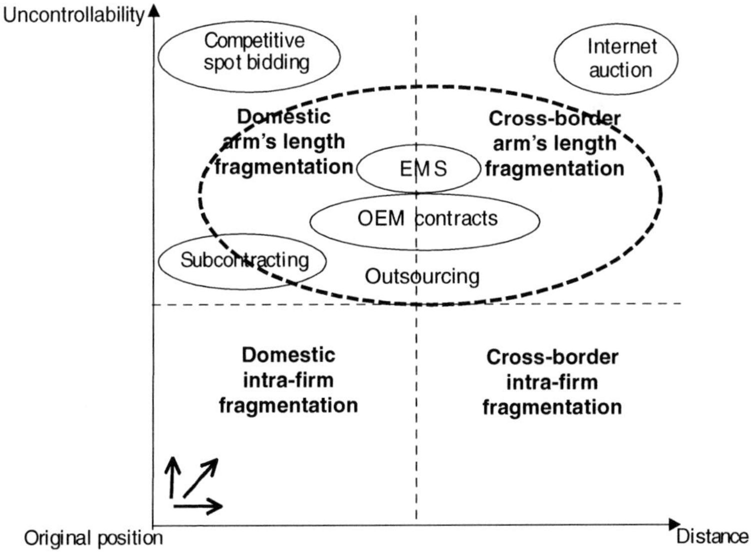

Source: Kimura and Ando (2005).

Table 1.1: Cost structure of two-dimensional fragmentation

	Service link cost	Production cost *per se*
Fragmentation (distance)	cost due to geographical distance	location advantages
Fragmentation (uncontrollability)	cost due to weaker controllability	"de-internalization" advantages (counterpart's ownership advantages)

Source: Kimura and Ando (2005).

in-house, arm's-length fragmentation or outsourcing may make the whole production system more efficient.

Second, service link cost for the connection between fragmented production blocks should not be too high. Fragmentation beyond national borders and/or the boundary of a firm is inevitably accompanied by substantial service link cost, but such cost must be low enough to enjoy total cost reduction.

Figure 1.2: Total cost reduction with fragmentation

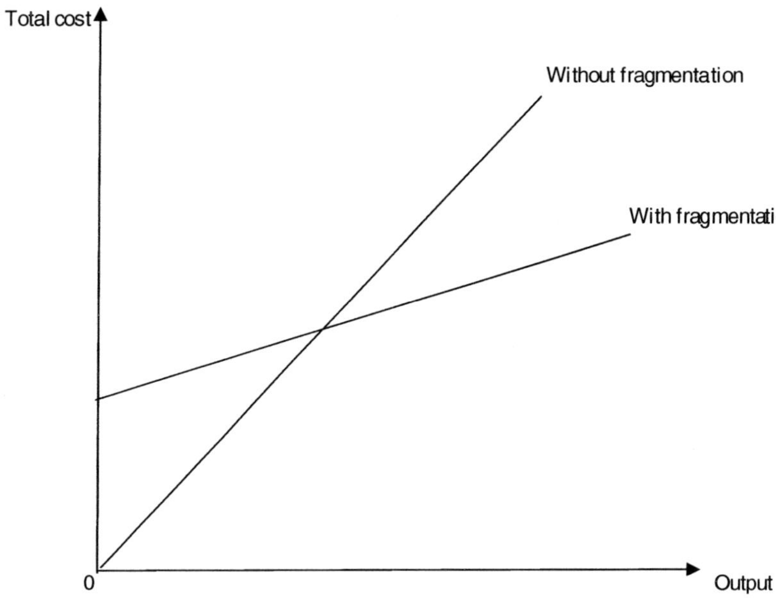

Source: Kimura and Ando (2005).

Figure 1.2 illustrates the relationship between the saving of production cost *per se* and the cost of service links. For simplicity, the cost structure of production is represented by a constant variable cost without fixed cost, displayed as an upward-sloping line as output increases. Production cost saving *per se* is found in the difference in slope between production with and without fragmentation. The service link cost comes in only in the case of fragmentation, which explains the higher intercept. The larger the production cost saving, the flatter the slope of the cost curve in the case of fragmentation, and the more likely fragmentation occurs. The smaller the service link cost, the lower the intercept of the cost curve in the case of fragmentation, and again the more likely fragmentation occurs. This argument can apply to both types of fragmentation.

In East Asia, because of the large diversity in income levels and development stages across countries/regions, there exist various opportunities to explore different location advantages through cross-border fragmentation. In addition, the tradition of Japanese *shitauke* and Taiwanese subcontracting in addition to innovative processing trade arrangements between Hong Kong and Guangdong provide a prototype model of arm's-length fragmentation. Two kinds of service link cost have lowered due to both technological innovation of transportation/telecommunication systems and policy effort in facilitating trade/FDI and improving governance.

In East Asia, geographical fragmentation and agglomeration go hand in hand. In contrast with market-oriented agglomeration in Europe, agglomeration in East Asia is typically motivated by production-side logic. One channel is the nature of increasing returns to service links; fragmented production blocks tend to concentrate in some specific location with low service link cost. Another channel is the desired combination of geographical proximity and arm's-length fragmentation; close communication between upstream and downstream firms facilitates inter-firm arrangements in the vertical production division of labor. In contrast with agglomeration in Europe where market-driven agglomeration of differentiated products is formulated, agglomeration in East Asia is often production-driven.

3 Evolving patterns of industrial location and international trade

The patterns of industrial location and international trade in East Asia have drastically evolved since the 1990s. Until the 1980s, these patterns were basically dictated by the traditional theory of comparative advantage. Developing countries specialized in resource-based and labor-intensive industries while Japan and some of the newly industrialized economies (NIEs) had capital- and human capital-intensive industries. The trade pattern in East Asia was typical of North–South trade, based on industry-wise location patterns. In the 1990s, however, the relative importance of such one-way trade declined, and instead intra-industry trade, particularly in machinery, expanded in share. In particular, back-and-forth international trade in machinery parts and components increased explosively as production-process-wise division of labor gained in importance.

Figures 1.3 and 1.4 present the drastic changes in the importance of machinery/machinery parts trade in East Asia.[4] In 1990, Japan was a predominant exporter of machinery, particularly for finished products.

Figure 1.3: Machinery goods and machinery parts and components: shares in total exports and imports in 1990–1994

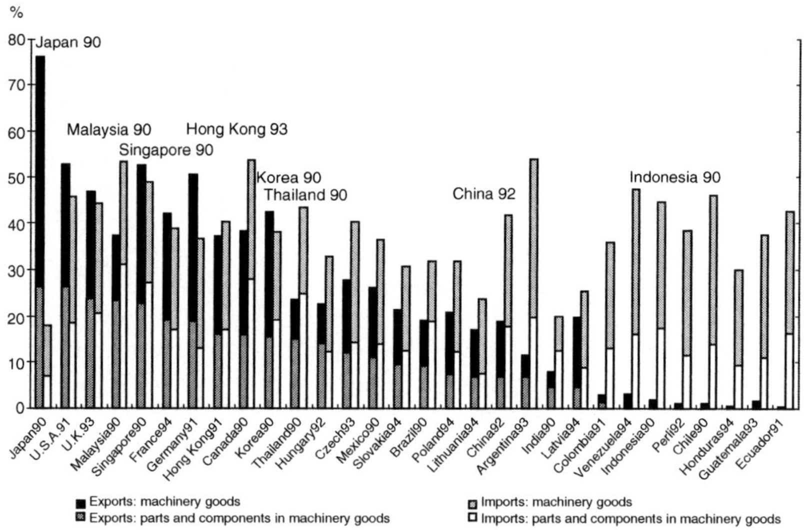

Note: data is of 1990 or close to 1990. For instance Japan 90 and USA 91 indicate that data is of 1990 for Japan and 1991 for USA. Estonia, Philippines and Russia are not included in Figure 1.3 though included in Figure 1.4 due to the lack of available data for 1990–1994.
Source: Ando (2004). Original data source: author's calculation based on UN COMTRADE online.

Figure 1.4: Machinery goods and machinery parts and components: shares in total exports and imports in 2000

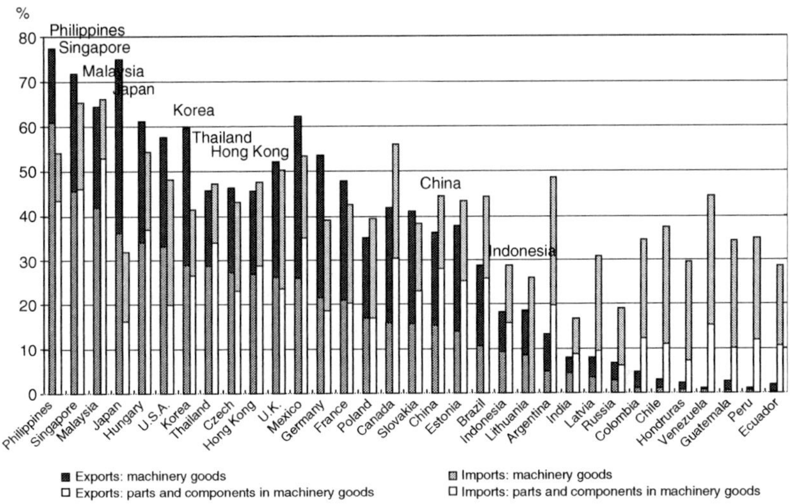

Note: Data for Russia and Slovakia is of 1999 due to the lack of data for 2000.
Source: Ando and Kimura (2004). Original data source: author's calculation, based on UN COMTRADE for exports of Hong Kong and exports and imports for Russia and Slovakia and UN PC-TAS for others.

By 2000, however, Japan became an important exporter of the machinery parts and components as well as one of the major importers of both finished products and parts. The ASEAN forerunners, notably the Philippines, Malaysia, Singapore and Thailand, became active back-and-forth traders of machinery parts and components. China was a bit behind as of the year 2000 but was moving rapidly to the left-hand side. We observe similar trade patterns between the US and Mexico and between Germany and the Czech Republic/Slovakia/Hungary/Poland, but the extensiveness of production networking is distinctive in East Asia.

The nature of current intra-industry trade in East Asia is obviously different from that of Europe. In the case of Europe, particularly in core EU countries, horizontal intra-industry trade, defined by comparable unit prices of exports and imports, occupies 15–25 percent of total intra-regional trade.[5] In contrast, in East Asia horizontal intra-industry trade is still minimal while vertical intra-industry trade, i.e. intra-industry trade with large differentials in export and import unit prices, is rapidly increasing. More importantly, vertical intra-industry trade in East Asia does not follow a systemic pattern of "quality ladders"; i.e. high-income countries do not necessarily export more expensive products and vice versa.[6] This means that vertical intra-industry trade in East Asia is mainly due not to vertical product differentiation but rather to production-process-wise division of labor.

An analysis of the behavior of Japanese firm affiliates in East Asia suggests that arm's-length transactions instead of intra-firm transactions increase the share in international production/distribution networks. We observe vigorous FDI in East Asia by Japanese manufacturing small and medium enterprises (SMEs), which indicates vertical production networking and agglomeration formation among Japanese firms. In addition, numerous case studies suggest that transactions among firms with different nationalities also become active as local indigenous entrepreneurs gain competitiveness. This provides new channels for fostering local industries/firms, not through infant industry protection but by penetrating into international production/distribution networks developed by MNEs.

4 Policy background and the implication for regional integration

How was the formation of international production/distribution networks realized in East Asia? Why were production/distribution networks not formulated in other regions such as Latin America? As the *East Asian Miracle* report (World Bank 1993) emphasized, the stability of macroeconomic fundamentals and solid initial conditions such as abundant human capital were of course essential elements. The international competitiveness of East Asian firms in machinery industries was obviously another important factor. In addition, we claim that development strategies applied in East Asian developing economies were also crucial in the development of international production/distribution networks.

The ASEAN forerunners applied a so-called dual-track strategic approach to industrialization, fostering both import-substituting industries and export-oriented industries at the same time. One sharp contrast to the cases of Japan, Korea and partially Taiwan was these countries' active use of FDI from abroad. Initially, heavier weights were placed on import-substituting industries where trade protection was provided so as to yield sufficient incentive for either immature domestic industries or foreign companies to start producing and serving the domestic market. Typical import-substituting industries were automobiles, domestic electric appliances, iron and steel, petrochemicals, pharmaceuticals and others. Export-oriented industries, on the other hand, were either resource-based/labor-intensive industries such as food processing and garments, or MNEs' operations in textiles and garments and electronics industries, which were typically located in export processing zones carefully insulated from the domestic economy.

Major policy reforms in the ASEAN forerunners occurred in the latter half of the 1980s and the early 1990s and were triggered by serious recessions in the mid-1980s and the emerging threat of China in the 1990s as a massive FDI attractor. Policy-makers in the ASEAN forerunners realized that foreign companies were already in the core of their manufacturing sector, and their strong fear of losing FDI made them change their FDI policy from selective acceptance to essentially an "accept everybody" policy with aggressive FDI facilitation. To avoid potential flight of strategic MNEs, host countries faced a number of urgent tasks, including the improvement of the investment climate, effective connection with domestic industries, and the formulation of agglomeration. Well-planned, deliberate policy packages did not seem to exist initially, but as a result of cumulative efforts towards attracting FDI, the policy environment for accelerating the formulation of international production/distribution networks was prepared.

These countries still kept trade protection for import-substituting industries. Trade protection contradicts the policy of attracting network-forming FDI. To invite outward-oriented foreign companies, host countries must convince investors that they have the best or second-best location advantages in the world. Import levies on parts and components are surely negative factors for them. To partially solve this policy contradiction, countries extensively applied duty drawback systems as well as various trade/FDI facilitation measures.

The formation of international production/distribution networks created new channels for technology transfer from developed to developing economies. The production-process-wise division of labor instead of the old-style industry-wise location choice allows various types of production sharing between developed and developing countries, even in high-tech industries. The development of sophisticated vertical division of labor provides opportunities for local indigenous firms to participate in international production networks, which accelerates further technology transfer. The policy package for industrial promotion started to be fundamentally revised. The traditional infant industry protection argument gradually lost its charm, and fostering local supporting industries became more clearly emphasized.

Were these changes special to East Asia? We would like to claim "yes." Most of the developing countries outside East Asia still apply import-substituting policies for industrialization. The fear of notorious MNEs is not yet overcome, the acceptance of FDI is still picky and selective, and policy-makers do not understand the existence of harsh competition in attracting FDI in the world. Mexico and Central and Eastern European countries (CEECs) are perhaps exceptions. Even in Mexico, however, efforts to foster local supporting industries are weak, and most of the cross-border production sharing between the US and Mexico still consists of simple intra-firm fragmentation. CEECs are not very successful in formulating agglomeration because of relatively low population densities and decentralized policies for industry location. The relatively small wage gap with Western Europe and infrastructure development in the near future may intensify the footloose behavior of MNEs located in Czech, Hungary, Poland and other CEECs.

Admitting that the East Asian economy followed its own path of de facto integration, does de jure integration of East Asia require a special design? Yes, certainly. Free trade agreements (FTAs) are flexible policy tools in terms of speed, scope and sequencing. In contrast to rigorous WTO rules, FTAs can be designed with large degrees of freedom so as to accommodate the policy issues of participating countries.

There are two issues for policy reform through FTAs which are common to the ASEAN forerunners and China. One is to restructure inefficient import-substituting industries in the framework of international competition. Despite the voices of skeptics such as the World Bank (1993) and Noland and Pack (2003), there surely exist cases in which industries became competitive because of temporary import protection and other government interventions; i.e. at least Mill's criterion for infant industry protection argument holds. Of course, Bastable's criterion – i.e. that the inter-temporal cost–benefit balance must be favorable – may or may not be met, depending on the case. In the ASEAN forerunners and China, there are examples in which inward FDI is utilized in the import-substitution schemes. Automobiles in Thailand and cellular phones in China are such examples. But, of course, import-substitution-type industrial promotion policy requires complicated fine-tuning, and has experienced numerous failures. How to clean up such interventions and to make import-substituting industries competitive is one of the most important policy issues for the ASEAN forerunners and China.

To restructure the import-substituting industries, simple removal of trade impediments will certainly be effective. These industries, whether they are run by domestic or foreign companies, are typically under heavy border protection, and the removal of tariffs and other trade impediments will substantially alter the competitive environment. Restructuring is important in East Asia not only for making import-substituting industries more efficient, but also for solving policy contradiction by promoting international networking. Furthermore, local supporting industries attached to import-substituting industries are not necessarily hopeless so that a proper soft-landing scenario can perhaps be documented for some sectors in East Asia. FTAs can contribute to the restructuring of import-substituting industries by eliminating tariffs and other trade impediments in the appropriate time framework.

The other issue around policy formation via FTAs is to further activate international production/distribution networks. Due to trade liberalization for semiconductor-related parts and components in the 1990s as well as the extensive use of the duty drawback system, network-forming firms barely pay tariffs these days. But international transactions are still far from friction-free; national border effects are substantially high. East Asian trade effectively utilizes the logic of fragmentation, but there is a lot of room for reducing service link cost. In particular, the strength of the East Asian economy is to serve sophisticated markets with flexible small-lot/wide-variety supplies. Therefore, lowering service link cost and speeding up feedback between upstream and downstream inputs are fundamental issues for the East Asian economy. Indeed, some firms in certain sectors such as Dell successfully develop an efficient supply chain management (SCM) system and manage the whole production chain with abundant cash flows. How far such a system is workable depends on the industry, but it indicates a general direction to pursue.

More concrete policy items that should be included in East Asian FTA in order to further activate international production/distribution networks are suggested by examining Table 1.1. In each dimension of fragmentation, either along the distance axis or along the uncontrollability axis, fragmentation can further be activated by (i) reducing the service link cost and/or (ii) saving the production cost *per se* in fragmented production blocks. In the distance fragmentation, the reduction of service link cost could be realized by policies overcoming geographical distance and national border effect. Examples of such policies are the removal of explicit and implicit trade impediments, trade facilitation, the development of transport and distribution services, the betterment of transport and telecommunication infrastructure, the facilitation of personnel mobility, and the reduction in investment cost for constructing production/distribution networks. The saving of production cost *per se*, on the other hand, would come from policies strengthening location advantages. Such policies include the development of human capital through education and vocational training, the establishment of stable and flexible labor regulation, the development of a healthy and efficient domestic/international financial sector, the reduction in infrastructure services cost for energy procurement, industrial estates and others, the formation of agglomeration facilitating vertical division of labor, and the establishment of a transparent and accountable business environment through investment rule and intellectual property rights.

In the uncontrollability fragmentation, the reduction of service link cost may be realized by institutional building for reducing transaction cost in arm's length transactions. Examples of such policies are policies reducing informational cost in searching and monitoring business partners and providing the stability of contracts, policies promoting modulation technology, and policies securing intellectual property rights. The saving of production cost *per se* could come from policies keeping and strengthening various types of potential business partners, which include hosting foreign firms as well as fostering local entrepreneurs in industrial agglomeration. A policy environment allowing various types of contracts is also important.

Most of these policies are not covered by WTO policy discipline and thus must be taken care of by regional trade arrangements. FTAs with enlarged policy agendas are appropriate flexible channels to pursue such policy initiatives. The ASEAN latecomers may also take advantage of the existence of international production/distribution networks in the region; rather than providing an overdose of near-sighted poverty alleviation aid, we must try to integrate these economies in the networks. These are policy agenda items that we should incorporate in the designing of East Asian de jure integration.

5 Conclusion

This chapter claims that East Asia is experiencing an unprecedented path of de facto integration and therefore requires its own proper designing of policy-level economic integration. De facto integration is represented by the formation of international production/distribution networks, aggressively exploiting non-integrated elements, e.g. wage differences, in globalizing corporate activities. The formation of international production/distribution networks has been backed up by the drastic transformation of development strategies of developing countries. In this context, there are two policy agenda items to be incorporated in the designing of the East Asian FTA. One is to make a solid commitment to the proper elimination of tariffs and other trade impediments. The other is to incorporate an innovative policy package to reduce the two kinds of service link costs and to reinforce the production basis *per se* so as to further activate international production/distribution networks.

The role of Japan is crucial in designing the East Asian FTA. We should say that countries other than Japan do not have capability to create a model FTA for the whole of East Asia, at least at this point in time. In November 2004, China and ASEAN concluded the good trade portion of China-ASEAN FTA.[7] This agreement presents a tariff elimination scheme in detail but unfortunately is not successful in accelerating the industrial adjustment of major import-substituting industries such as automobiles, certain chemicals, and iron & steel. Regrettably, it is a much looser agreement than the ASEAN Free Trade Area (AFTA). Talks between China and ASEAN do not seem to address urgent issues in further activating international production/distribution networks. China is thus far not very successful in presenting a model FTA. Korea is a bit behind in concluding FTAs with East Asian countries. Japan is in a responsible position in constructing high-quality FTAs in East Asia.

There are also, however, a lot of problems on the Japanese side. So far Japan has not been successful in showing a strong will to reform itself. It is good news that the agricultural lobby is now cooperating in negotiating FTAs. However, the committed liberalization is not impressive enough to prove Japan's strong will for liberalizing trade. The frequent use of preferential allocation of quotas is another problem because such concessions are more distortive than simple preferential tariff elimination and are not internationally regarded as "free trade." The largely negative responses to the requests facilitating the movement of persons also do not indicate any willingness to promote economic integration. Only after presenting a strong will and vision, will East Asian countries accept Japan's requests penetrating into their domestic policies. Further effort is called for if Japan wishes to be a part of the leadership in East Asia.

Notes

1. For the core–periphery model and the agglomeration literature, see Fujita et al. (1999) and Baldwin et al. (2003).
2. See Ando and Kimura (2004).
3. Also see Arndt and Kierzkowski (2001), Deardorff (2001) and Cheng and Kierzkowski (2001) for the fragmentation theory.
4. "Machinery" includes general machinery, electric machinery, transport equipment and precision machinery. "Machinery parts" are defined at the 6-digit level of HS classification. See Ando and Kimura (2004) for the detail.
5. See, for example, the estimates by Fontagne and Freudenberg (2002).
6. See Ando (2004).
7. The whole text of the agreement is in http://www.aseansec.org/16646.htm.

References

Ando, Mitsuyo (2004) "Fragmentation and Vertical Intra-Industry Trade in East Asia," originally presented at the Western Economic Association International, 79th Annual Conference. Forthcoming in *North American Journal of Economics and Finance.*

Ando, Mitsuyo and Fukunari Kimura (2004) "The Formation of International Production and Distribution Networks in East Asia," *NBER Working Paper No. 10167*, December. Forthcoming in *International Trade* (NBER-East Asia Seminar on Economics, Volume 14), ed. T. Ito and A. Rose, Chicago: University of Chicago Press.

Arndt, S. W. and Kierzkowski, H. (2001) *Fragmentation: New Production Patterns in the World Economy*, Oxford: Oxford University Press.

Baldwin, Richard, Forslid, Rikard, Martin, Philippe, Ottaviano, Gianmarco and Robert-Nicoud, Fredric (2003) *Economic Geography and Public Policy*, Princeton: Princeton University Press.

Cheng, L. K. and Kierzkowski, H. (2001) *Global Production and Trade in East Asia*, Boston: Kluwer Academic Publishers.

Deardorff, A. V. (2001) "Fragmentation in Simple Trade Models," *North American Journal of Economics and Finance*, 12: 121–37.

Fontagne, Lionel and Freudenberg, Michael (2002) "Long-term Trends in Intra-industry Trade," in *Frontiers of Research in Intra-industry Trade*, ed. P. J. Lloyd and Hyun-Hoon Lee, Basingstoke and New York: Palgrave Macmillan.

Fujita, M., Krugman, P. R. and Venables, A. J. (1999) *The Spatial Economy: Cities, Regions, and International Trade*, Cambridge, Mass: MIT Press.

Jones, R. W. and Kierzkowski, H. (1990) "The Role of Services in Production and International Trade: a Theoretical Framework," in *The Political Economy of International Trade: Essays in Honor of R. E. Baldwin*, ed. R. W. Jones and A. O. Krueger, Oxford: Basil Blackwell.

Kimura, Fukunari and Mitsuyo Ando (2005) "Two-Dimensional Fragmentation in East Asia: Conceptual Framework and Empirics," *International Review of Economics and Finance*, 14, 3: 317–48.

Noland, Marcus and Pack, Howard (2003) *Industrial Policy in an Era of Globalization: Lessons from Asia*, Washington, DC: Institute for International Economics.

World Bank (1993) *The East Asian Miracle: Economic Growth and Public Policy*, Oxford: Oxford University Press.

2

Intra-Industry Trade and Economic Integration

Pierre Ecochard, Lionel Fontagné, Guillaume Gaulier and Soledad Zignago

1 Introduction

In a world where trade is subject to significant tariffs, an industrial core is likely to develop in every country to satisfy home demand, whatever the initial allocation of factors. Conversely, in an integrated zone, and when transportation costs are not too high, production is concentrated to benefit from economies of scale, as Krugman argues from the example of the United States (Krugman 1991b). In consequence, trade liberalization may cause a sudden reallocation of production. This raises concerns that integration processes will prompt harsh adjustments, the cost of which will affect asymmetrically industries and countries engaged in the liberalization effort. In contradiction with these conclusions, European integration was accompanied by an increase in intra-industry trade (IIT) between member countries. The "mezzogiornification" of southern Europe did not take place, and it is doubtful that the "true US-style industrial specialization" Krugman forecasted will eventually take hold. The European integration process was followed by changes in trade patterns in Europe that generated interest from trade economists, who were led to think that the observed increase in similar product exchanges could be a result of this regional economic integration. The size of IIT in Europe suggests that in spite of almost fifty years of integration, European countries are still less specialized than US regions, or are specialized in a different fashion. Instead of concentration, integration resulted in a quality layered market; the share of vertically differentiated intra-industry trade has been increasing since the mid-1980s (Fontagné et al. 1997). It aPpears that countries are specializing along a quality range. A textbook example of this phenomenon is the car industry. The French firm

Renault recently launched the Dacia Logan, a low-cost car built in Romania (which is set to join the EU in 2007). The purpose of this chapter is to clarify this matter by exploring the empirical relationship between IIT and economic integration, through a worldwide study of the determinants of IIT in four de jure or de facto integration zones: NAFTA, East Asia, Europe and Mercosur. Our contribution is to provide updated information comparable across countries, on a worldwide basis.

As the traditional Heckscher-Ohlin-Samuelson (HOS) model is inappropriate to account for IIT, several models were developed in the 1980s to provide a theoretical basis for the trade of similar goods. Horizontal IIT arises between countries with similar endowments and in industries where a small minimum efficient scale of production permits the existence of a great number of varieties (Lancaster 1980; Krugman 1981). The case of vertical IIT is not clear-cut; Falvey (1981) shows that vertical IIT may arise when there are no increasing returns and a large number of firms are producing varieties, while Shaked and Sutton (1984) find that it can arise when a small number of firms are confronted with increasing returns. Among the determinants of IIT, economic integration turns out to be one of the most difficult to assess. Wong (1995) introduces free factor mobility in his model and finds that IIT is then lowered; IIT occurs only if there are considerable differences in endowments. Based on these models, many studies have investigated the determinants of IIT, including Balassa (1986a), Balassa and Bauwens (1987), Bergstrand (1990), Stone and Lee (1995) and Fontagné et al. (1997), to name just a few. However, little or no attempt has been made to realize a worldwide study at a highly disaggregated level. This is probably due to the difficulty in gathering coherent data at a detailed level. Thanks to a large international trade database, in this chapter we are able to take into account four dimensions: industry, time, the importing and exporting country, and product level; the last category captures data for every country in the world, at the 6-digit level, that is, with more than 5000 product categories.

The rest of the chapter is organized as follows. The next section deals with the harmonization of the COMTRADE database and the methodology used to measure IIT and quality range. The third section consists of a descriptive study of trade patterns in each of the four considered integration zones. The fourth section lists the determinants of IIT and their economic justifications. We then expose the estimated model in section 5, and regression results in section 6. Section 7 concludes.

2 Measurement of intra-industry trade

The phrase "intra-industry trade" was coined by Balassa (1966) to name a phenomenon that had been described for the first time by Verdoorn in a study about Benelux (Verdoorn 1960). IIT refers to simultaneous export and import of similar goods in a given time. Thus, any measure of IIT must be based on a classification of products precise enough so that within one category, commodities can be assumed to be similar. Grubel and Lloyd (1975) proposed considering similar goods that share a common production process and/or assignment. Many studies conduct analysis at a rather aggregated level, which makes little sense, since classifications with less than a few hundred categories bring together very different products. Bergstrand (1982) pointed out that category 363 of the US Standard Industrial Classification contains such household appliances as washing machines, freezers and stoves; these products involve very different production processes, and cannot be considered close substitutes. Some even raised doubts about the very existence of IIT, arguing it was a mere artifact caused by the aggregation process (Finger 1975; Lipsey 1976).

2.1 Harmonization of data

To conduct a worldwide analysis of the determinants of IIT, we need an appropriate data set. We used the BACI database, which brings together and renders consistent various levels of analysis and classifications, drawing on the most detailed information available. This data set, based on COMTRADE (United Nations), covers every country in the world from the beginning of the 1990s to 2002 and provides the quantity as well as value of traded goods. Products are classified according to the Harmonized System (HS), at the 6-digit level, representing 5017 categories of products. In BACI, trade flows are reported to the United Nations in value and quantity by both exporting and importing countries (using mirror flows, when available) and are harmonized,[1] this operation being necessary given the huge discrepancies between reported mirror flows. (At the 6-digit level, the gap between mirror flows exceeds 100 percent for half of the observations in COMTRADE.) Original procedures have been developed to harmonize data, which use an evaluation of the quality of country declarations, the conversion into tons of the other units of quantities exchanged and the evaluation of CIF rates which reconcile import and export declarations. Indeed, in COMTRADE import values are reported CIF (cost, insurance and freight) and the exports are reported FOB (free on board). In order to remove CIF, we have to estimate freight costs. Being plagued with large measurement errors, mirror flow ratios cannot be directly identified with freight costs. We use predicted mirror flow ratios from a gravity-type equation as an estimate of CIF. We compute the IIT indexes at the 6-digit level, and then aggregate data at the industry-level according to the ISIC Rev. 2 classification, to allow sectoral analysis. In order to avoid confusion between products and industries, throughout this chapter we use the letter k for the former and c for the latter. We restrict our sample to 6-digit products for which we consider the reliability of data to be sufficient. Concretely, we compute for each product-year pair the standard deviation and kurtosis of the logarithm of unit values (UV). The pairs for which the standard deviation falls within 5 percent of the largest values (large errors) or for which the kurtosis is within 5 percent of the lowest values (very skewed at distribution of UV) are rejected.[2] Our hypothesis is that a very large dispersion of UV signals a high probability of classification failure due to the heterogeneity of the HS 6-digit heading (that is, heterogeneous products are grouped together), or due to measurement error. Within the selected pairs we further restrict the sample to those being selected in all years in the sample. This restriction avoids breaks in time series due to products entering or leaving the sample. In the text we point out cases where differences are large between results obtained with the restricted sample and the whole available data set. Globally, results are more stable with the restricted sample, which represents 44 percent of world trade value, and 67 percent of the total number of flows. Large divergences arise only for some specific countries (often known as poor declaring countries) and industries (such as diamonds).[3] With the restricted sample we obtain better correlations between total IIT share and the Grubel and Lloyd index (weighted average of the product level GL indexes) for some important country pairs; for US–Canada trade (1991–2002) the correlation increases from 0.86 on the full sample to 0.99 on the restricted sample. Also, with the restricted sample we override the counterintuitive result that the number of traded products declines.[4]

2.2 Measurement of intra-industry trade

There are two main indicators commonly used to measure IIT: the Grubel–Lloyd index and the threshold-based method. The first indicator consists of measuring the extent of the overlap in a given flow (for given year, product, importer and exporter), while the other classifies flows as either inter- or intra-industry using a threshold. The literature stresses the importance of the distinction between vertically and horizontally differentiated intra-industry trade, since those two phenomena follow different rules. Thus, both methods provide means to distinguish between the trade of goods of similar quality (and therefore similar price) and the trade of goods with different quality. Understandably, such a distinction can only be made using a threshold; if the difference in price is below that threshold, goods are considered to be of the same quality, otherwise they are considered to be vertically differentiated. Following most of the literature, we set the threshold to $\alpha = 0.25$. It is important to note that this distinction between vertically and horizontally differentiated products is different from the quality ranges discussed below, which involve the world average unit price.

2.2.1 *The Grubel–Lloyd index*

Grubel and Lloyd (1975) proposed the most widely used intra-industry trade index, which measures the overlap between exports and imports for a given flow:

$$GL_{ijtk} = 1 - \frac{[X_{ijtk} - M_{ijtk}]}{X_{ijtk} + M_{ijtk}}$$

where M stands for imports, X for exports, i and j for the countries and k for the product. The aggregation procedure is simple. The average Grubel and Lloyd indicator for countries i and j, year t and ISIC industry c is calculated as follows:

$$IIT_{ijtc} = 1 - \Sigma_{i;j;t;c} \frac{[X_{ijtc} - M_{ijtc}]}{X_{ijtc} + M_{ijtc}}$$

This index of IIT varies between 0 (complete inter-industry trade) and 1 (complete intra-industry trade).

2.2.2 *The threshold-based method*

The Grubel–Lloyd approach does not permit us to break IIT into vertical and horizontal trade, which is necessary as those two types of trade differ in their determinants. Greenaway et al. (1994, 1995) proposed a methodology to characterize trade flows as horizontally or vertically differentiated using Grubel–Lloyd indexes. However, Fontagné and Freudenberg (1997) underlined the shortcomings of this methodology, and proposed a new methodology based on Abd-El-Rahman (1986). Recent studies have used this method (Fontagné et al. 1997; Fukao et al. 2003). Flows are classified in three categories: one-way trade (OWT), two-way trade horizontally differentiated (TWTH), and two-way trade vertically differentiated (TWTV). This is a two-stepped classification:

(a) Flows are classified as OWT if the following equation holds:

$$\frac{Min(M_{ijtk}, M_{jitk})}{Max(M_{ijtk}, M_{jitk})} \leq \sigma$$

where σ is a threshold (here $\sigma = 0.1$).

(b) Remaining flows are considered vertically differentiated if:

$$1 - \alpha \leq \frac{UV_{ijtk}}{UV_{jitk}} \leq 1 + \alpha$$

where UV_{ijk} is the unit value of product k, and α is a threshold (here $\alpha = 0.25$).

Remaining flows are classified as horizontally differentiated.

We classify flows according to this procedure and then aggregate the data, to obtain the share of each trade type for a given i, j, year and ISIC Rev. 2 industry. For a large number of data, particularly in North America (see below), quantity data are missing from the observations, so unit values cannot be calculated. We were therefore obliged to introduce a fourth "type of trade" into our breakdown, corresponding to non-classified trade flows, denoted TWTnc. In addition, some bilateral trade flows with available unit values are still not classified. Indeed, we consider that when unit values differ by a ratio higher than 10, the probability of one (or both) partner(s) having "misclassified" the trade flow, possibly due to the existence of an HS 6-digit heading which groups together products which are too heterogeneous, cannot be ignored. In that case the bilateral trade flow may be OWT rather than TWTV. Although this method cannot replace the Grubel and Lloyd indicator, it is a useful complement. While GL evaluates the intensity of overlap in trade, the threshold approach measures the relative importance of the three trade types (see Fontagné and Freudenberg 1997 for more details). More specifically, it permits an analysis of specialization along the quality range.

The threshold method has recently been subject to criticism, on the ground that its applicability within the Chamberlin–Heckscher–Ohlin–Samuelson model (CHOS) is doubtful (Gullstrand 2002). There is also debate about the arbitrariness of chosen thresholds; it is doubtful whether there exists such thing as a non-arbitrary threshold. The case is not yet clear-cut; no method appears able to gather a consensus (Table 2.1). As our intention is not to prove the CHOS model right or

Table 2.1: Decomposition of trade (adapted from Fontagné and Freudenberg 2002)

Does the minority flow represent at least 10% of the majority flow?	Do export and import unit values differ less than 25%?	
	Yes	No
Yes	Two-way trade in horizontally differentiated products	Two-way trade in vertically differentiated products
No	One-way trade	

wrong, but to study the determinants of the repartition of trade between these three categories, we use the threshold-based method. Furthermore, this allows us to keep the possibility of comparing results with previous studies.

2.3 Quality range

To test the hypothesis that holds that regional integration is followed by a specialization along a quality range, we need to measure the quality of traded goods. We use unit value[5] as a proxy for quality, and define three ranges: low, medium and high quality. For each HS-6 product and for each year, we compute the world unit value average (noted $\overline{UV}$). We then classify each flow:

- Flows with unit values verifying $UV \in [\overline{UV} - 15\%, \overline{UV} + 15\%]$ belong to the medium range, along with the last decile of $]min, \overline{UV} - 15\%]$ and the first decile of $[\overline{UV} + 15\%, max]$.
- The first nine deciles of $[min, \overline{UV} - 15\%]$ are considered low range.
- The last nine deciles of $[\overline{UV} + 15\%, max[$ are considered high range.

This method permits us to take into account the high variability of unit values, and to have a significant share of trade in the medium range.

It is theoretically possible to classify any flow using this procedure, as long as the unit value is available. However, it appears wise to avoid associating flows with ranges when it was not possible to ascertain the validity of such a classification. Thus, when the variance of the unit value was too high for a product, flows were not classified.

Table 2.2: Worldwide share of the three trade types, 1989–2002 (%)

	OWT	TWTnc	TWTH	TWTV
1989	67.6	3.4	11.5	17.5
1990	65.7	3.0	12.1	19.1
1991	66.4	3.0	11.1	19.6
1992	65.0	2.9	11.9	20.2
1993	67.1	2.8	10.9	19.2
1994	65.1	2.5	12.4	20.0
1995	64.5	2.1	13.1	20.3
1996	64.0	2.2	12.9	20.9
1997	63.6	2.3	13.1	21.1
1998	61.8	2.5	13.5	22.2
1999	60.9	2.8	13.6	22.8
2000	61.8	2.9	13.1	22.3
2001	61.5	3.0	12.9	22.6
2002	62.7	2.8	12.6	21.9

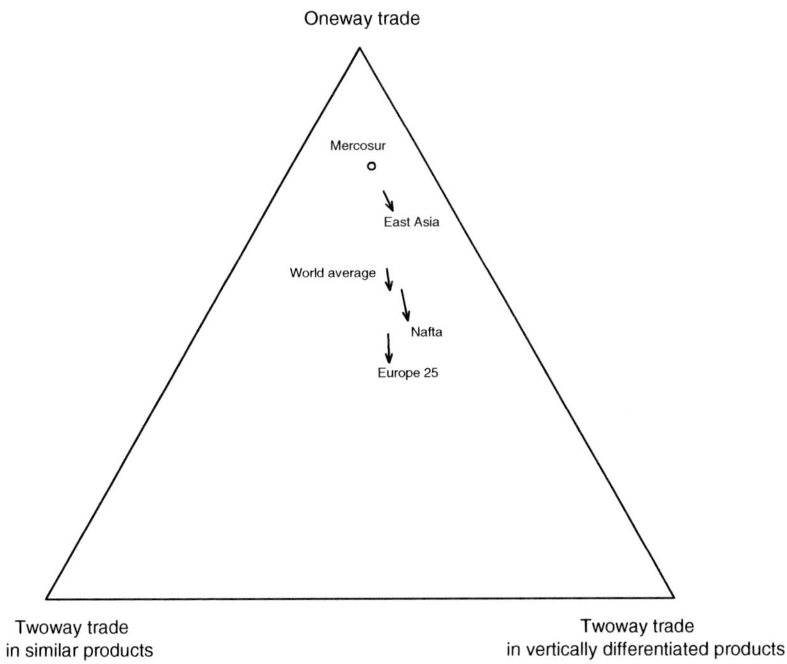

Figure 2.1: Evolution of the shares of the three trade types by integration zone, 1993–2002

3 Empirics of intra-industry trade

As can be seen in Table 2.2, there is a world trend towards the increase of IIT. The share of OWT in world trade has been falling regularly from 1989 to 1999, and has been stable since then, with the exception of 2002. OWT accounts for around 60 percent of world trade, vertically differentiated IIT constitutes two-thirds of remaining flows, and horizontally differentiated IIT one-third. If we adopt a strict definition of the similarity of goods by restricting IIT to horizontal IIT, then inter-industry trade accounts for almost 90 percent of overall trade.

This evolution of international trade towards IIT is mainly driven by Europe, NAFTA and East Asia. Figure 2.1 shows the evolution of the composition of trade of the four studied zones, using a triangle-shaped graph; each point is the center of mass, and vertices are weighted according to the respective share of each trade type. Arrows denote an evolution (since Mercosur's trade remained stable, it is represented by a point). As expected, Europe has the highest IIT level among the four studied integration zones, followed closely by NAFTA. East Asia and Mercosur have significantly lower IIT levels.

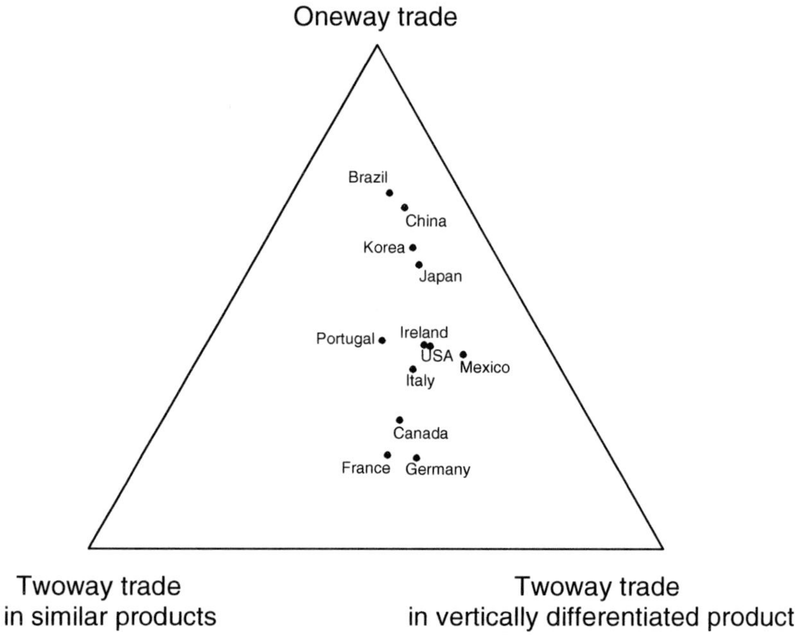

Figure 2.2: Trade types for various countries, 2002

As seen in Figure 2.2, IIT is quite unevenly distributed among countries. In most developing countries, OWT makes up more than 90 percent of trade. Not surprisingly, Brazil and China have the highest share of OWT in the set of countries selected for this graph. Korea and Japan, belonging to the least integrated zone, follow closely. European countries and members of NAFTA have a high level of IIT, with Germany and France being world leaders (along with Belgium, which is not shown in the figure).

3.1 Trade patterns in the European Union

We first focus on the EU, for which trade patterns have been extensively studied. Europe is a textbook case of intensive IIT trade; it has economies of comparable sizes, high standards of living, small distances between partners, and strong integration. As discussed above,

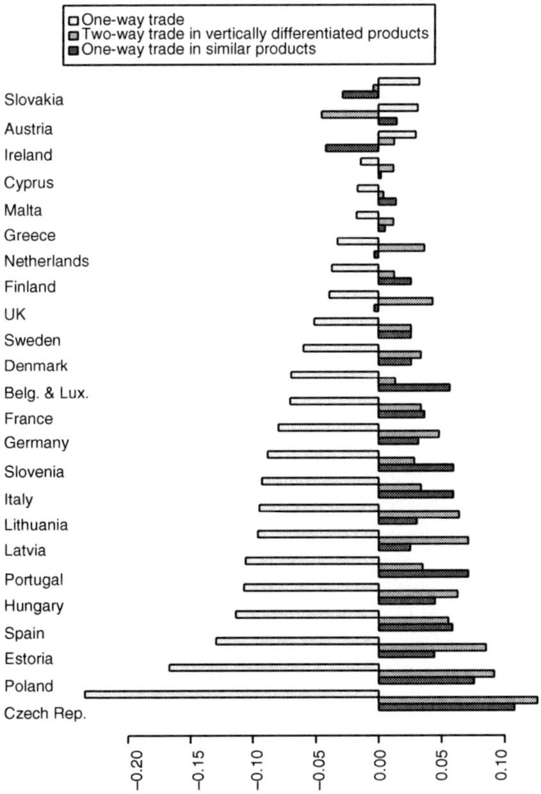

Figure 2.3: Evolution of the shares of trade types in Europe, 1993–2002

the share of IIT has been increasing since the beginning of the integration process. We are able to confirm previous results with updated information, and compare them with other regions (Figure 2.3).

Note that there are no declarations for Belgium before 1995 and France before 1994; therefore their trade flows are derived indirectly by using the declarations of their trade partners. In consequence, there is no bilateral trade flow between Belgium and France in 1994. These missing flows call for caution when interpreting the results for intra-EU trade before 1995.

3.1.1 EU trade with non-members

Shares of trade by type are given for total EU trade and trade of individual member countries for 2002 (Table 2.3), 1993 (Table 2.14) and 1995 (Table 2.15). Trade is further decomposed into extra- and intra-EU for 1995 and 2002. Looking first at total trade in 2002, Germany and France show the highest share of IIT, with the lowest shares of OWT, 40 percent and 41 percent, respectively. Belgium and Austria follow closely. The Netherlands and the UK have OWT of around 49 percent. One newcomer in the EU does more IIT than OWT: the Czech Republic (46 percent for OWT in 2002). Some other EU countries also have a large share of IIT; Spain is close to 50 percent, with Italy and Denmark not far behind. In contrast, for Greece, Ireland and, to a lesser extent, Portugal, trade is largely dominated by inter-industry flows. OWT is also largely dominant for the vast majority of new EU members.

From 1995 to 2002 IIT increased in the overwhelming majority of countries (24 out of 25). This rise is the most striking for Poland (+13 percent in IIT), Portugal (+11 percent), Hungary (+8 percent), Slovakia (+6 percent) and Czech Republic (+6 percent). Spain (+5 percent) continued its catching up with core EU countries (according to Fontagné et al. 1998, Spain's IIT share gained 12 percent from 1980 to 1994) whereas Greece increased its inter-industry specialization, as the 1980–1994 trend did not change. Also highly specialized, Ireland was one of the rare EU countries that did not increase its share of TWTH, in spite of its tremendous economic growth during the period. The Celtic Dragon rather oriented its specialization towards trade in quality (TWTV increased by four points). Among the newcomers, the rise in IIT is very marked for the Central and Eastern European countries (CEECs). The Mediterranean and Baltic countries stayed relatively apart. The newcomers contributed to the rise in IIT of the EU 25, with the trade patterns of the largest among them quickly converging towards the typical trade pattern for the core countries.

Table 2.3: Trade types, EU 25, 2002

	Extra-zone				Intra-zone				All			
	OWT	TWTnc	TWTH	TWTV	OWT	TWTnc	TWTH	TWTV	OWT	TWTnc	TWTH	TWTV
Austria	74.5	2.7	7.1	15.8	35.2	0.6	29.0	35.2	43.5	1.0	24.3	31.1
Belg. & Lux.	82.4	1.6	4.2	11.8	29.1	0.7	36.9	33.3	40.8	0.9	20.7	28.6
Cyprus	97.1	0.8	0.8	1.4	88.3	1.2	3.3	7.2	91.5	1.0	2.4	5.1
Czech Rep.	86.0	2.3	2.2	9.5	38.7	0.8	19.8	40.6	45.8	1.1	17.2	36.0
Denmark	83.0	1.6	3.6	11.8	47.7	1.2	19.0	32.1	58.9	1.3	14.1	25.6
Estonia	93.6	0.7	0.5	5.1	70.8	1.1	8.1	20.0	77.9	1.0	5.7	15.4
Finland	88.8	1.3	2.6	7.2	67.1	0.7	11.9	20.3	74.5	0.9	8.8	15.9
France	75.1	1.3	6.1	17.5	27.6	0.4	35.4	36.6	40.8	0.7	27.2	31.3
Germany	65.9	1.1	9.0	24.0	28.5	0.3	30.4	40.9	40.4	0.6	23.6	35.5
Greece	92.4	0.8	1.5	5.4	82.5	0.6	6.0	10.8	85.9	0.7	4.5	8.9
Hungary	85.0	1.6	3.9	9.5	55.2	0.8	13.7	30.4	62.1	1.0	11.4	25.5
Ireland	84.5	2.6	3.1	9.8	51.0	2.0	15.4	31.6	59.7	2.2	12.2	26.0
Italy	78.7	1.1	5.1	15.2	44.0	0.3	22.1	33.6	56.4	0.6	16.0	27.0
Latvia	91.7	1.1	2.0	5.2	82.2	1.1	4.7	12.0	84.4	1.1	4.1	10.5
Lithuania	87.2	0.9	3.8	8.1	83.9	0.6	4.7	10.8	84.8	0.7	4.4	10.1
Malta	97.4	0.6	0.0	2.0	85.4	3.6	3.1	7.9	87.9	3.0	2.4	6.7
Netherlands	82.4	1.8	3.4	12.4	34.1	1.1	28.2	36.7	48.5	1.3	20.8	29.5
Poland	90.9	1.3	1.6	6.2	57.1	0.5	13.8	28.6	64.1	0.7	11.2	24.0
Portugal	93.9	0.9	1.2	4.0	53.8	2.5	20.8	23.0	60.5	2.2	17.5	19.8
Slovakia	92.8	1.2	1.4	4.6	57.2	0.7	13.6	28.5	62.4	0.8	11.8	25.0
Slovenia	83.3	1.0	5.6	10.1	59.4	0.8	12.4	27.5	65.7	0.8	10.6	22.9
Spain	85.1	2.6	2.7	9.6	39.9	1.1	27.5	31.6	51.7	1.5	21.0	25.8
Sweden	71.1	1.6	9.4	17.9	52.2	1.0	17.1	29.7	58.0	1.2	14.7	26.1
UK	66.6	2.5	6.2	24.8	38.1	1.1	23.1	37.8	48.8	1.6	16.7	32.9
All	75.4	1.6	5.8	17.2	37.7	0.7	26.7	34.9	48.9	1.0	20.5	29.7

3.1.2 Intra-EU trade

Two-way-trade in horizontally differentiated products is essentially a regional type of trade; it is relatively minor at 6 percent of total trade when extra-EU trade is considered, except perhaps for Germany and Sweden with shares close to 10 percent. Two-way trade in vertically differentiated products is twice as high for trade within the EU 25 (35 percent in 2002) than for extra-EU trade (17 percent). One-way trade is around one-third of total intra-EU trade for eight countries, with the lowest shares (28 percent) in France and Germany. Most of the rise in TWTV stems from intra-EU trade.

Two-way trade in horizontally differentiated products is usually found between core countries, such Germany, France and Belgium (the world leaders for that trade type in 2002). After OWT, TWTV largely dominates in more peripheral countries, including the UK.

Not a single EU 25 country experienced a decrease in regional IIT from 1995 to 2002. For the whole EU, the IIT rise was mainly due to the rise in two-way trade in vertically differentiated products (+3 percent) whereas two-way trade in horizontally differentiated products stagnated. Within the EU, countries went into more specialization in quality ranges. From 1995 to 2002, TWTH stagnated or declined in a majority of industries, particularly in those where it was already highest. For instance, in the transport industry, TWTV rose at the expense of TWTH.

There is evidence of a specialization along quality ranges in intra-Europe trade (Table 2.4). The trade of Ireland, as stated above, is made up of a lot of high-quality OWT, which represents 43 percent of its intra-zone trade. Malta specialized in export-oriented high value-added products like pharmaceuticals and electronics, thanks to foreign investments; almost one-half of the country's exports are high-quality products. Specialization along the quality range is also very clear in vertical IIT; almost two-thirds of Czech TWTV is low-quality. Low-range specialization is also predominant in TWTV in Estonia, Poland, Slovakia, Slovenia and, to a lesser extent, Spain. The converse is true of Western countries like Germany, France, Denmark and Sweden.

3.2 Trade patterns in NAFTA

Trade among members of the North American Free Trade Agreement (NAFTA), which is composed of Canada, the USA and Mexico, contains further evidence that there is a link between IIT and economic integration (see Table 2.5 for IIT data for 2002, Table 2.17 for 1993 and

Table 2.4: Share of trade types in intra-Europe trade, taking into account quality range (1995–2002 average)

	OWT Range			TWTH Range			TWTV Range		
	Low	Medium	High	Low	Medium	High	Low	Medium	High
Austria	7.7	15.8	14.1	3.3	13.3	8.6	9.7	11.3	16.2
Belg. & Lux.	5.6	12.5	11.2	4.8	19.8	8.5	10.0	13.3	14.3
Cyprus	21.4	17.2	20.4	1.6	5.8	2.6	9.3	10.0	11.8
Czech Rep.	19.7	13.0	6.5	9.0	7.8	2.4	26.2	9.9	5.4
Denmark	11.3	18.9	20.0	2.4	8.5	6.5	7.8	9.7	14.9
Estonia	29.5	19.8	13.8	3.6	3.5	2.8	12.7	4.8	9.6
Finland	13.9	32.1	22.5	1.6	4.9	3.5	5.4	5.9	10.3
France	5.8	11.3	11.0	5.1	19.0	9.3	10.4	12.8	15.4
Germany	5.6	11.4	12.7	3.9	15.0	9.8	10.7	13.9	17.1
Greece	22.0	25.8	23.7	1.6	4.9	3.2	6.0	4.9	7.9
Hungary	17.4	20.2	15.4	4.2	6.2	3.8	13.1	7.3	12.4
Ireland	11.2	9.5	42.6	1.6	3.7	4.3	7.7	5.5	13.9
Italy	11.7	16.1	16.4	4.6	11.0	3.3	14.4	10.2	10.4
Latvia	43.1	29.6	8.8	1.7	1.5	1.5	8.6	2.8	2.5
Lithuania	35.8	32.4	12.0	2.6	2.3	1.0	8.4	3.3	2.4
Malta	16.8	16.1	31.3	0.8	2.0	1.2	8.2	8.6	15.0
Netherlands	6.5	18.3	16.1	4.2	13.6	6.8	9.1	10.9	14.6
Poland	25.1	20.3	11.7	5.4	5.4	2.1	18.6	6.4	5.1
Portugal	10.7	18.9	20.7	3.3	13.8	5.7	9.6	7.8	9.4
Slovakia	24.9	26.9	8.3	5.9	6.5	1.6	16.4	6.0	3.7
Slovenia	19.7	18.3	12.8	4.7	7.0	3.4	17.3	6.7	10.2
Spain	10.0	17.3	10.5	7.0	17.8	5.1	14.0	9.9	8.4
Sweden	8.1	23.1	19.4	2.5	8.4	5.9	7.0	8.9	16.9
UK	6.8	14.2	11.4	3.5	13.4	7.7	11.9	14.4	17.9
All	8.4	14.9	14.3	4.2	13.8	7.4	11.2	11.6	14.3

Note: Unclassified flows are ignored.

Table 2.5: Trade types, NAFTA, 2002

	Extra-zone				Intra-zone				All			
	OWT	TWTnc	TWTH	TWTV	OWT	TWTnc	TWTH	TWTV	OWT	TWTnc	TWTH	TWTV
Canada	88.6	2.4	1.9	7.1	23.2	20.1	25.0	31.6	40.0	15.6	19.1	25.3
Mexico	91.0	1.8	1.5	5.8	41.1	13.1	8.9	37.0	53.2	10.4	7.1	29.4
USA	70.4	3.2	6.1	20.2	28.9	17.5	19.4	34.3	55.9	8.2	10.8	25.2
All	73.5	3.0	5.4	18.1	29.4	17.5	19.2	33.9	52.3	10.0	12.0	25.7

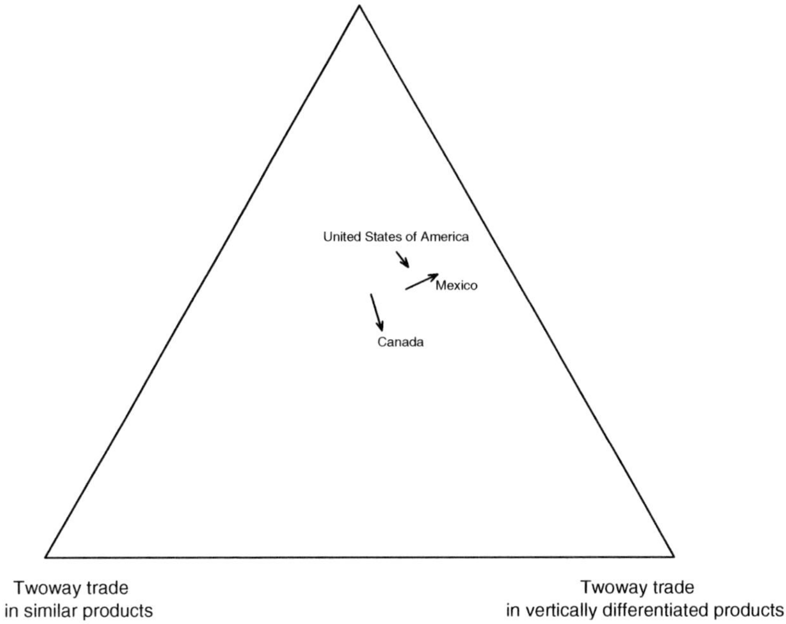

Figure 2.4: Evolution of the shares of the three trade types in NAFTA, 1993–2002

Table 2.18 for 1995). Since 1995, OWT has made up less than one-third of total regional trade. In 2002 it stood at 29 percent, but increased from a lower point in 1999. However, non-classified trade is very high within NAFTA because of the lack of reported quantities (and therefore unit values) between the US and Canada. Finally, we can be quite confident that NAFTA trade patterns are similar to EU trade patterns.

Two-way trade in horizontally differentiated products is the more important between the US and Canada, which does not come as a surprise given the proximity of these two high-income countries. Mexico does more two-way trade in vertically differentiated products. Given the non-classified trade problem, we should not over-analyze the change in TWTH and TWTV; from 1995 to 2002 non-classified trade for Mexico within NAFTA rose by 10 points, at the expense of TWTH. It seems that IIT reached a peak in the late 1990s, thanks to a surge in TWTV as Mexico entered NAFTA, driven by regional segmentation of production along quality ranges which obviously occurred in the car industry, for example. From then on, NAFTA countries may have been respecializing.

As in other regions, extra-zone trade is largely dominated by inter-industry trade. Thanks to its size and development, the US carries out between one-quarter and one-third of its trade in IIT, but Mexico and Canada carry out around 90 percent of their extra-NAFTA trade as OWT.

3.3 Trade patterns in East Asia

The breakdown into intra-zone and extra-zone trade is particularly insightful for East Asia (China, Hong Kong, Indonesia, Japan, South Korea, Malaysia, Taiwan, the Philippines, Singapore and Thailand). Indeed, Asian countries do almost all of their IIT with their East Asian partners (see Table 2.6 for IIT in 2002, Table 2.20 for 1993, and Table 2.21 for 1995).

Two-way trade in horizontally differentiated products is insignificant in extra-East Asia trade, reaching only 3 percent in 2002 for the whole zone, and 8 percent for Japan. Within Asia, it remains very limited, reaching 5 percent in 2002, compared to 27 percent within the EU. Korea and Singapore are slight exceptions, at 8 percent and 9

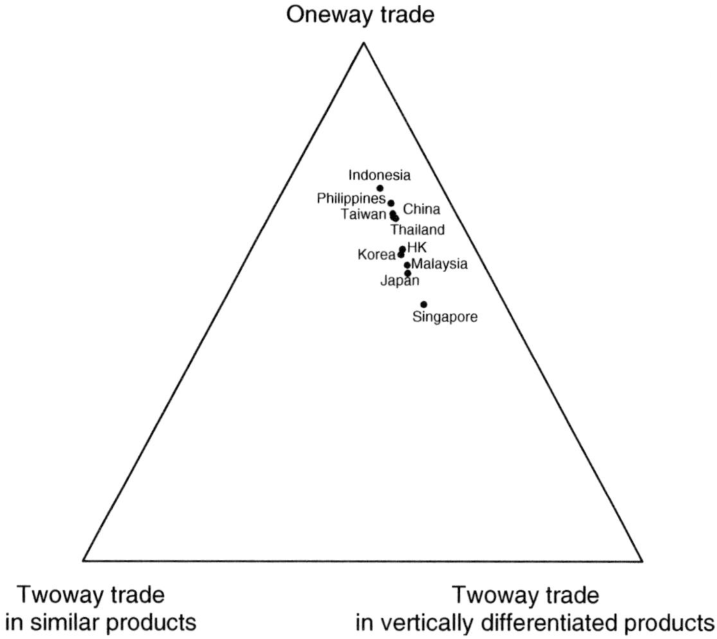

Figure 2.5: Trade types in East Asia, 2002

Table 2.6: Trade types, East Asia, 2002

	Extra-zone				Intra-zone				All			
	OWT	TWTnc	TWTH	TWTV	OWT	TWTnc	TWTH	TWTV	OWT	TWTnc	TWTH	TWTV
China	90.3	2.4	1.0	6.2	76.0	1.2	5.0	17.8	81.3	1.9	2.7	11.1
Hong Kong	85.0	3.3	1.7	10.0	74.5	1.2	5.9	18.4	78.2	1.9	4.5	15.5
Indonesia	95.0	0.6	1.0	3.4	83.3	0.8	3.9	12.0	89.7	0.7	2.3	7.3
Japan	74.3	1.2	7.6	16.8	75.0	1.4	3.6	20.0	74.6	1.3	5.8	18.3
Korea	84.6	1.4	3.0	11.1	70.2	1.0	7.6	21.2	77.9	1.2	5.1	15.8
Malaysia	86.1	2.5	2.4	9.0	63.1	4.7	7.5	24.7	74.2	3.6	5.1	17.1
Taiwan	86.1	4.9	1.4	7.6	79.4	1.5	4.2	14.9	82.6	3.1	2.9	11.4
Philippines	92.9	1.5	1.2	4.5	79.1	2.0	3.0	15.9	86.2	1.8	2.0	10.0
Singapore	78.4	2.9	3.2	15.5	59.0	3.6	8.7	28.7	67.8	3.3	6.2	22.7
Thailand	91.0	2.4	1.4	5.2	76.4	1.4	3.9	18.2	83.4	1.9	2.7	11.9
All	85.0	2.2	3.0	9.8	74.2	1.6	5.2	19.1	79.8	1.9	4.1	14.3

percent, respectively. All this is to be expected, given the relatively large per capita income gaps within the zone and the large geographical distances between the East Asian industrialized countries and their counterparts in the Western hemisphere. The continuous growth in East Asia should fuel further TWTH in the future. However, past growth in China has not yielded additional TWTH as a share of total trade.

Two-way trade in vertically differentiated products is not very developed for extra-East Asian trade; it reached 10 percent in 2002, compared with 17 percent for the EU. In contrast, almost all the East Asian countries do a very significant share of their intra-zone trade in TWTV. Within East Asia, TWTV rose by 4 percentage points between 1995 and 2002, to reach 19 percent. It increased by 5 percentage points or more in all countries except China, Taiwan and Hong Kong. This trade type was particularly dynamic for the ASEAN countries.

Singapore, Malaysia and Korea are the leading Asian countries in IIT. Nonetheless, IIT accounts for more than one-fifth of intra-zone trade for the Philippines, which is a poorer country. Within the world's major economic regions – the US, the EU and Japan – the last region is by far the most specialized.

This high level (and growth) of TWTV goes hand-in-hand with the deep regional division of production processes in East Asia. The integration of production networks within East Asia goes beyond segmentation at the stage of production level (e.g. intermediate goods versus final goods)[6] to trade in quality ranges within products.

China and to a lesser extent other countries in Greater China (Taiwan and Hong Kong) seem to be left aside from the development of TWTV in East Asia. However, if we keep in the database products for which data are considered to be unreliable (see below), China is found to have increased its regional TWTV share by 5 percentage points. It is common knowledge among trade data specialists that Chinese and Hong Kong trade data are unreliable, particularly because of re-exportation. Concerning Taiwan, trade flows are only reported by its partners (mirror flows) since this country does not belong to the UN, to which the trade flows are reported. Consequently we should be cautious with the results for these countries. However, the integration of China into the East Asian production and trade networks seems to have more to do with a division of labor across stages of production than with intra-industry trade, including trade in quality (see Gaulier et al. 2004).

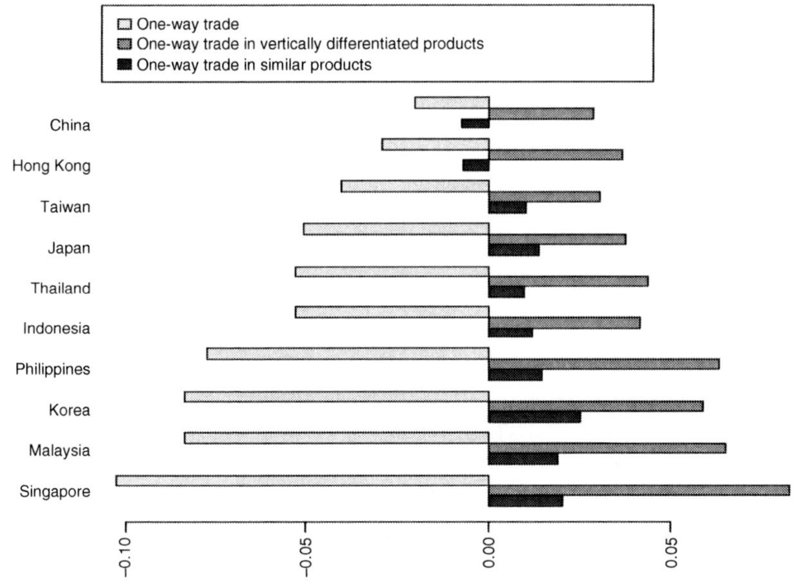

Figure 2.6: Evolution of the shares of trade types in East Asia, 1993–2002

3.4 Trade patterns in Mercosur

Among the studied zones, Mercosur (Argentina, Brazil, Paraguay and Uruguay) is the one where the share of IIT is the lowest by far, and the shares of the three trade types have been stable since 1993, as seen in Figure 2.1. More precisely, comparing Table 2.7 for 2002 and Table 2.24 for 1995, it is clear that stability prevails. The only

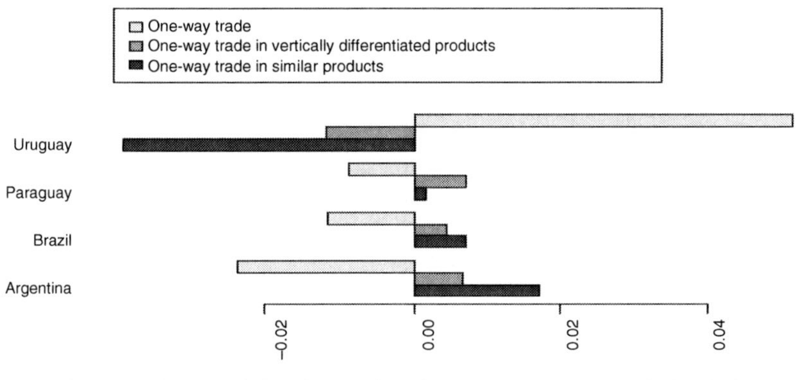

Figure 2.7: Evolution of the shares of trade types in Mercosur, 1993–2002

Table 2.7: Trade types, Mercosur, 2002

	Extra-zone				Intra-zone				All			
	OWT	TWTnc	TWTH	TWTV	OWT	TWTnc	TWTH	TWTV	OWT	TWTnc	TWTH	TWTV
Argentina	95.2	0.4	1.0	3.4	67.1	0.2	16.5	16.2	88.9	0.4	4.5	6.2
Brazil	89.6	1.0	2.2	7.2	71.3	0.3	14.4	14.0	87.7	0.9	3.5	7.9
Paraguay	99.3	0.3	0.3	0.1	96.2	1.0	0.5	2.4	97.5	0.7	0.4	1.4
Uruguay	97.5	0.5	0.8	1.3	85.1	0.4	4.2	10.2	92.4	0.5	2.2	5.0
All	91.3	0.8	1.9	6.0	73.2	0.3	13.0	13.5	88.5	0.8	3.6	7.2

significant change that can be noted is the 5 percentage point fall of Uruguayan IIT. This drop is mainly a drop of intra-zone IIT, and extra-zone IIT remains unaffected.

Most IIT in Mercosur occurs between Argentina and Brazil. Brazil enjoys the world's tenth biggest economy, with probably the most advanced industrial sector in South America. Still, Brazil's trade is mostly OWT, at 88.9 percent of total trade. Intra-zone trade represents a small part of Brazilian trade, and is more IIT-oriented, with TWTV and TWTH each representing more than 14 percent of intra-Mercosur trade. Argentina follows the same pattern, with intra-zone IIT as high as 33 percent, equally divided between TWTH and TWTV. Further disaggregation shows that most intra-industry trade between Argentina and Brazil takes place within the automobile industry.

Paraguay and Uruguay offer a different picture. Among the four members of Mercosur, IIT is at its lowest in Paraguay, where OWT represents 97.5 percent of total trade; intra-zone trade is also mostly OWT, at 96 percent. Paraguay also has the lowest per capita GDP. The agricultural sector is significant, and mostly export-oriented. There is a large informal sector featuring re-exportation of imported goods to Argentina or Brazil: IIT may therefore be under-estimated. Although agriculture is less important in Uruguay, it makes up more than half of the country's exports. Uruguayan trade is mainly OWT (92 percent), although the country developed intra-industry trade within Mercosur, as 10 percent of intra-zone trade is TWTV. Yet, as stated above, both TWTV and TWTH in intra-zone trade have fallen since 1995, which may be a consequence of the integration process. This fact does not fit in the scheme proposed in this chapter; it could be explained by the great difference in size and endowments between Uruguay and its patterns.

3.5 Trade types by industries and stages of production

In the EU, as elsewhere in the world, the vast majority of new TWTV flows were concentrated in machinery (including electrical, electronic and transportation machinery) and precision apparatus. Chemical products, which are also often sold on an intra-industry basis, especially within the EU and NAFTA, contributed negatively to the growth of TWTH and moderately to the growth of TWTV. Table 2.8 shows the distribution of world trade by types for product sections. The highest TWTH share is found in transportation machinery (further disaggregation would point to the car industry as a major contributor to TWTH).

Table 2.8: Trade types by sector, 1995–2002

	1995				2002			
	OWT	TWTnc	TWTH	TWTV	OWT	TWT	TWTH	TWTV
Agriculture	86.4	0.2	6.0	7.3	84.5	0.3	6.3	8.9
Food and beverages	74.8	0.2	11.1	13.8	69.3	0.4	12.4	17.8
Mining products	39.0	0.3	5.7	5.1	86.1	0.5	5.5	7.9
Chemicals	57.9	1.6	17.3	23.2	57.6	2.3	15.4	24.8
Light industry	68.1	3.3	8.0	20.5	72.2	3.5	7.1	17.2
Wood and paper	65.6	1.2	15.0	18.2	62.0	2.2	15.1	20.7
Textile and clothing	73.0	0.6	9.1	17.3	75.6	0.9	7.4	16.1
Pottery products	65.4	2.5	9.0	23.1	64.4	3.0	8.4	24.2
Basic metals	62.2	1.5	16.7	19.6	61.7	1.9	15.4	21.0
General machinery	57.8	4.1	10.9	27.1	53.3	5.4	10.7	30.6
Electrical machinery	54.4	4.9	11.6	29.1	55.6	6.1	8.9	29.5
Precision apparatus	44.4	6.4	11.9	37.4	42.2	9.2	9.7	39.0
Transport machinery	46.2	4.8	29.3	19.7	43.1	3.8	30.5	22.5
Others	65.3	9.3	5.1	20.2	67.4	10.6	8.1	14.0
All	64.5	2.1	13.1	20.3	62.7	2.8	12.6	21.9

Table 2.9: Trade types by stage of production, 1995–2002

	1995				2002			
	OWT	TWTnc	TWTH	TWTV	OWT	TWT	TWTH	TWTV
Consumption	68.5	1.5	12.1	18.0	66.5	2.0	12.8	18.7
Investment	60.6	3.1	11.5	24.9	58.3	4.7	10.2	26.8
Primary	87.4	0.4	5.7	6.5	87.1	0.7	6.3	6.0
Parts and components	43.3	8.1	14.9	33.6	40.0	8.5	14.5	36.9
Transformed	64.9	1.4	14.8	19.2	64.2	1.6	13.4	20.8
All	64.5	2.1	13.1	20.3	62.7	2.8	12.6	21.9

General and electrical machinery and precision apparatus have very large shares of TWTV. Consequently, the increase in IIT for aggregate trade is partly due to composition effects: IIT increases as the share of IIT-intensive industries increases. Trade in agriculture or mining is generally OWT. More differentiated products in the food and textile industries have a significant share of IIT.

As shown in Table 2.9, among stages of production, "Parts and components" are the most IIT intensive (TWTV = 37 percent, TWTH = 15 percent for world trade in 2002), followed by "Investment goods" (27 percent and 10 percent). "Transformed goods" and "Consumption goods" have medium levels of IIT. Trade in "Primary goods" is overwhelming dominated by OWT. The main contributor to the growth in

IIT is two-way trade in vertically differentiated industries, in intermediate products and among them parts and components.

4 Determinants of intra-industry trade

In a Ricardian or Hecksher–Ohlin model, it is expected that trade occurs between countries with different endowments and different economic structures. However, trade between developed countries with similar endowments and structures accounts for a great part of world trade, and it is often intra-industry trade. This kind of trade cannot be explained by classic comparative advantage theory, because there is no such effect in this case. According to the monopolistic competition model, the appearance of intra-industry trade is caused by the desire for variety. Consumers in every country have a preference for variety. But it is not efficient to produce every variety at home: in order to benefit from economies of scale, each country produces only a small number of varieties. Intra-industry trade then occurs so that consumers can enjoy the choice between similar products. The costs of such trade, made up of transportation and other transactions costs, are lower than the benefit for the consumer. This phenomenon has been modeled by Lancaster (1980) and Krugman (1979). Helpman and Krugman (1985) developed a model to account simultaneously for inter- and intra-industry trade. This model features two countries (North and South), two factors (labor and capital), and two goods. It incorporates horizontal product differentiation, factor endowments, decreasing costs and preference for variety. Greenaway et al. (1994), using the same assumptions, and assuming that trade is balanced, show that IIT increases when differences in market size and in the labor/capital ratio are lower. It is generally accepted that the determinants of vertical and horizontal IIT are different. Horizontal IIT is often found to be more sensitive to efficient scale and monopolistic competition, while vertical IIT responds mainly to factor endowments. To quote Fontagné and Freudenberg (1997: 5), "different countries will engage in IIT in vertically differentiated products whereas similar ones will engage in IIT of varieties within similar qualities." To test the validity of this assumption, we compute the determinants of IIT for each trade type with a different equation.

4.1 Country characteristics

Country-related determinants of IIT can be divided into two categories. The first is the market size and endowments of the two partners. The second includes the geographical distance, the usual variable in gravity models.

We have the following expectations concerning market size and endowments:

(1) IIT is positively correlated with average country size; the larger the market size, the larger the demand for differentiated products (Lancaster 1980). Since the analysis takes place on a bilateral basis, the arithmetic mean of the GDPs is used as an indicator of country size, following the methodology proposed by Bergstrand (1990). GDPs come from the CHELEM database.[7]

(2) IIT is negatively correlated with country size difference: countries with similar size will trade similar goods. In contrast, countries with different sizes will have different abilities to produce differentiated products (Dixit and Norman 1980; Helpman 1981). Following Balassa (1986a) and Balassa and Bauwens (1987) we use the normalized difference in GDPs:

$$GDPD_{ij} = 1 + \frac{wln(w) + (1 - w)\,ln(1 - w)}{ln(2)}$$

where $w \equiv \frac{GDP_i}{GDP_i + GDP_i}$. The advantage of this indicator over the absolute difference in GDPs is its insensitivity to the absolute size of the partners. However, the results are similar whichever indicator is used in the regression.

(3) IIT is positively correlated with standard of living: demand for differentiated products grows as per capita income increases (Linder 1961). PCIs come from the CHELEM database.

(4) Economic distance is negatively correlated with horizontal IIT and positively correlated with vertical IIT; absolute differences in per capita income stands for differences in resource endowments (Dixit and Norman 1980; Helpman 1981) and differences in demand structure (Linder 1961).

We also introduce distance indicators that are commonly used in gravity models:

(1) IIT is negatively correlated with the average level of trade barriers. Tariffs can be measured at the bilateral level and for each product of the HS-6 nomenclature in the TRAINS database from UNCTAD.

We base our investigation on this rather crude measurement of tariffs, namely considering weighted averages of MFN tariffs among the three partners. These tariffs are aggregated from Jon Haveman's treatment of TRAINS data (UTBC Database[8]) in order to match our ISIC Rev. 2 industry classification using the world imports as weights for HS-6 products.

(2) The participation in regional integration schemes has a positive impact on IIT. A large literature has tried to provide evidence that integration schemes and trade liberalization have a positive impact on IIT. Globerman (1992) suggested from the example of NAFTA that free trade agreements could increase IIT, and Ocampo and Esguerra (1994) relate the trade liberalization of the 1980s and the rise of IIT. PTA is a dummy variable that takes one as value when both trading countries belong to the same Preferential Trade Agreement at the year t, zero otherwise.[9]

(3) Geographic distance has a negative impact on IIT, as it increases transport, communication and transactions costs; consumers are likely to trade diversity for price (see for example Balassa 1986b). We use CEPII-calculated weighted bilateral distances.[10] As geographic distance is not a perfect proxy of these costs, we introduce two more variables from the same data set:
    (a) countries sharing a common border will have a greater share of IIT, taking account of locational advantages (Grubel and Lloyd 1975);
    (b) the use of a common language reduces transaction costs and thus has a positive impact on IIT.

4.2 Industry characteristics

We introduce two sector-specific variables to test the relationship between product differentiation, scale and IIT.

(1) Product differentiation allows consumers to satisfy their preference for variety (Krugman 1979; Lancaster 1980; Helpman 1981), and favors higher levels of IIT. In accordance with Fontagné and Freudenberg (1997) we use the following ratio to measure product differentiation:

$$Diff_{ijtc} = \frac{\sum_{k \in c} V_{ijtk} \dfrac{MAX(UV_{ijtk}, UV_{..k})}{MIN(UV_{ijtk}, UV_{..k})}}{\sum_{k \in c} V_{ijtk}}$$

This ratio can be computed at any level of aggregation and is available for any country and industry.

(2) Economies of scale increase specialization and lower production costs, and therefore have a positive impact on IIT. Several variables are proposed in the literature to measure scale economies. In this study, average establishment sizes are used as a proxy for scale economies. Those come from the Trade and Production 1976–1999 database made available by Alessandro Nicita and Marcelo Olarreaga at the World Bank, which compiles this data for 67 developing and developed countries at the ISIC Rev. 2 3-digit industry level over the period 1976–99. The original data comes principally from United Nations statistical sources, COMTRADE database for trade and UNIDO industrial statistics for production.

5 Estimated model

The model is a panel data model with four dimensions: reference countries (*i*), partner countries (*j*), time (*t*) and industry (*c*). We use the Generalized Linear Model (GLM). The estimated equation is as follow, using a logit-log specification:

$$\begin{aligned} Sh_{ijtc} = {} & \alpha_1 GDP_{ijt} + \alpha_2 GDPD_{ijt} + \alpha_3 PCI_{ijt} + \alpha_4 PCID_{ijt} \\ & + \alpha_5 TARIFF_{ijtc} + \alpha_6 DIST_{ij} + \alpha_7 CONTIG_{ij} \\ & + \alpha_8 COMLANG_{ij} + \alpha_9 DIFF_{ijtc} + \alpha_{10} ESIZE_{itc} \end{aligned}$$

where *Sh* is the share of OWT, the share of TWTV or the share of TWTH. This model is similar to a gravity model, as it relates in a multiplicative manner the dependent variable to the distance between partners and their economic size. The main difference is that this model does not have a value as dependent variable, but a share; the purpose is to distinguish the effect of these determinants on different types of trade.

Table 2.10 presents the variables used and their expected signification. Independent variables, including dummies, are standardized thus allowing comparison of their respective impact on IIT; their mean is set to zero and their standard deviation to one.

As seen in Figure 2.8, variables of interest are not homoscedastic: when a logarithm specification is used, the variance of residuals is dependent on predicted values. Variances and standard errors are understated when using OLS, and observations with high shares are not given due weight. In order to stabilize the variance of dependent

Table 2.10: Determinants of the share of one-way trade and their expected sign

Variable	Exp. sign	Indicator
Country-specific determinants		
Size (GDP)	–	Average GDP of the two countries
Difference in size (GDPD)	+	Normalized difference of GDPs
Income per capita (PCI)	–	Average PCI of the two partners
Economic distance (PCID)	+	Differences of PCIs
Tariffs (TARIFF)	+	Bilateral tariffs
Geographic distance (DIST)	+	Weighted bilateral distances
Contiguity (CONTIG)	–	Dummy
Common language (COMLANG)	–	Dummy
Common integration zone (IZONE)	–	Dummy
Industry-specific determinants		
Product differentiation (DIFF)	–	Differentiation indicator
Economies of scale (ESIZE)	–	Average establishment size

variables, we transform them using a logit link function (see the result in Figure 2.8). This specification is also more accurate theoretically; by construction, the shares of the three trade types follow a binomial distribution (the parameter being the probability of belonging to a given type); the canonical link function for binomial distributions is the logit. When all trade is completely inter-industry, it is obviously impossible to use the logit of vertical or horizontal IIT share. In these cases, we use *logit*(0.005) (checking that $0.005 < \min(TWTf)$, where *TWTf* is the share of vertical or horizontal intra-industry trade for flow *f*).

Countries report imports and exports to the United Nations. During the harmonization of the data, values are transformed to ensure that exports from country *a* to country *b* are equal to import of country *b* from country *a*. However, both flows are included in the database; every bit of information is reported twice. In order to avoid underestimating standard errors, we only use flows verifying $i < j$.

We introduce four fixed effects: *i*, *j*, *t*, *c*, for each dimension of our panel data. Although some studies found that controlling for country effect was not useful when analyzing a homogeneous group of countries (e.g. Fontagné et al. 1997 in the case of the European Union), it appears that in the case of a worldwide study, the heterogeneity bias due to countries is not negligible. It turned out that introducing those four effects as random effects did not have a major impact on the

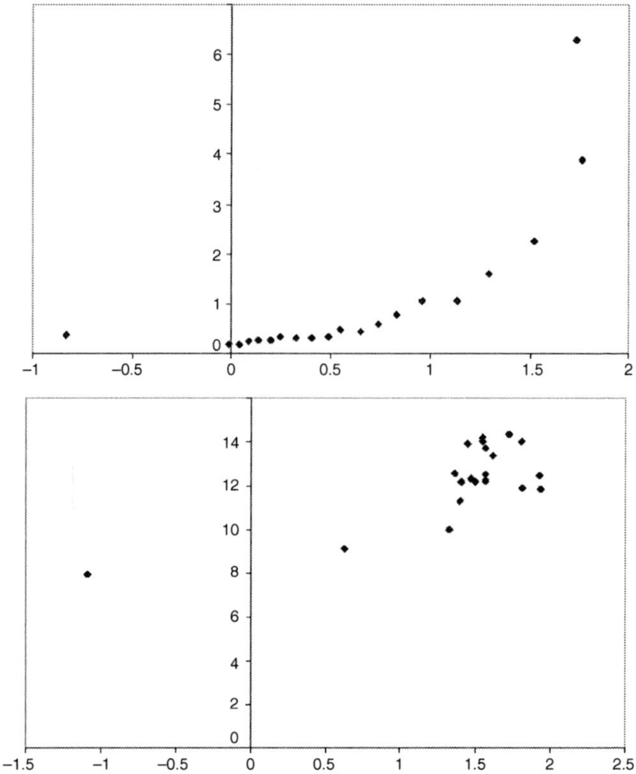

Figure 2.8: Homoscedasticity plots for the share of OWT

results; consequently, regressions presented here are not mixed models. In order to measure the impact of country-specific effect on IIT, we also compute the regression with only two fixed effects: *t* and *c*.

It could have been desirable to introduce more variables, or to use better proxies. For example, it is expected that IIT is negatively correlated with the degree of product standardization. Fukao et al. (2003) among others also proposed a theoretical model to link foreign direct investments and IIT, and some studies find empirical support for this view (see Aturupane et al. 1997 for the case of trade between Eastern and Western Europe). However, there is a trade-off between more variables and more observations, as most variables do not cover all countries in the world on a bilateral basis; any worldwide study of the determinants of IIT is doomed to be plagued with missing values. We settled on a compromise that accounts for most of world trade in value, and nevertheless introduces what we considered the most important variables.

6 Estimation results

As stated above, different kinds of IIT have different kind of determinants. To take this fact into account, we computed regressions for the share of OWT, the share of TWTH and the share of TWTV.

Table 2.11 presents the results of the regression 11, without fixed effects *i* and *j*. All coefficients were statistically very significant

Table 2.11: Results for main regressions without fixed effects for *i* and *j*

	OWT	TWTV	TWTH
Intercept	9.306[a]	-8.412[a]	-10.234[a]
	(0.030)	(0.029)	(0.030)
GDP	-1.664[a]	1.157[a]	0.955[a]
	(0.008)	(0.008)	(0.008)
GDPD	0.731[a]	-0.391[a]	-0.570[a]
	(0.005)	(0.005)	(0.005)
PCI	-0.616[a]	0.504[a]	0.183[a]
	(0.010)	(0.010)	(0.010)
PCID	0.519[a]	-0.406[a]	-0.377[a]
	(0.006)	(0.005)	(0.006)
Tariff	-0.088[a]	0.136[a]	-0.148[a]
	(0.005)	(0.005)	(0.005)
Dist	1.115[a]	-0.808[a]	-0.821[a]
	(0.006)	(0.006)	(0.007)
Contig	-0.094[a]	-0.018[a]	0.265[a]
	(0.003)	(0.003)	(0.003)
Comlang	-0.350[a]	0.050[a]	0.074[a]
	(0.004)	(0.004)	(0.004)
Izone	-0.357[a]	0.220[a]	0.227[a]
	(0.003)	(0.003)	(0.003)
Diff	-0.147[a]	0.163[a]	0.045[a]
	(0.007)	(0.006)	(0.007)
Esize	-0.120[a]	0.074[a]	-0.230[a]
	(0.007)	(0.007)	(0.007)
N	635,973	635,973	635,973
R^2	0.51	0.37	0.36
Root MSE	486.8	469.8	495.6

($p<0.001$). A comparison with Table 2.10 shows that for OWT all signs fit with what was expected, except for tariffs; the coefficient is significantly negative, although a positive coefficient was expected. Yet, it is quite small compared to other coefficients. The coefficient associated with tariffs was positive for TWTV, suggesting that tariffs tend to favor vertical differentiation, for which price elasticity is arguably lower. In contrast, the coefficient on tariffs for TWTH is negative, suggesting that an increase in tariffs made the trade of horizontally differentiated products harder, probably because the consumer then trades diversity for price. Indicators of economic distance (geographic distance, contiguity, share of a common language) have a strong impact on IIT. The coefficient for contiguity is negative for OWT and TWTV and positive for TWTH; this is coherent with predictions of Grubel and Lloyd (1975). Small trade costs, in particular low tariffs and participation in a preferential trade agreement, unambiguously favor TWTH.

Results for the model with fixed effects for *i* and *j* are shown in Table 2.12. If we compare Table 2.12 and Table 2.11, we note a lot of similarities, but also striking differences. It appears that distance indicators are very robust and have similar behavior in both tables. Distance, contiguity and share of a common language have the same sign in both regressions, and the size of their coefficients remains comparable. This is also true for tariffs and participation in a common integration zone. Most of the literature also finds that distance is the most robust determinant of IIT. Determinants related to factor endowments and market structure are affected by the introduction of country fixed effects. GDP and per capita income are the clearest examples: both have their signs reversed. This result is expected, as dummies for countries attracted most of the country-specific effects. The difference in GDPs has no significant impact on OWT; however, it is positively linked with TWTV. Once country effects are taken into account, countries with different GDPs tend to trade vertically differentiated products, and countries with similar GDPs tend to trade horizontally differentiated products. The difference in per capita income has the same sign in both models, its effect being smaller when country effects are introduced.

Krugman and Venables (1990) have argued that as transportation costs fall, three different allocation patterns may exist in a two-country economy: high shipping costs lead to production in both countries, medium shipping costs lead to production in the country with high wages but good access to markets, and low shipping costs prompt allo-

Table 2.12: Results for main regressions with fixed effects for *i* and *j*

	OWT	TWTV	TWTH
Intercept	7.640[a]	−8.180[a]	−6.128[a]
	(1.238)	(1.211)	(1.293)
GDP	0.752[a]	−1.301[a]	−0.275[a]
	(0.038)	(0.037)	(0.040)
GDPD	−0.001	0.336[a]	−0.351[a]
	(0.013)	(0.012)	(0.013)
PCI	0.556[a]	−0.481[a]	−0.143[a]
	(0.026)	(0.025)	(0.027)
PCID	0.247[a]	−0.234[a]	−0.276[a]
	(0.008)	(0.008)	(0.008)
Tariff	−0.111[a]	0.195[a]	−0.011
	(0.006)	(0.006)	(0.007)
Dist	1.101[a]	−0.904[a]	−0.397[a]
	(0.009)	(0.008)	(0.009)
Contig	−0.128[a]	−0.045[a]	0.281[a]
	(0.003)	(0.003)	(0.003)
Comlang	−0.195[a]	0.135[a]	0.084[a]
	(0.006)	(0.006)	(0.006)
Izone	−0.299[a]	0.121[a]	0.489[a]
	(0.005)	(0.005)	(0.005)
Diff	0.014[a]	0.093[a]	0.074[a]
	(0.006)	(0.006)	(0.007)
Esize	−0.396[a]	0.133[a]	0.207[a]
	(0.010)	(0.009)	(0.010)
N	635,973	635,973	635,973
R^2	0.57	0.44	0.41
Root MSE	453.6	443.6	474.0

cation of production in the country with low wages but worse access to markets. There would be a U-shaped relationship between transport costs and industrial output of peripheral countries. In an attempt to test this relationship, we introduce square distance in the model. We find support for such a hypothesis in Table 2.13. Results are very similar to those obtained in Table 2.12. Distance has a significant positive impact on TWTV, while square distance has a strongly negative impact, suggesting that there is a U-shaped relationship between distance and vertically differentiated IIT. For horizontally differentiated IIT, square distance appears statistically insignificant; the relationship is linear.

Table 2.13: Results for main regressions with one additional variable: square distance (Dist2)

	OWT	TWTV	TWTH
Intercept	7.684[a]	-8.285[a]	-6.128[a]
	(1.238)	(1.210)	(1.294)
GDP	0.723[a]	-1.222[a]	-0.276[a]
	(0.039)	(0.038)	(0.041)
GDPD	0.011	0.305[a]	-0.351[a]
	(0.013)	(0.013)	(0.014)
PCI	0.552[a]	-0.469[a]	-0.142[a]
	(0.026)	(0.026)	(0.027)
PCID	0.252[a]	-0.246[a]	-0.277[a]
	(0.008)	(0.008)	(0.009)
Tariff	-0.118[a]	0.220[a]	-0.015[b]
	(0.006)	(0.006)	(0.007)
Dist	0.573[a]	0.441[a]	-0.367[a]
	(0.062)	(0.061)	(0.065)
Dist2	0.565[a]	-1.439[a]	-0.033
	(0.066)	(0.065)	(0.069)
Contig	-0.137[a]	-0.022[a]	0.282[a]
	(0.004)	(0.004)	(0.004)
Comlang	-0.199[a]	0.146[a]	0.084[a]
	(0.006)	(0.006)	(0.007)
Izone	-0.282[a]	0.077[a]	0.487[a]
	(0.006)	(0.006)	(0.006)
Diff	0.017[a]	0.089[a]	0.075[a]
	(0.007)	(0.007)	(0.007)
Esize	-0.397[a]	0.136[a]	0.208[a]
	(0.010)	(0.010)	(0.010)
N	635,973	635,973	635,973
R^2	0.58	0.44	0.41
Root MSE	453.6	443.3	474.0

Note: Fixed effect for *i* and *j* are included.

Before concluding, we discuss the main results and their implications regarding economic integration. High share of intra-industry, besides being an indicator for integration (and industrialization since it concerns mainly manufactured goods), can be viewed as desirable by promoters of currency areas as it implies a lower frequency of asymmetric shocks. Industry specific shocks are not present if the specialization is intra-industry and "intra-quality" (TWTH). As regards asymmetry of shocks, vertical intra-industry could be intermediary between horizontal intra-industry and inter-industry. Short distances are necessary for horizontal intra-industry to take a significant share of trade. A common border is also important, particularly by allowing cross-border trade of products which usually are not internationally traded (such as cement or other heavy materials).

Vertical intra-industry is also very sensitive to distance. The quadratic relationship between distance and TWTV implies a very high response to distance of this type of trade. The inverted U-curve is of less practical significance since its declining part is attained for very short distances. The contiguity is not significant in that case. On the contrary, the existence of a common language favors greatly vertical intra-industry: business networks and good communications may have an important role.

Institutional integration (more generally preferential trade agreements; variable Izone) seem to boost TWTH and TWTV, but to a lesser extent in the latter case, making trade integrated areas good candidates for being Optimal Currency Areas. However, low tariffs, generally associated with PTA, are more ambiguous: they depress TWTV without having much impact on TWTH. In fact, what is required for intra-industry to develop is deep integration, stable business networks, good mutual knowledge of partners, etc. Proximity in all senses is essential, leaving only a limited impact to policies. Vertical intra-industry can develop without strong formal integration; it can accommodate barriers to trade. Within regions (in a geographical sense, notwithstanding any formal integration) a division of labor by quality emerges when firms specialize in different market segments. Proximity is crucial because it facilitates the exchange of information about the supply but, once established, the specialization by quality is less sensitive to transactions costs (products of different qualities are not substitutes, therefore the price elasticity is low).

The EU is the only region that combines short distances and deep integration of industrialized countries. The intra-industry potential of Asia is less because of longer distances and heterogeneity of development levels. Yet, vertical intra-industry has been dynamic in this region, certainly taking profit of business networks (Chinese diaspora, etc.) and of the capacity of multinational firms to exploit comparative advantages along the quality range.

7 Concluding remarks

Theory does not yet provide a framework to explain unequivocally the relationship between economic integration and the level of intra-industry trade. While early models based on monopolistic competition (Krugman 1979) or oligopolistic competition (Brander 1981; Shaked and Sutton 1984) predict a positive correlation between the two phenomena, other models expect the contrary (Wong 1995). Transportation costs certainly play a key role and affect the outcome of integration (Krugman 1991a). In this chapter, trade flows were classified as inter- or intra-industry and IIT was broken down into horizontal and vertical components. The analysis of trade patterns in the European Union, NAFTA, East Asia and Mercosur suggest that there is a positive link between IIT and regional integration, although the case of Mercosur is not clear-cut. In Europe, contrary to Brülhart and Torstensson (1996), we do not observe an increase of OWT in intra-zone trade, suggesting a concentration of production in central countries. The determinants of the share of vertical and horizontal IIT were investigated. Results support the conclusion that countries with similar endowments and sizes tend to trade similar goods, that there is a non-linear negative relationship between IIT and geographic distance, and that belonging to a preferential trade agreement favors IIT between member countries. Further research will determine if the observed trend towards the increase of IIT within integrated zones will be followed by a concentration of production in economic cores and a drop of IIT, as predicted by some models.

Annex

Table 2.14: Trade types, EU 25, 1993

	Extra-zone				Intra-zone				All			
	OWT	TWTnc	TWTH	TWTV	OWT	TWTnc	TWTH	TWTV	OWT	TWTnc	TWTH	TWTV
Austria	67.0	3.8	10.2	19.1	33.7	0.5	26.2	39.7	40.5	1.1	22.9	35.5
Belg. & Lux.	84.4	3.9	2.9	8.9	35.3	0.6	31.0	33.1	47.5	1.4	24.0	27.1
Cyprus	97.0	0.2	1.0	1.8	90.9	1.2	2.8	5.0	93.0	0.9	2.2	3.9
Czech Rep.	94.8	1.1	0.7	3.4	62.7	1.6	7.8	27.9	68.7	1.5	6.5	23.3
Denmark	82.7	1.2	4.2	11.9	57.4	0.8	14.8	26.9	65.0	1.0	11.6	22.4
Estonia	99.5	0.1	0.1	0.2	87.9	0.9	1.8	9.5	91.0	0.7	1.4	7.0
Finland	89.5	1.3	2.0	7.2	71.7	1.1	8.5	18.7	78.0	1.2	6.2	14.6
France	72.4	5.8	6.0	15.8	36.2	0.6	30.7	32.5	47.1	2.2	23.3	27.5
Germany	69.1	0.9	9.3	20.7	37.5	0.3	26.3	36.0	48.3	0.5	20.4	30.7
Greece	94.6	0.5	0.9	4.0	85.5	0.4	5.0	9.1	87.8	0.4	4.0	7.8
Hungary	91.6	1.1	1.6	5.8	65.6	0.8	9.0	24.6	72.9	0.8	7.0	19.4
Ireland	85.4	2.8	2.1	9.8	50.0	1.4	19.9	28.7	57.1	1.7	16.4	24.9
Italy	80.2	4.5	3.6	11.8	54.9	0.6	13.9	30.5	64.5	2.1	10.0	23.4
Latvia	98.6	0.9	.	0.5	92.8	0.8	2.1	4.3	94.1	0.8	1.6	3.5
Lithuania	99.9	0.0	0.0	0.1	93.4	0.5	1.7	4.4	94.4	0.4	1.4	3.7
Malta	98.8	0.9	0.0	0.3	90.0	0.7	1.4	7.9	91.6	0.7	1.2	6.5
Netherlands	84.2	0.9	4.1	10.8	38.9	0.4	28.3	32.4	52.1	0.6	21.3	26.1
Poland	97.1	1.1	0.4	1.4	76.2	1.1	4.6	18.1	80.4	1.1	3.7	14.8
Portugal	95.5	0.7	0.8	3.1	66.8	0.8	12.8	19.6	71.9	0.8	10.7	16.6
Slovakia	97.5	0.4	0.2	1.9	57.2	1.2	15.3	26.4	58.9	1.2	14.6	25.3
Slovenia	71.1	2.9	6.2	19.8	75.3	0.8	4.0	20.0	74.0	1.4	4.7	19.9
Spain	90.8	0.7	1.9	6.6	52.1	0.6	20.9	26.4	63.4	0.6	15.4	20.6
Sweden	76.3	1.8	6.8	15.2	55.7	1.0	15.2	28.1	63.1	1.3	12.2	23.5
UK	70.5	1.7	7.3	20.5	41.8	0.8	23.3	34.1	52.9	1.2	17.1	28.8
All	76.3	2.1	6.1	15.5	44.8	0.6	23.0	31.6	54.8	1.1	17.6	26.5

Table 2.15: Trade types, EU 25, 1995

	Extra-zone				Intra-zone				All			
	OWT	TWTnc	TWTH	TWTV	OWT	TWTnc	TWTH	TWTV	OWT	TWTnc	TWTH	TWTV
Austria	75.5	1.5	7.3	15.7	41.1	0.6	23.8	34.5	49.0	0.8	20.0	30.2
Belg. & Lux.	84.8	1.5	3.8	9.8	30.9	0.3	35.3	33.5	41.4	0.5	29.2	28.9
Cyprus	97.8	0.9	0.3	1.1	91.6	1.1	1.2	6.2	93.8	1.0	0.9	4.4
Czech Rep.	87.0	1.4	4.5	7.1	45.4	1.1	16.1	37.4	51.7	1.1	14.4	32.8
Denmark	83.1	1.1	4.9	11.0	56.2	0.5	15.9	27.4	64.3	0.7	12.6	22.4
Estonia	88.8	0.6	1.6	8.9	72.7	1.3	8.1	17.9	76.7	1.2	6.5	15.7
Finland	90.3	1.1	2.1	6.5	71.3	0.7	9.9	18.1	77.6	0.8	7.3	14.3
France	75.8	1.1	6.0	17.0	30.4	0.4	34.3	34.9	42.5	0.6	26.8	30.1
Germany	68.4	0.8	8.7	22.0	34.0	0.3	29.9	35.9	45.3	0.5	22.9	31.3
Greece	92.9	0.5	1.3	5.3	83.9	0.5	5.9	9.8	86.3	0.5	4.7	8.6
Hungary	93.6	0.8	1.2	4.5	61.6	0.9	12.0	25.4	69.6	0.9	9.3	20.2
Ireland	84.6	2.9	2.7	9.8	57.3	1.1	16.6	25.1	63.5	1.5	13.5	21.6
Italy	81.4	1.1	4.3	13.3	48.9	0.3	20.8	30.0	59.9	0.6	15.2	24.3
Latvia	92.9	0.5	2.2	4.4	86.0	1.3	3.0	9.6	88.4	1.0	2.8	7.9
Lithuania	87.8	1.1	3.2	7.9	87.0	1.2	2.5	9.4	87.3	1.2	2.8	8.8
Malta	98.8	0.6	0.1	0.4	88.5	1.1	1.4	9.0	90.5	1.0	1.2	7.3
Netherlands	82.8	1.3	4.5	11.5	37.2	0.3	29.8	32.7	49.5	0.6	23.0	26.9
Poland	88.5	0.6	2.6	8.3	73.7	0.8	6.6	19.0	77.2	0.8	5.7	16.4
Portugal	95.6	0.6	0.9	2.9	65.7	0.4	13.4	20.6	71.2	0.5	11.1	17.3
Slovakia	96.6	0.6	0.8	2.0	03.6	1.0	11.9	23.5	68.4	1.0	10.3	20.3
Slovenia1	82.4	0.9	5.1	11.6	65.0	0.9	9.1	25.1	69.1	0.9	8.1	21.9
Spain	87.3	0.9	4.9	6.9	46.1	0.4	26.2	27.3	57.0	0.5	20.6	21.9
Sweden	69.1	1.7	9.5	19.7	55.5	0.7	16.5	27.4	59.5	1.0	14.4	25.1
UK	69.0	1.9	7.6	21.6	39.2	0.5	26.3	34.1	50.2	1.0	19.4	29.5
All	76.5	1.2	6.2	16.1	41.5	0.4	26.3	31.8	51.7	0.7	20.4	27.2

Table 2.16: Trade types by ISIC industry, EU 25, 1995–2002

	Extra-zone				Intra-zone				All			
	OWT	TWTnc	TWTH	TWTV	OWT	TWTnc	TWTH	TWTV	OWT	TWTnc	TWTH	TWTV
Agriculture	96.51	0.19	1.3	1.99	64.51	0.17	16.61	18.72	73.26	0.18	12.42	14.14
Food and beverages	91.01	0.51	2.55	5.92	50.2	0.3	22.47	27.04	61.97	0.36	16.73	20.95
Mining products	94.31	0.41	1.65	3.64	68.33	0.5	11.33	19.85	79.22	0.46	7.27	13.05
Chemicals	70.07	1.23	8.23	20.48	33.51	0.58	30.53	35.37	43.36	0.76	24.52	31.36
Light industry	77.39	1.22	4.78	16.62	42.65	0.56	19.31	37.48	54.6	0.78	14.31	30.31
Wood and paper	75.84	0.8	7.3	16.1	46.0	0.4	25.8	27.8	53.3	0.5	21.3	25.0
Textile and clothing	85.0	0.9	3.8	10.3	43.9	1.3	19.4	35.4	59.0	1.1	13.7	26.2
Pottery products	80.8	1.8	3.3	14.1	47.4	0.6	17.1	34.9	56.8	0.9	13.3	29.1
Basic metals	75.7	1.1	6.9	16.4	35.5	0.3	32.4	31.8	46.7	0.5	25.3	27.5
General machinery	64.4	2.1	8.2	25.3	33.7	0.7	21.4	44.3	44.6	1.2	16.7	37.5
Electrical machinery	67.9	2.8	6.3	23.0	31.1	1.6	20.3	47.1	43.4	2.0	15.6	39.0
Precision apparatus	42.3	5.2	10.8	41.8	28.8	2.6	17.8	50.9	35.0	3.8	14.5	46.7
Transport machinery	74.6	2.5	8.5	14.4	28.1	0.4	45.8	25.7	35.6	0.7	39.8	23.9
Others	59.0	12.7	7.5	20.8	48.5	5.6	13.1	32.9	54.1	9.3	10.2	26.5
All	75.0	1.5	6.3	17.3	39.5	0.6	26.3	33.6	50.0	0.9	20.4	28.7

Table 2.17: Trade types, NAFTA, 1993

	Extra-zone				Intra-zone				All			
	OWT	TWTnc	TWTH	TWTV	OWT	TWTnc	TWTH	TWTV	OWT	TWTnc	TWTH	TWTV
Canada	90.6	2.8	1.6	5.0	33.8	22.5	17.0	26.7	49.2	17.2	12.8	20.8
Mexico	92.9	0.6	1.5	5.0	42.2	1.7	16.4	39.6	54.4	1.5	12.8	31.3
USA	73.2	4.2	5.5	17.1	35.6	16.2	17.1	31.1	62.1	7.8	8.9	21.2
All	75.5	3.9	5.0	15.5	36.0	16.2	16.9	30.9	58.8	9.1	10.1	22.0

Table 2.18: Trade types, NAFTA, 1995

	Extra-zone				Intra-zone				All			
	OWT	TWTnc	TWTH	TWTV	OWT	TWTnc	TWTH	TWTV	OWT	TWTnc	TWTH	TWTV
Canada	90.2	1.9	1.9	6.0	29.8	19.6	23.9	26.7	47.2	14.5	17.6	20.8
Mexico	92.3	0.8	1.6	5.3	42.8	3.4	18.0	35.8	54.7	2.8	14.1	28.5
USA	71.5	2.6	6.6	19.3	32.6	15.0	22.6	29.8	60.0	6.3	11.3	22.4
All	74.2	2.5	6.0	17.4	33.1	14.9	22.4	29.6	56.9	7.7	12.9	22.5

Table 2.19: Trade types by ISIC industry, NAFTA, 1995–2002

	Extra-zone				Intra-zone				All			
	OWT	TWTnc	TWTH	TWTV	OWT	TWTnc	TWTH	TWTV	OWT	TWTnc	TWTH	TWTV
Agriculture	97.0	0.2	0.7	2.2	63.4	1.1	16.5	19.0	83.9	0.6	6.8	8.7
Food and beverages	86.6	1.0	3.0	9.4	39.2	0.2	33.7	26.9	65.2	0.7	16.9	17.3
Mining products	95.7	0.3	0.7	3.3	51.9	0.1	36.4	11.6	78.4	0.3	14.8	6.5
Chemicals	62.9	2.2	9.5	25.5	26.1	12.8	29.6	31.5	44.3	7.5	19.7	28.6
Light industry	85.3	2.9	2.3	9.5	21.7	41.0	7.4	29.9	60.9	17.6	4.2	17.4
Wood and paper	79.1	0.9	3.9	16.2	48.1	8.7	18.3	25.0	59.2	5.9	13.1	21.8
Textile and clothing	82.7	0.5	5.2	11.7	22.9	1.4	31.9	43.9	59.7	0.8	15.4	24.1
Pottery products	75.0	3.6	4.4	17.1	32.6	16.9	11.1	39.3	53.8	10.3	7.8	28.2
Basic metals	75.3	2.7	5.0	17.0	26.0	5.7	27.7	40.6	46.9	4.4	18.1	30.6
General machinery	55.4	5.8	8.7	30.1	17.2	33.8	11.4	37.5	39.1	17.8	9.9	33.2
Electrical machinery	61.4	6.9	5.5	26.2	17.2	29.1	11.4	42.4	38.2	18.5	8.6	34.7
Precision apparatus	32.9	12.2	11.4	43.5	15.4	47.8	7.4	29.5	28.1	21.9	10.3	39.7
Transport machinery	67.3	2.9	11.9	18.0	16.5	32.7	9.5	41.3	37.3	20.5	10.5	31.7
Others	67.6	7.3	6.5	18.6	16.9	30.9	8.6	43.6	57.6	12.0	6.9	23.6
All	71.7	3.1	6.1	19.1	29.2	16.1	20.7	34.0	51.4	9.3	13.1	26.2

Table 2.20: Trade types, East Asia, 1993

	Extra-zone				Intra-zone				All			
	OWT	TWTnc	TWTH	TWTV	OWT	TWTnc	TWTH	TWTV	OWT	TWTnc	TWTH	TWTV
China	94.4	1.9	0.7	3.0	77.9	3.4	5.9	12.8	85.6	2.7	3.5	8.2
Hong Kong	86.9	3.2	1.2	8.7	75.6	3.8	7.3	13.3	79.7	3.6	5.1	11.7
Indonesia	97.9	0.3	0.3	1.5	91.9	0.5	2.3	5.3	95.2	0.4	1.2	3.2
Japan	77.2	0.8	5.6	16.3	83.3	1.4	3.0	12.4	79.8	1.1	4.5	14.6
Korea	89.7	1.2	1.6	7.5	81.8	1.2	4.0	13.0	86.1	1.2	2.7	10.0
Malaysia	92.7	2.7	0.9	3.8	71.5	8.0	4.9	15.5	80.5	5.8	3.2	10.6
Taiwan	88.2	5.1	1.1	5.6	84.2	2.6	2.6	10.7	86.0	3.7	1.9	8.4
Philippines	95.6	1.6	0.4	2.4	92.3	1.3	0.9	5.5	94.1	1.5	0.6	3.8
Singapore	83.0	6.6	1.8	8.7	66.9	9.2	5.7	18.2	74.0	8.0	4.0	14.0
Thailand	93.9	1.4	0.6	4.2	83.2	2.4	3.0	11.4	88.7	1.9	1.8	7.7
All	86.4	2.1	2.6	9.0	80.0	3.1	4.3	12.6	83.2	2.6	3.5	10.8

Table 2.21: Trade types, East Asia, 1995

	Extra-zone				Intra-zone				All			
	OWT	TWTnc	TWTH	TWTV	OWT	TWTnc	TWTH	TWTV	OWT	TWTnc	TWTH	TWTV
China	92.7	1.4	1.1	4.8	74.4	1.2	6.9	17.6	82.8	1.3	4.2	11.7
Hong Kong	87.5	2.5	1.7	8.3	74.9	2.0	7.5	15.6	79.6	2.2	5.3	12.9
Indonesia	96.4	0.7	0.6	2.3	90.7	0.6	2.7	6.1	93.8	0.6	1.6	4.0
Japan	75.3	0.8	6.4	17.5	81.4	1.0	3.2	14.4	78.1	0.9	4.9	16.1
Korea	88.5	0.9	2.3	8.3	78.5	0.9	5.3	15.3	83.8	0.9	3.7	11.5
Malaysia	92.0	2.7	1.0	4.3	70.6	8.3	6.9	14.3	79.5	5.9	4.4	10.1
Taiwan	87.4	4.3	1.7	6.6	81.3	2.1	3.9	12.7	84.1	3.1	2.9	10.0
Philippines	95.4	1.7	0.5	2.4	91.3	1.4	1.2	6.1	93.5	1.6	0.8	4.1
Singapore	82.2	5.5	3.0	9.3	64.6	9.7	7.5	18.3	72.3	7.9	5.6	14.4
Thailand	93.7	1.0	0.9	4.4	84.0	1.8	2.2	12.0	88.9	1.4	1.6	8.2
All	85.6	1.8	3.0	9.6	78.0	2.3	5.1	14.7	81.7	2.1	4.1	12.2

Table 2.22: Trade types by ISIC industry, East Asia, 1995–2002

	Extra-zone				Intra-zone				All			
	OWT	TWTnc	TWTH	TWTV	OWT	TWTnc	TWTH	TWTV	OWT	TWTnc	TWTH	TWTV
Agriculture	97.7	0.2	0.5	1.6	91.8	0.1	2.1	5.8	95.6	0.3	1.0	3.1
Food and beverages	90.9	0.2	2.0	6.9	84.7	0.4	3.8	11.2	88.2	0.3	2.8	8.7
Mining products	97.9	0.4	0.3	1.4	87.0	1.8	4.0	7.1	93.2	1.0	1.9	3.9
Chemicals	77.1	1.6	5.6	15.7	75.7	1.1	6.7	16.6	76.3	1.3	6.2	16.2
Light industry	91.9	1.5	1.0	5.6	82.7	1.3	3.7	12.3	88.1	1.4	2.2	8.4
Wood and paper	85.1	1.2	1.9	11.9	78.9	1.9	6.4	12.9	81.9	1.5	4.2	12.4
Textile and clothing	94.5	0.7	0.9	3.9	77.0	0.6	6.0	16.5	84.4	0.6	3.8	11.2
Pottery products	80.3	2.9	2.9	13.9	74.8	3.9	3.0	18.3	77.7	3.4	2.9	16.0
Basic metals	86.6	2.0	2.4	9.1	73.3	1.5	7.3	17.9	79.4	1.7	5.0	13.8
General machinery	74.8	4.9	3.8	16.5	67.9	5.0	3.0	24.0	71.7	5.0	3.5	19.9
Electrical machinery	75.8	4.7	3.1	16.5	54.9	5.5	8.7	31.0	64.8	5.1	6.0	24.1
Precision apparatus	53.1	11.3	6.1	29.6	57.9	8.5	4.3	29.4	54.6	10.4	5.5	29.6
Transport machinery	86.0	0.8	5.3	8.0	82.2	1.3	4.9	11.6	84.9	1.0	5.2	9.0
Others	89.2	5.1	0.8	4.9	95.9	2.2	0.5	1.4	89.8	4.8	0.8	4.6
All	84.2	2.3	2.9	10.6	74.8	2.0	5.6	17.6	79.5	2.2	4.2	14.1

Table 2.23: Trade types, Mercosur, 1993

	Extra-zone				Intra-zone				All			
	OWT	TWTnc	TWTH	TWTV	OWT	TWTnc	TWTH	TWTV	OWT	TWTnc	TWTH	TWTV
Argentina	95.4	0.6	0.8	3.2	77.6	0.5	8.9	12.9	91.2	0.6	2.7	5.5
Brazil	90.0	1.0	2.1	6.9	82.9	0.4	6.6	10.1	88.9	0.9	2.8	7.4
Paraguay	99.5	0.1	0.0	0.3	98.4	0.1	0.4	1.1	98.9	0.1	0.2	0.7
Uruguay	98.1	0.4	0.9	0.7	78.1	0.5	10.6	10.8	87.2	0.5	6.2	6.2
All	92.1	0.8	1.6	5.5	81.9	0.4	7.3	10.4	89.9	0.7	2.8	6.5

Table 2.24: Trade types, Mercosur, 1995

	Extra-zone				Intra-zone				All			
	OWT	TWTnc	TWTH	TWTV	OWT	TWTnc	TWTH	TWTV	OWT	TWTnc	TWTH	TWTV
Argentina	95.3	0.3	1.2	3.2	67.9	0.3	15.6	16.2	88.3	0.3	4.9	6.5
Brazil	88.7	0.6	2.4	8.3	72.8	0.3	13.3	13.5	86.3	0.6	4.0	9.1
Paraguay	99.6	0.1	0.0	0.4	97.0	0.2	0.6	2.3	98.2	0.1	0.3	1.4
Uruguay	98.2	0.4	0.6	0.8	74.8	1.3	7.5	16.4	87.5	0.8	3.8	7.9
All	91.1	0.5	2.0	6.5	73.5	0.4	12.4	13.7	87.4	0.5	4.1	8.0

Table 2.25: Trade types by ISIC industry, Mercosur, 1995–2002

	Extra-zone				Intra-zone				All			
	OWT	TWTnc	TWTH	TWTV	OWT	TWTnc	TWTH	TWTV	OWT	TWTnc	TWTH	TWTV
Agriculture	98.9	0.0	0.5	0.5	98.1	0.1	0.5	1.3	98.7	0.1	0.5	0.8
Food and beverages	97.7	0.1	0.7	1.6	78.1	0.1	7.8	13.9	95.4	0.1	1.6	3.0
Mining products	96.5	0.2	0.3	3.1	98.1	0.0	4.7	2.2	96.0	0.2	0.9	2.9
Chemicals	86.0	0.7	4.2	9.2	51.3	0.2	29.4	19.0	77.2	0.6	10.6	11.7
Light industry	93.9	0.7	1.0	4.5	81.6	0.3	5.4	12.6	91.7	0.6	1.8	5.9
Wood and paper	93.0	0.6	1.7	4.7	76.7	0.1	7.7	15.4	89.5	0.5	3.0	7.0
Textile and clothing	91.9	0.5	1.3	3.3	74.1	0.5	14.2	11.2	87.7	0.5	5.8	6.1
Pottery products	86.8	1.3	1.0	10.0	72.3	0.2	8.7	18.8	83.5	1.1	3.4	12.0
Basic metals	91.4	0.8	2.1	5.8	64.4	0.3	16.2	19.1	87.6	0.7	4.1	7.6
General machinery	79.4	1.6	3.9	15.1	54.5	0.4	14.7	30.4	75.8	1.4	5.5	17.4
Electrical machinery	83.2	1.9	3.0	11.8	57.9	0.7	15.8	25.6	78.6	1.7	5.4	14.3
Precision apparatus	86.8	3.0	1.4	8.9	73.9	2.7	5.2	18.2	86.1	3.0	1.6	9.4
Transport machinery	83.7	1.1	4.2	10.9	55.2	0.0	20.8	24.0	72.8	0.7	10.5	15.9
Others	90.1	1.7	1.1	7.0	91.7	0.3	–	8.0	90.3	1.6	1.0	7.2
All	91.0	0.7	2.1	6.2	72.8	0.2	12.9	11.0	87.1	0.6	1.5	7.9

Notes

1. See the detailed note available at http://www.cepii.fr/anglaisgraph/bdd/baci/baci.pdf.
2. Pairs with less than 50 observations (bilateral flows) are also rejected.
3. The oil and gas industries are excluded.
4. Changes in nomenclatures can explain this decline obtained with raw data.
5. Unit values in the BACI database are corrected so as not to take into account transportation costs.
6. Chapter 5 analyzes the rapid progress of the integration of Asian production networks, focusing on China.
7. See http://www.cepii.fr/anglaisgraph/bdd/chelem.htm for more details.
8. http://www.eiit.org/Protection/extracts.html.
9. 105 preferential trade agreements (including bilateral trade agreements) are taken into account. EU, NAFTA, Mercosur and ASEAN are the major multilateral preferential trade agreements.
10. Available at: http://www.cepii.fr/anglaisgraph/bdd/distances.htm.

References

Abd-El-Rahman, Kamal (1986) "Réexamen de la définition et mesure des échanges croisés de produits similaires entre les nations," *Revue Economique*, 37: 89–115.

Aturupane, Chomira, Djankov, Simeon and Hoekman, Bernard (1997) "Determinants of Intra-industry Trade between East and West Europe," *World Bank Working Paper*, no. 1850, November.

Balassa, Bela (1966) "Tariff Reductions and Trade in Manufactures among the Industrial Countries," *American Economic Review*, 56: 466–73.

Balassa, Bela (1986a) "The Determinants of Intra-industry Specialization in United States Trade," *Oxford Economic Papers*, 38: 220–33.

Balassa, Bela (1986b) "Intra-industry Trade among Exporters of Manufactured Goods," in *Imperfect Competition and International Trade*, ed. D. Greenaway and P. K. M. Tharakan, Brighton: Wheatsheaf.

Balassa, Bela and Bauwens, Luc (1987) "Intra-industry Specialization in a Multi-country and Multi-industry Framework," *Economic Journal*, 97: 923–39.

Bergstrand, Jeffrey H. (1982) "The Scope, Growth, and Causes of Intra-industry International Trade," *New England Economic Review*, September/October: 45–61.

Bergstrand, Jeffrey H. (1990) "The Heckscher–Ohlin–Samuelson Model, the Linder Hypothesis and the Determinants of Bilateral Intra-industry Trade," *Economic Journal*, 3: 1216–29.

Brander, J. (1981) "Intra-industry Trade in Identical Commodities," *Journal of International Economics*, 11: 1–14.

Brülhart, Marius and Torstensson, Johan (1996) "Regional Integration, Scale Economies and Industry Location in the European Union," *CEPR Discussion Paper*, no. 1435.

Dixit, Avinash and Norman, Victor (1980) *Theory of International Trade: a Dual General Equilibrium Approach*, Cambridge: Cambridge University Press.

Falvey, Rod (1981) "Commercial Policy and Intra-industry Trade," *Journal of International Economics*, 11: 495–511.

Finger, J. Michael (1975) "Trade Overlap and Intra-industry Trade," *Economic Inquiry*, 13, 4: 581–9.

Fontagné, Lionel and Freudenberg, Michael (1997) "Intra-industry Trade: Methodological Issues Reconsidered," *CEPII Working Paper*, no. 1.

Fontagné, Lionel and Freudenberg, Michael (2002) "Long-term Trends in IIT," In *Frontiers of Research on Intra-industry Trade*, ed. P. Lloyd and H. Lee, Basingstoke: Palgrave Macmillan.

Fontagné, Lionel, Freudenberg, Michael and Péridy, Nicolas (1997) "Trade Patterns inside the Single Market," *CEPII Working Paper*, no. 7.

Fontagné, Lionel, Freudenberg, Michael and Péridy, Nicolas (1998) "Intra-industry Trade and the Single Market: Quality Matters," *CEPR Discussion Paper*, no. 1959.

Fukao, K., Hikari Ishido and Keiko Ito (2003) "Vertical Intra-industry Trade and Foreign Direct Investment in East Asia," *Discussion Paper Series* a434, Institute of Economic Research, Hitotsubashi University.

Gaulier, Guillaume, Lemoine, Françoise and Unal-Kesenci, Deniz (2004) "China's Integration in Asian Production Networks and Its Implications," Mimeo, June.

Globerman, Steven (1992) "North American Trade Liberalisation and Intra-industry Trade," *Weltwirtschaftliches Archiv*, 128: 487–97.

Greenaway, David, Hine, R. and Milner, C. (1994) "Country-specific Factors and the Pattern of Horizontal and Vertical Intra-industry Trade in the UK," *Welwirtschaftliches Archiv*, 130, 1.

Greenaway, David, Hine, R. and Milner, C. (1995) "Vertical and Horizontal Intra-industry Trade: a Cross Industry Analysis for the United Kingdom," *Economic Journal*, 105, 433: 1505–18.

Grubel, Herbert G. and Lloyd, Peter J. (1975) *Intra-industry Trade, the Theory and Measurement of International Trade in Differentiated Products*, Basingstoke: Macmillan.

Gullstrand, Joakim (2002) "Does the Measurement of Intra-industry Trade Matter?" *Weltwirtschaftliches Archiv*, 138: 317–39.

Helpman, Elhanan (1981) "International Trade in the Presence of Product Differentiation, Economies of Scale and Monopolistic Competition: a Chamberlain–Heckscher–Ohlin Approach," *Journal of International Economics*, 11: 305–40.

Helpman, Elhanan and Krugman, Paul (1985) *Market Structure and Foreign Trade: Increasing Returns, Imperfect Competition, and the International Economy*, Cambridge, Mass.: MIT Press.

Krugman, Paul (1979) "Scale Economies, Product Differentiation, and the Pattern of Trade," *American Economic Review*, 70: 950–9.

Krugman, Paul (1981) "Intra-industry Specialization and the Gains from Trade," *Journal of Political Economy*, 89: 959–73.

Krugman, Paul (1991a) "Increasing Returns and Economic Geography," *Journal of Political Economy*, 99, 3: 483–99.

Krugman, Paul (1991b) *Geography and Trade*, Cambridge, Mass.: MIT Press.

Krugman, Paul and Venables, Anthony (1990) "Integration and the Competitiveness of Peripheral Industry," in *Unity with Diversity in the European Community*, ed. C. Bliss and J. B. de Macedo, Cambridge: Cambridge University Press.

Lancaster, Kelvin (1980) "Intra-industry Trade under Perfect Monopolistic Competition," *Journal of International Economics*, 10: 151–75.
Linder, Sephan B. (1961) *An Essay on Trade and Transformation*, New York: John Wiley and Sons.
Lipsey, Robert E. (1976) "Review of Grubel and Lloyd (1975)," *Journal of International Economics*, 6: 312–14.
Ocampo, Jose Antonio and Esguerra, Pilar (1994) "The Andean Group and Latin American Integration," in *Economic Integration in the Western Hemisphere*, ed. Roberto Bouzas and Jaime Ros, Notre Dame: University of Notre Dame Press.
Shaked, Avner and Sutton, John (1984) "Natural Oligopolies and International Trade," in *Monopolistic Competition and International Trade*, ed. Riccardo Faini and R. Portes, Oxford: Oxford University Press.
Stone, Joe A. and Lee, Hyun-Hoon (1995) "Determinants of Intra-industry Trade: a Longitudinal, Cross-country Analysis," *Weltwirtschaftliches Archiv*, 131: 67–85.
Verdoorn, Petrus Johannes (1960) "The Intra Block Trade of Benelux," in *Economic Consequences of the Size of Nations*, ed. E. Robinson, Basingstoke: Palgrave Macmillan.
Wong, Kar-yiu (1995) *International Trade in Goods and Factor Mobility*, Cambridge, Mass: MIT Press.

3

Production Networks and Spatial Linkages in East Asia

Ikuo Kuroiwa

1 Introduction

In East Asia, international production sharing or fragmentation, where stages of production leading to final goods are fragmented and located in more than one country, has been a driving force of economic integration. Therefore, it would be appropriate to analyze trade in East Asia from the viewpoint of a production network and to focus on trade in intermediate goods rather than in final goods.

On the other hand, it is an important contribution of inter-industry economics to investigate the process of production from the material to final goods and to develop this idea into a theory from the perspective of production technology. In inter-industry economics, for example, "clusters of industries" and "channels of roundabout production" are identified by an analysis of inter-industry linkages and permutations of sectors (such as triangulation) of the national input–output table. In East Asia, however, parts of the stages of production that used to be undertaken by domestic industries have relocated to other countries, particularly driven by the activities of multinational firms, and hence input–output structures of industries, as well as clusters of industries and channels of roundabout production, have been reshaped across national borders accordingly.

Because of the expansion of production networks throughout East Asia, it is becoming inappropriate to rely on the conventional input–output analysis, which is mostly concerned with domestic issues. Overcoming this limitation requires a different analytical tool and methodology that captures not only domestic transactions but also cross-border transactions in East Asia. In this chapter, I will analyze trade in East Asia and inter-industry linkages over borders (i.e.

spatial linkages) with the use of the Asian international input–output tables. For the latter topic, I will, in particular, focus on the machinery industry because of its leading role in establishing a production network in East Asia.

This chapter is structured as follows. In section 2, trade in East Asia will be analyzed with particular emphasis on intermediate goods. Also the Grubel–Lloyd index will be calculated to examine the progress of intra-industry trade. In section 3, the structure of spatial linkages will be explored, followed by an analysis of clusters in the machinery industry.

2 Trade in East Asia

2.1 Trend of trade in intermediate goods

First, let us examine how the trade in intermediate goods has evolved in East Asia by looking at the Asian international input–output tables for 1985 and 1995. Table 3.1 shows total inputs of all the industries in eight East Asian countries, the US and Japan – endogenous countries covered in the Asian tables – as well as their inputs from the region[1] (i.e. inputs from all the endogenous countries excluding its own country). Transactions of intermediate goods, consumption goods and investment goods are respectively derived in the Asian tables from the matrices or vectors of intermediate transactions, private plus government consumption, and gross capital formation, so that these data are consistent with the national accounts of all the endogenous countries.[2]

Table 3.1 shows that total intermediate (goods) inputs in the eight East Asian countries increased from US$741.5 billion in 1985 to US$2757 billion in 1995. The volume of total intermediate inputs nearly reflects the scale of economic activities. China, for example, had the largest total intermediate inputs among the eight East Asian countries at US$1154.7 billion. Furthermore, although Japan and the US had much larger total intermediate inputs, the eight East Asian countries had relatively large shares of total intermediate inputs. This is because industries such as manufacturing tend to have a long process of roundabout production and thereby a higher intermediate input ratio. East Asian countries have a higher share of such industries, as compared to, for example, the US where the service sector is dominant.[3]

Next, intermediate inputs from the region in the eight East Asian countries increased from US$51.8 billion in 1985 to US$265.8 billion in 1995. However, the volume of such intermediate inputs in each country did not correspond to the scale of economic activities. For

Table 3.1: Total input and input from the region (1 billion dollars)

	Intermediate goods				Consumption goods				Capital goods			
	85		95		85		95		85		95	
	Total	Region	Total	Region	Total	Region	Total	Region	Total	Region	Total	Region
China	346.0	9.6	1,154.7	45.5	190.1	2.2	428.7	4.3	92.7	7.3	243.1	14.4
Korea	121.3	12.2	570.9	54.0	64.0	1.1	312.2	5.4	27.3	2.5	190.2	15.9
Taiwan	87.7	7.9	310.8	44.9	39.7	0.9	195.3	7.2	11.6	1.4	62.3	11.1
Singapore	29.6	8.1	140.4	42.7	10.5	1.5	41.8	4.0	7.5	1.5	27.6	7.4
Malaysia	31.1	5.0	118.3	28.0	20.2	2.0	51.7	7.7	9.3	1.8	38.2	15.7
Thailand	37.5	3.1	189.5	29.0	30.0	0.7	114.2	2.4	8.8	1.2	74.4	11.1
Philippines	26.2	1.8	68.6	9.6	24.7	0.3	63.8	1.9	5.0	0.3	16.2	3.4
Indonesia	62.1	4.2	203.8	12.0	61.6	0.4	175.9	4.2	19.6	1.1	62.4	5.4
East Asia 8	741.5	51.8	2,757.0	265.8	440.8	9.1	1,383.6	37.1	181.7	17.0	714.3	84.3
Japan	1,446.4	44.4	4,580.9	105.0	915.5	5.7	3,616.6	43.4	360.2	4.0	1,484.3	24.4
US	3,395.2	42.4	6,378.1	123.9	3,430.0	45.0	5,916.9	68.7	657.9	23.3	1,286.9	61.2
Total	5,583.1	138.6	13,716.0	494.8	4,786.3	59.9	10,917.1	149.2	1,199.8	44.3	3,485.5	169.8

*1) Total input is a total of intermediate inputs, private + government consumptions, and gross capital formation in all the industries in each country.

*2) Input from the region is a total amount of input from all the endogenous countries excluding its own country.

*3) East Asia 8 is a subtotal of the eight East Asian countries from China through Indonesia.

Source: Asian International Input-Output Tables (1985, 1995).

example, inputs in China in 1995 (US$45.5 billion) were below those of Korea (US$54 billion) and slightly exceeded those of Taiwan and Singapore. Furthermore, the US and Japan, which were of larger economic size, had much lower inputs from the region than the subtotal of the eight East Asian countries.

The above relationships will be further clarified by comparing the regional input ratios of those countries, which are the ratios of inputs from the region to total inputs. Table 3.2 shows the overseas dependency ratios, which are the ratios of total inputs minus domestic inputs (= overseas inputs) to the total inputs, as well as the regional input ratios. According to Table 3.2, the regional input and overseas dependency ratios of intermediate goods in the eight East Asian countries in 1995 were 9.6 percent and 19.8 percent respectively, and they both vastly exceeded the ratios of the US and Japan. Furthermore, those countries which had extremely high dependency ratios were countries with small populations, such as Singapore and Malaysia, while large counties like China and Indonesia had lower dependency rations. These facts seem to reflect the fact that large economies as well as mature economies tend to have high self-sufficiency of intermediate goods.

Over the period 1985–95, the regional input ratio of intermediate goods in the eight East Asian countries increased by 38 percent (from 7.0 percent to 9.6 percent), while the overseas dependency ratio grew only by 21 percent (from 16.4 percent to 19.8 percent). The overall dependency on regional inputs, therefore, increased in this period. Ozaki (2004) pointed out that the EC, which was composed of smaller economies than the US, increased self-sufficiency of intermediate goods by expanding inter-regional trade faster than trade with non-EC countries. It is interesting to find that a similar process was occurring in East Asia with the US and Japan deeply involved. Also, it is notable that in many countries, with the exceptions of Korea, Singapore, Indonesia and Japan, regional input and overseas dependency ratios of intermediate goods simultaneously increased in this period.[4]

Regarding final goods, total consumption goods inputs in the US were overwhelmingly large (US$5916.9 billion in 1995), while the eight East Asian countries and Japan had relatively large total capital goods inputs. Similarly, consumption goods inputs from the region in the US were significantly large (US$68.7 billion), while those in the eight East Asian countries were relatively small (US$37.1 billion), and no single country exceeded US$10 billion. Therefore the regional input and overseas dependency ratios of consumption goods in the eight

Table 3.2: Overseas dependency and regional input ratios (%)

	Intermediate goods				Consumption goods				Capital goods			
	85		95		85		95		85		95	
	Overseas	Regional	Overseas	Regional	Overseas	Regional	Overseas	Regional	Overseas	Regional	Overseas	Regional
China	7.7	2.8	10.0	3.9	4.1	1.1	2.5	1.0	16.1	7.9	15.1	5.9
Korea	22.5	10.0	20.7	9.5	3.5	1.7	5.6	1.7	14.5	9.3	15.4	8.4
Taiwan	22.9	9.0	29.5	14.5	9.3	2.4	11.8	3.7	21.2	12.0	26.2	17.9
Singapore	53.0	27.2	45.5	30.4	28.3	14.6	17.4	9.6	30.4	19.9	35.1	26.8
Malaysia	33.8	16.1	41.5	23.7	18.6	10.1	29.8	15.0	33.4	19.1	56.9	41.1
Thailand	19.6	8.1	30.1	15.3	6.9	2.3	13.6	2.1	26.5	13.5	29.5	14.9
Philippines	17.2	7.0	30.0	14.0	6.0	1.0	10.5	3.0	11.6	5.8	32.8	20.9
Indonesia	15.1	6.7	15.0	5.9	3.8	0.6	9.6	2.4	13.6	5.4	19.0	8.6
East Asia 8	16.4	7.0	19.8	9.6	6.0	2.1	8.2	2.7	17.8	9.4	21.4	11.8
Japan	9.2	3.1	6.5	2.3	1.9	0.6	3.2	1.2	1.7	1.1	2.5	1.6
US	5.9	1.2	7.6	1.9	4.7	1.3	4.5	1.2	8.5	3.5	10.6	4.8
Total	8.1	2.5	9.7	3.6	4.3	1.3	4.5	1.4	7.8	3.7	9.4	4.9

*1) Overseas dependency ratio = (Total input–Input from the domestic industries)/Total input × 100.
*2) Regional input ratio = Input from the region (i.e. input from the endogenous countries excluding its own country) / Total input × 100

Source: Asian International Input-Output Tables (1985, 1995).

East Asian countries were both extremely low (2.7 percent and 8.2 percent respectively in 1995). In 1995, on the other hand, capital goods inputs from the region in the eight East Asian countries amounted to US$84.3 billion, exceeding those of the US and Japan. Consequently, the regional input and overseas dependency ratios of capital goods in the eight East Asian countries (11.8 percent and 21.4 percent respectively) were both higher than those of intermediate goods, although the latter had grown faster in regional input ratios.[5] Singapore and Malaysia were especially highly dependent on the procurement of capital goods from the other endogenous countries (26.8 percent and 41.1 percent respectively). The structure of high dependency, which is biased towards intermediate and capital goods and against consumption goods, implies that the main purpose of trade with other countries in the region was procurement of production goods (and much less the procurement of consumption goods), and economic integration in production goods had preceded that in consumption goods.

On the other hand, Table 3.1 shows that intermediate inputs from the region in the eight East Asian countries were much greater than those of capital and consumption goods and had grown faster than them – in 1995 intermediate goods, consumption goods and capital goods inputs from the region were respectively 5.13, 4.08 and 4.96 times as large as those in 1985. Also, an increase in the intermediate inputs from the region over the period 1985–95, US$214 billion, held 69 percent of all the increases in inputs, US$309.3 billion. Hence, we may conclude that intra-regional trade for the eight East Asian countries was driven by the trade in intermediate goods.

2.2 Intra-industry trade

It was established in the 1960s that intra-regional trade in the EC countries was driven by intra-industry trade rather than inter-industry trade (Balassa 1966; Grubel 1967). In this section, we calculate the Grubel–Lloyd (GL) index using the data from the Asian international input–output tables for 1975, 1985 and 1995, which are all convertible into the uniform sector classification (56 sectors), and then examine the progress of intra-industry trade.[6] In this analysis, traded goods will be classified into intermediate inputs, consumption goods and investment goods, according to the purpose of usage of traded goods (for the details of methodology, see the Technical Note).

Table 3.3 clearly indicates the rising tendency of the average GL index in all the endogenous countries. The weighted average GL index

Table 3.3: Grubel-Lloyd index

	Intermediate goods			Consumption goods			Capital goods		
	75	90	95	75	90	95	75	90	95
China		0.47	0.66		0.04	0.20		0.35	0.51
Korea	0.39	0.59	0.66	0.19	0.19	0.43	0.20	0.45	0.55
Taiwan		0.60	0.75		0.32	0.64		0.69	0.76
Singapore	0.37	0.58	0.63	0.44	0.51	0.56	0.41	0.43	0.39
Malaysia	0.23	0.34	0.58	0.44	0.55	0.63	0.35	0.26	0.52
Thailand	0.19	0.45	0.55	0.25	0.25	0.31	0.04	0.38	0.39
Philippines	0.12	0.42	0.52	0.30	0.32	0.37	0.03	0.31	0.31
Indonesia	0.11	0.19	0.29	0.25	0.40	0.43	0.02	0.05	0.25
Japan	0.22	0.41	0.50	0.31	0.26	0.40	0.45	0.36	0.44
US	0.30	0.46	0.57	0.29	0.19	0.33	0.50	0.56	0.61
Average	0.25	0.46	0.57	0.30	0.25	0.39	0.38	0.45	0.52

*1) Average is an average GL index weighted by the shares of gross trade (=export+import) for the 10 countries.

Source: Asian International Input-Output Tables (1975, 1990, 1995).

of intermediate goods notably increased from the lowest (0.25) among the three types of traded goods in 1975 to the highest (0.57) in 1995. On the other hand, the weighted average GL index of consumption goods was relatively high (0.30) in 1975, but it did not grow thereafter. This fact suggests that intra-industry trade within the eight East Asian countries, the US and Japan has been driven by production goods, especially intermediate goods. Among the countries which had high GL indexes were industrialized countries such as Taiwan, Korea, Singapore and Malaysia, while Indonesia and the Philippines still had low GL indexes due to the vertical structure of trade in these countries.

Table 3.4 lists the top eight intermediate goods in terms of the GL index. Because the GL indexes of primary goods were generally low, Table 3.4 lists manufactured goods only. Light manufacturing industries, such as Meat and Dairy Products, Leather Products, and Other Made-up Textile Products, had the highest GL index ranks in 1975. Since 1990, however, the GL indexes of material industries, such as Glass Products, Other Non-metallic Mineral Products and Non-ferrous Metals, have risen, along with Printing and Publishing. Further, in 1995 machinery industries, in particular, Precision Machinery, Other Transport Equipment and Electric Machinery, had sharply increased GL indexes.[7]

Table 3.4: Grubel-Lloyd index (intermediate goods)

	75		90		95	
1	Meat and dairy products	0.70	Glass products	0.81	Non-ferrous metal	0.77
2	Leather products	0.65	Printing and publishing	0.80	Other non-metallic mineral products	0.76
3	Other textile products	0.60	Other non-metallic mineral products	0.73	Precision machinery	0.75
4	Non-ferrous metal	0.59	Other manufacturing products	0.65	Printing and publishing	0.70
5	Printing and publishing	0.58	Electric machinery	0.63	Other transport equipment	0.69
6	Electric machinery	0.57	Other rubber products	0.62	Other manufacturing products	0.68
7	Glass products	0.52	Non-ferrous metal	0.62	Glass products	0.68
8	Basic industrial chemical	0.51	Leather products	0.60	Electric machinery	0.66

*) Sector classification in the above table is based upon the 56 basic sector classification for the 1975 input-output table. (see IDE Statistical Data Series No.39, 1982, pp. 502–3).

Source: Asian International Input-Output Tables (1975, 1990, 1995)

3 Spatial linkages in East Asia

3.1 Input–output structure and spatial linkages

As shown in section 2, intra-regional trade within the eight East Asian countries, the US and Japan was driven by the intermediate goods trade, and the overall dependency on regional inputs increased correspondingly. At the same time, the intra-industry trade of intermediate goods, especially those of material and machinery industries, gained weight as the East Asian economies industrialized. The next question of interest is how these facts are relevant to the establishment of production networks in East Asia. In order to answer this question, I will first examine the spatial linkages in East Asia and then the clusters of machinery industry.

The input–output structures of industries are determined by their technologies. For example, the process of roundabout production from the material to final products can be depicted as follows (Ozaki and Ishida 1970, Ozaki 2004):

Figure 3.1 shows the process of roundabout production starting from the raw material, then going through several stages of processing, and finally reaching the final output. When such interdependency exists among different stages of production, an increase in demand for the final output, i.e. vinylon products, would induce an increase in demand for its main input, i.e. vinylon yarn. This in turn would induce an increase in demand for its main input, i.e. vinylon resin, followed by an increase in demand for the most upstream industry, i.e. raw material – crude petroleum. On the other hand, an increase in supply of upstream industries, such as crude petroleum, would increase the production capacity of downstream industries (i.e. vinylon resin, vinylon yarn and vinylon products), and thereby would induce an increase in the production of these industries. These effects of inducement on production (on demand and supply sides) are respectively called the "backward linkage effects" and "forward linkage effects."

Figure 3.1: Process of roundabout production

Raw Material ⟶ [(Main Input ⟶ Output)] ⟶ [(Main Input ⟶ Output) . . .] ⟶ [Final Output]

1st Processing stage 2nd Processing stage . . .

(Example)

Crude petroleum ⟶ [Vinylon resin ⟶ Vinylon yarn] ⟶ [Vinylon products]

Source: Ozaki 2004.

As can be inferred from the above discussion, backward linkage effects are strongly induced by industries with high intermediate input coefficients, such as manufacturing industries, while forward linkage effects are induced by the primary and material industries, whose outputs are utilized by the other industries as intermediate goods. In fact, Chenery and Watanabe (1958) investigated the structure of inter-industry linkages of the domestic industries in Japan, the US, Italy and Norway, and they found that (i) intermediate primary industries, such as agriculture and mining, had high forward and low backward linkage effects, (ii) intermediate manufacturing industries, such as metals and chemicals, had high forward and high backward linkage effects, (iii) final manufacturing industries, such as foods and machinery, had low forward and high backward linkage effects, and (iv) final primary industries, such as transportation, trade and services, had low forward and low backward linkage effects.

However, the actual process of production is more complex than described above. For example, in addition to main inputs, inputs processed from other materials will be utilized as well as energy, transportation, telecommunication, trade, finance and other miscellaneous services. All these inputs either directly or indirectly induce production of the relevant industries. Furthermore, some intermediate goods cannot be produced domestically and need to be imported from abroad. Especially in small developing countries with an immature industrial structure, a large amount of intermediate goods needs to be imported, and hence strong spatial linkages will be generated.

Here it is convenient for us to clarify the definition of spatial linkage: a spatial linkage represents interdependency of industries over the space (or borders) which are linked through transactions of intermediate goods. For example, when intermediate goods produced by industries in Country A are utilized by industries in Country B, spatial linkages will occur. In this case, as the outputs of the industries in Country B increase, production of the industries in Country A will be induced both directly and indirectly by the spatial backward linkage effects. On the other hand, an increase in the outputs of the industries in Country A will increase supply of intermediate goods and thereby enhance the production capacity of the industries in Country B through the spatial forward linkage effects.

3.2 Interdependency and spatial linkages in East Asia

As shown above, there is a distinct regularity with regard to the interdependency of industries, which is largely determined by the production technology and industrial structure of each economy. It is therefore expected that the position of a certain industry (in a certain country) relative to the entire production process can be known by investigating such interdependency. Focusing on the interdependency of industries across borders, the magnitudes of spatial forward and backward linkage effects were computed by using the Asian international input–output tables, which had been converted (from the 56 sectors in Tables 3.3 and 3.4) into the uniform 23 sectors. Table 3.5 indicates the numbers of spatial linkages with magnitudes exceeding 5 percent, i.e. those spatial linkages through which output of the recipient industry increased by more than 5 percent of output of the inducing industry (see the Technical Note for details of the methodology). Due to limited space, Table 3.5 neglects the names of countries that either induce or receive the strong linkage effects, and only the combinations of industries are indicated.

As might be expected, Table 3.5 reflects the production technology of industries. For example, Crude Petroleum and Natural Gas had strong forward linkage effects on Petroleum Products (4), which then had similar effects on Basic Chemicals (1). Also, looking at Table 3.5 column-wise, we notice that primary industries, such as Crude Petroleum and Natural Gas and Mining, had strong forward linkage effects, and the numbers of combinations of spatial linkages with magnitudes exceeding 5 percent were 11 and 9 respectively. Similarly, intermediate manufacturing industries, such as Basic Chemicals, and Iron and Non-ferrous Metal, had both strong backward and forward linkage effects (backward 7, forward 6 and backward 6, forward 10), while final manufacturing industries, such as Industrial Machinery, Electric Machinery and Motor Vehicles, had strong backward linkage effects (10, 18, 12). Interestingly, these structures of spatial linkages are similar to those of the domestic industries that were examined intensively by the above-mentioned study by Chenery and Watanabe (1958), and it may be inferred that similar technology is being applied whether the goods are produced domestically or through the production networks across borders. However, Electric Machinery had strong spatial forward linkage effects (22) as well as backward linkage effects (18), and hence its usage as intermediate input goods (i.e. parts and components) for other industries was strengthened accordingly. This corresponds to the fact that Electric Machinery has expanded its production network throughout East Asia, as shown below.

Looking at Table 3.5 row-wise, it is seen that industries that received strong backward linkage effects (i.e. those industries whose outputs

Table 3.5: Spatial linkages, 1995 (industry X industry)

	Agriculture	Crude petroleum	Mining	Food	Spinning	Textile	Wooden prod.	Paper & pulp	Basic chemicals	Chemical prod.	Refined petroleum	Rubber prod.	Non-metallic min.	Iron & non-ferrous	Metal prod.	Industrial machinery	Electric machinery	Motor vehicles	Other trans. equip.	Precision machinery	Other manuf. prod.	Trade & trans.	Services and others	Total
Agriculture				1			1																	2
Crude petroleum											2													2
Mining																								
Food	<1>			**1**																				1<1>
Spinning					**1<1>**	2			<2>															3<3>
Textile																								
Wooden prod.	<1>						**3<2>**																	3<3>
Paper & pulp								**3**																3
Basic chemical					1				**7<2>**	5	<1>										5			18<3>
Chemical prod.																								
Refined petroleum		<4>									**1<1>**													1<5>
Rubber prod.												**<1>**											<1>	
Non-metallic min.													**1**											1
Iron & non-ferrous			<3>											**6<5>**	6	3		2	2					19<8>
Metal prod.			<1>											<1>										<2>
Industrial machinery			<1>													**5**								5<1>
Electric machinery											<1>			<1>		2<1>	**16<15>**			1				19<18>
Motor vehicles			1<1>									<1>					<1>	**6<1>**						7<4>
Other trans. equip.																			**2**					2
Precision machinery																				**2**				2
Other manuf. prod.														<1>						<1>				<2>
Trade & trans.		<2>									<2>							2		1				3<4>
Services and others	<2>	<5>	<3>				<6>		<2>		<1>	<2>		<2>	<2>	<3>	2<6>	2	<1>	1<4>	<2>	<1>		5<42>
Total	<4>	<11>	1<9>	2	2<1>	2	4<8>	3	7<6>	5<1>	3<5>	<4>	1	6<10>	6<2>	10<4>	18<22>	12<1>	4<1>	5<5>	5<2>	<1>		96<97>

*1) Looking at the table column-wise (i.e. vertically), we can find what origin sectors (in columns) give strong spatial linkage effects on what destination sectors (in rows).
*2) Figures with and without the parentheses respectively indicate the numbers of industry pairs with magnitudes of spatial forward and backward linkage effects exceeding 5%.
*3) Motor vehicles are comprised of automobiles, motor cycles, and bicycles.
*4) Services and others are comprised of services, electricity, gas, water supply, construction; and public administration.

Source: Asian International Input-Output Tables (1995).

were strongly induced by backward linkage effects) were mostly material industries, such as Basic Chemicals, Iron and Non-ferrous Metal (18, 19). On the other hand, Services and Others received nearly a half number of strong forward linkage effects (42), and Electric Machinery was a recipient of strong forward linkage effects as well as of backward linkage effects (forward 18, backward 19).

Using the same results of analysis as Table 3.5, Table 3.6 indicates the names of countries that either induce or receive strong linkage effects, but the combinations of industries are neglected. According to Table 3.6, no large economies like the US and Japan had an industry that induced production of another country's industry by more than 5 percent of its output – note that columns of the US and Japan are all blank. This is because they had high self-sufficiency, and the outputs of the US and Japanese industries were so large that the ratios of induced production to outputs became negligible (even though absolute values of induced production were significantly large). In a similar vein, China had only four combinations of spatial linkages exceeding 5 percent. On the other hand, Taiwan and Southeast Asian countries, with the exception of Indonesia, had more than twenty combinations of strong spatial linkage effects. Malaysia and the Philippines were outstanding in creating forward linkage effects (25, 22), and so were Taiwan and the Philippines in backward linkage effects (22, 20). These facts reflect the general tendency that developing countries, with relatively small economies and immature industrial structures, are marked by an imbalance in the demand for and supply of intermediate goods in the domestic markets, so that these countries need to trade with other countries, especially with developed countries.

Next, looking at Table 3.6 row-wise, it can be seen that Japan received by far the largest number of strong backward linkage effects – Japan had 63 combinations, holding 65.6 percent of the total number of backward linkages. Regarding the forward linkage effects, the US has increased its presence (35), and the difference from Japan has narrowed to only five. These results suggest that, compared with East Asian industries, Japanese industries were located in the upstream of roundabout production and hence became recipients of backward linkage effects (or suppliers of intermediate goods for East Asia), while the US industries became recipients of forward linkage effects (or demanders of intermediate goods from East Asia). In any event, Japan and the US received strong spatial linkage effects from all the eight East Asian countries, and their shares as a recipient of linkage effects were very large, with a combined share as much as 79.3 percent of all spatial

Table 3.6: Spatial linkages, 1995 (country X country)

	China	Korea	Taiwan	Singapore	Malaysia	Thailand	Philippines	Indonesia	Japan	US	Total
China		<1>		<1>	<2>	1					1<4>
Korea				1<1>	<2>		2<1>	<1>			3<5>
Taiwan					1		2				3
Singapore					1<2>	1<1>	1<1>				3<4>
Malaysia			2	3<4>		1		<1>			6<5>
Thailand				<1>	<2>		<1>				<4>
Philippines											
Indonesia			2								2
Japan	1<2>	4<1>	14<2>	10<2>	7<11>	9<4>	12<10>	6<8>			63<40>
US	<1>	1<2>	4<5>	3<9>	2<6>	1<3>	3<9>	1			15<35>
Total	1<3>	5<4>	22<7>	17<18>	11<25>	13<8>	20<22>	7<10>	0<0>	0<0>	96<97>

*1) Looking at the table column-wise (i.e. vertically), we can find what origin countries (in columns) give strong spatial linkage effects on what destination countries (in rows).
*2) Figures with and without the parentheses respectively indicate the numbers of country pairs with magnitudes of spatial forward and backward linkage effects exceeding 5%.

Source: Asian International Input-Output Tables (1995).

linkage effects. As shown above, the interdependency between the eight East Asian countries and the US and Japan was not balanced, with much greater dependency of the former on the latter. Such a relationship, however, will be changed gradually, as the East Asian economies further industrialize, although one-sided relationships will remain in countries with small populations.[8]

3.3 Intra-industry spatial linkages

Returning to Table 3.5, we notice that the spatial linkage effects that are located on the diagonal of the table hold a large portion of all the linkage effects. These spatial linkage effects represent the linkage effects within the same industry but between different countries (hereafter we call them "intra-industry spatial linkages"), and therefore reflect the progress of international division of labor between different stages of production (where international production sharing or fragmentation can be considered as a driving force of this development). On the other hand, it was shown in Table 3.4 that the intra-industry trade of intermediate goods, especially those of material and machinery industries, gained weight. However, it does not demonstrate how the intra-industry trade of intermediate goods was slotted into the production network in East Asia. In order to address this problem, the analysis of intra-industry spatial linkage effects will be useful because it clarifies how the industries in each country were situated (i.e. whether upstream or downstream) in the entire production process and how the intra-industry trade of intermediate goods connected different stages of production within the same industry. Further, in order to see the progress over time, the same methodology was applied to the 1975, 1990 and 1995 tables.

Table 3.7 indicates the numbers for these intra-industry spatial linkage effects (only the top four are listed) and their percentages of all the linkage effects. In 1975, the percentages of such forward and backward linkage effects were 15.5 percent and 29.6 percent respectively. But they increased drastically in the 1990s and reached 28.9 percent and 56.3 percent respectively in 1995 – namely more than a half of strong backward linkage effects occurred within the same industry across borders. As shown above, the division of labor between different stages of production had progressed rapidly within the eight East Asian countries, the US and Japan. Further, Table 3.7 shows that Electric Machinery had been at the top of the list (in both forward and backward linkage effects) since 1990, implying that a new model of international division of labor, such as fragmentation, had proceeded

Table 3.7: Intra-industry spatial linkage effects

		1	2	3	4	Total (share %)
1975	Backward	Basic chemicals (8)	Motor vehicles (7)	Iron and non-ferrous (6)	Electric machinery (5)	46(29.6%)
	Forward	Iron and non-ferrous (6)	Basic chemicals (1)	Chemical products (1)	Wooden products (1) etc.	13(15.5%)
1990	Backward	Electric machinery (12)	Basic chemicals (9)	Motor vehicles (7)	Precision machinery (6)	57(51.8%)
	Forward	Electric machinery (9)	Iron and non-ferrous (6)	Basic chemicals (3)	Wooden products (1) etc.	25(21.9%)
1995	Backward	Electric machinery (16)	Basic chemicals (7)	Iron and non-ferrous (6)	Motor vehicles (6)	54(56.3%)
	Forward	Electric machinery (15)	Iron and non-ferrous (5)	Chemical products (2)	Wooden products (2)	28(28.9%)

*1) Figures in the parentheses are diagonal elements of Table 3.5 (only the top four items are listed), while the total is a sum of the diagonal elements. Also, the share is a ratio of the sum of the diagonal elements to the sum of all the strong spatial linkages.

Source: Asian International Input-Output Tables (1975, 1990, 1995).

particularly in this industry. Also, material industries, such as Iron and Non-ferrous Metal and Basic Chemicals, and the Motor Vehicles industry (in backward linkage effects only) had high percentages of intra-industry spatial linkage effects. Therefore, we may conclude that the machinery and material industries played a pivotal role in this development.

3.4 Clusters in the machinery industry

In Tables 3.5 and 3.6, industries and countries are treated separately, and hence names of industries and countries cannot be identified simultaneously. Here they will be treated together, in order to look at the development of clusters, especially those of the machinery industry. Due to limited space, the criterion for including a cluster in Figure 3.2 will be raised from 5 percent to 10 percent. That is, only clusters in the machinery industry, where output of the recipient industry increased by more than 10 percent of output of the inducing industry, appear in the figure, and extremely strong linkage effects that exceed 20 percent of output are indicated by bold lines.

According to Figure 3.2, the sizes of individual clusters in 1975 were relatively small, and they were independent from each other. It is also striking that in 1975, when the Japanese steel industry was at the peak of its export, spatial linkages between different industries, especially linkages between the East Asian machinery industries and Japanese Iron and Non-ferrous Metal, were as strong as intra-industry spatial linkages in the machinery industries.

Next, looking at the figure for 1990 that covers China and Taiwan, it is clear that spatial linkages between different industries had shrunk, and most of the strong linkage effects occurred within the same industry. Needless to say, this corresponds to the fact that the international division of labor between different stages of production had proceeded, as shown in Table 3.7. Regarding industrial clusters, the Electric Machinery cluster expanded significantly, while the Industrial Machinery, Precision Machinery and Other Transport Equipment clusters shrunk or disappeared. Above all, Electric Machinery in five East Asian countries (Korea, Taiwan, the Philippines, Singapore and Thailand) had strong backward linkage effects on the same industry in Japan, and Electric Machinery in three East Asian countries (Malaysia, Taiwan and the Philippines) had strong forward linkage effects on US Services and Others. This suggests that the production network of Electric Machinery expanded rapidly with industries in Japan, East Asia and the US respectively located in the upstream, midstream and downstream of roundabout production. Regarding the interdependency in this region, conventional wisdom suggests a picture in which Japan first provides parts and components for East Asia, and then East Asia manufactures them into the final products for export to the US. However, this study implies that, while the interdependency between Japan and East Asia was consistent with the above-mentioned picture, the linkages between East Asia and the US through the transactions of intermediate goods were strong as well.

In 1995 the size of cluster as a whole had expanded, and the Motor Vehicles and Electronic Machinery industries in particular had strengthened their linkages. Within the cluster of Motor Vehicles, Indonesia,

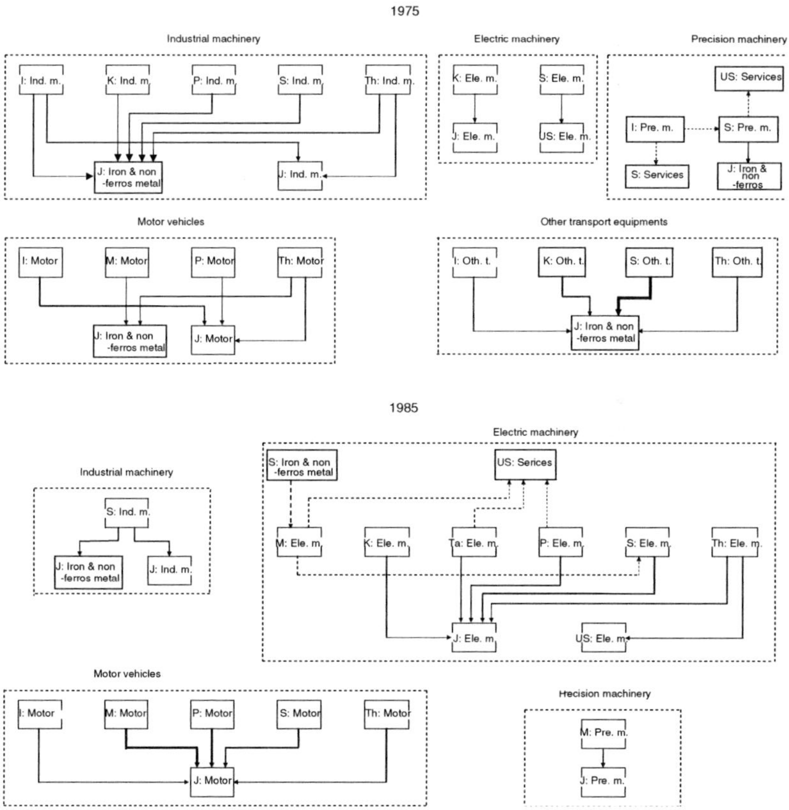

Figure 3.2: Clusters in the machinery industry

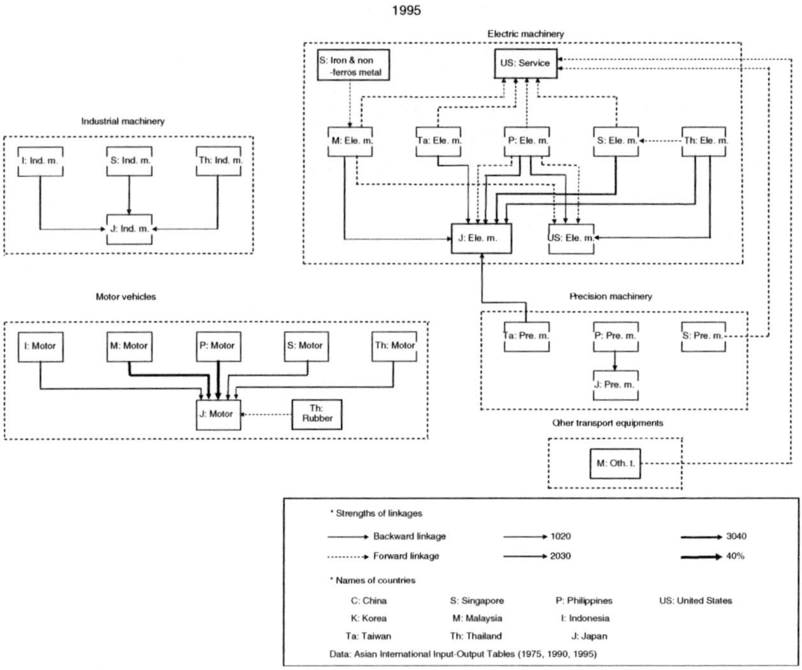

Figure 3.2: *Continued*

Malaysia, the Philippines, Singapore and Thailand (where Japanese automobiles are produced except for Singapore) continued to have strong backward linkage effects on the Japanese Motor Vehicles industries with the strength of linkages from Malaysia and the Philippines exceeding 30 percent and 40 percent respectively. On the other hand, the Electric Machinery industry in East Asia had strengthened its linkages with the US, while the linkages with Japan remained dominant. The Electric Machinery industry in the Philippines notably had both strong forward and backward linkage effects on the US and Japan, which in turn suggests that the Philippines came to play an important role in the production network of the Electric Machinery industry. Further, the Electric Machinery industry in Thailand had strong forward linkage effects on Singapore's Electric Machinery industry, while Singapore's Iron and Non-ferrous Metal industry had similar effects on the Malaysian Electric Machinery industry. These facts imply that spatial linkages had strengthened outside the US and Japan, and Singapore came to play a pivotal role in this development. Finally, East Asian industries had strengthened their forward linkage effects on the US Services and Others, and the latter made a significant contribution to the development of the machinery industry in East Asia.

4 Conclusion

In East Asia, intra-regional trade within the eight East Asian countries, the US and Japan has been driven by the intermediate goods trade, and the overall dependency on regional inputs increased correspondingly. At the same time, intermediate goods, especially those of the material and machinery industries, increased their proportion of intra-industry trade. These facts are consistent with the finding from spatial linkages analysis, which underpinned the progress of the international division of labor between different stages of production. This is because the expansion of production networks of multinational firms had spread different stages of production throughout East Asia, and these different stages of production were connected with each other through the intermediate goods trade. Therefore both intra-industry and intermediate goods trade had increased sharply.

On the other hand, although the structures of spatial linkages were more or less similar to those of domestic industries, the Electric Machinery industry had strong spatial forward linkage effects, implying that its usage as intermediate input goods (i.e. parts and components) for other industries was strengthened due to the expansion of production networks in Electric Machinery. Also it was shown that the interdependency between the eight East Asian countries and the US and Japan was not balanced with greater dependency of the former on the latter. Such a relationship will gradually change as the East Asian economies further industrialize, although unbalanced relationships will remain with regard to small economies. On the other hand, the percentage of intra-industry spatial linkages increased in the machinery and material industries, particularly in the Electric Machinery industry, implying that a new model of international division of labor, such as fragmentation, had proceeded in this industry.

Next, machinery industry clusters, especially those of the Motor Vehicles and Electric Machinery industries, expanded significantly, and most of the strong spatial linkage effects came to occur within the same industry. Further, it was shown that the production network of the Electric Machinery industry had expanded with industries in Japan,

East Asia and the US respectively located in the upstream, midstream and downstream of roundabout production; the Motor Vehicles industries in Malaysia and the Philippines had extremely strong backward linkage effects on the Japanese Motor Vehicles industry; the Electric Machinery industry in the Philippines notably had both strong forward and backward linkage effects on the US and Japan; spatial linkages had strengthened outside the US and Japan, and Singapore came to play an important role in this development; and East Asian industries had strengthened their forward linkage effects on the US Services and Others.

Technical note

1. Measurement of the Grubel–Lloyd index

The Grubel–Lloyd (GL) index is useful to examine whether the international division of labor is driven by inter-industry trade or intra-industry trade. In this study, the GL index was computed by using the data obtainable from the Asian international input–output tables. For example, the GL index on intermediate goods is obtained as follows:

$$GL_{i\bullet}^{r*} = 1 - \frac{\left|\sum_{j=1}^{n_1}\sum_{s\neq r}^{s=\varphi}(z_{ij}^{rs} - z_{ij}^{sr})\right|}{\sum_{j=1}^{n_1}\sum_{s\neq r}^{s=\varphi}(z_{ij}^{rs} + z_{ij}^{sr})}$$

where z_{ij}^{rs} represents the cross-border transaction of intermediate goods from Sector i in Country r to Sector j in Country s; n_1 and φ represent the numbers of sectors and of endogenous countries respectively (for the GL index on consumption and capital goods, it is just necessary to replace j in the above formula with the column vectors on private plus government consumption and on the fixed capital formation respectively).

Further, the GL index by country in Table 3.3 and by sector in Table 3.4 are obtained by calculating the average GL index weighted by the shares of gross trade (= export + import) for sectors and for countries respectively. Also, the GL index has values from zero to one, where the index becomes zero if there is no intra-industry trade, and one if there is 100 percent intra-industry trade.

2. Spatial linkages

Spatial linkages came to attract attention when Miller (1966) made an analysis of inter-regional feedback effects. In this chapter, I calculated the strengths of spatial linkages by applying the "hypothetical extraction method."

Backward linkage effects
Since Hirschman (1958) introduced the concepts of forward and backward linkage effects and his followers (Rasmussen 1956; Chenery and Watanabe 1958) presented the methods of measuring these linkage effects, the Leontief model has been used frequently. The Leontief model, which is theoretically consistent with Keynesian economics, is suitable for the analysis of backward linkage effects.[9]

Suppose $\mathbf{Z}$ is a square matrix representing intermediate transactions in the input–output table[10] and $\mathbf{x}$ is a column vector on outputs of the sectors. Then an input–output coefficient matrix is represented by $\mathbf{A} = \mathbf{Z}\hat{\mathbf{x}}^{-1}$, where $\hat{\mathbf{x}}$ is a diagonal matrix of $\mathbf{x}$. Next, since the relationship holds such that $\mathbf{x} = \mathbf{Zi} + \mathbf{f} = \mathbf{Ax} + \mathbf{f}$, where $\mathbf{i}$ is an identity matrix and $\mathbf{f}$ a vector on final demand, we obtain

$$\mathbf{x} = (\mathbf{I} - \mathbf{A})^{-1}\mathbf{f} \tag{1}$$

where $(\mathbf{I} - \mathbf{A})^{-1}$ is called the Leontief inverse matrix. Further, substituting $\Delta\mathbf{f}$ into Equation (1), it can be alternatively represented by $\Delta\mathbf{x} = (\mathbf{I} - \mathbf{A})^{-1}\,\Delta\mathbf{f} = \Delta\mathbf{f} + \mathbf{A}\,\Delta\mathbf{f} + \mathbf{A}^2\,\Delta\mathbf{f} + \mathbf{A}^3\,\Delta\mathbf{f} + \ldots$ This formula expresses the process in which output $\Delta\mathbf{f}$ is first induced by an increase in final demand, then is followed by an increase in demand for intermediate goods $\mathbf{A}\,\Delta\mathbf{f}$ (i.e. derived demand by $\Delta\mathbf{f}$), that is further followed by $\mathbf{A}^2\,\Delta\mathbf{f}$ (i.e. derived demand by $\mathbf{A}\,\Delta\mathbf{f}$)..., provided input coefficients are stable or fixed. Also, this is the process in which demand for intermediate goods spreads from downstream to upstream industries, corresponding to the concept of backward linkage effects. Further, this model captures a change in real output due to the assumption on the stability of prices in the model.[11]

Next, we explain the hypothetical extraction method. In this method, we suppose a case in which a column vector of Sector j in its own country is hypothetically extracted from the international input–output table (i.e. all the input coefficients of Sector j are replaced with zero and assume the case in which intermediate inputs for Sector j are all imported from the non-endogenous countries). Then the repercussion effects of Sector j are shut off, and consequently the outputs of the industries in the endogenous countries will be reduced. Here the reduced outputs are considered to represent the magnitude of backward linkage effects (Dietzenbacher and Van der Linden 1997).

Suppose that $\mathbf{A}(-sj)$ is a matrix in which a column vector of Sector j in Country s is hypothetically extracted. Then $\mathbf{x}(-sj) = [\mathbf{I} - \mathbf{A}(-sj)]^{-1}\mathbf{f}$ indicates the outputs induced in the hypothetical case. And the difference from Equation (1)

$$\mathbf{x} - \mathbf{x}(-sj) \tag{2}$$

represents the magnitude of backward linkage effects induced by Sector j in Country s.[12] In order to measure the relative strength of linkage, it is more convenient to use an index than an absolute value. Then dividing equation (2) by x_j^s, we obtain $BL(-sj) = [\mathbf{x} - \mathbf{x}(-sj)]/x_j^s$, which is considered to represent the strength of the backward linkage effects and that actually represents the output in each sector induced by one unit of output in an inducing sector, $x^s{}_j$.

Forward linkage effects

For the analysis of forward linkage effects, the Leontief model that corresponds to the concept of backward linkage is not appropriate. So an alternative methodology needed to be developed for measuring forward linkages, although it has been quite controversial due to some technical difficulties. In recent years, however, the hypothetical extraction method that utilizes the output coefficients rather than input coefficients has taken root as a prevailing methodology.

Suppose $\mathbf{v}$ is a row vector representing value added for each sector. Then the relationship holds such that $\mathbf{x}' = \mathbf{i}'\mathbf{Z} + \mathbf{v}'$. Next, by substituting an output coefficient matrix $\mathbf{B} = \hat{\mathbf{x}}^{-1}\mathbf{Z}$ into the above formula, we obtain $\mathbf{x}' = \mathbf{x}'\mathbf{B} + \mathbf{v}'$. Then solving for $\mathbf{x}'$, we get $\mathbf{x}' = \mathbf{v}' (\mathbf{I} - \mathbf{B})^{-1}$, where $(\mathbf{I} - \mathbf{B})^{-1}$ is called the Ghosh matrix. Further, substituting $\Delta\mathbf{v}'$ into the above formula, it can alternatively be represented by $\Delta\mathbf{x}' = \Delta\mathbf{v}' (\mathbf{I} - \mathbf{B})^{-1} = \Delta\mathbf{v}' + \Delta\mathbf{v}'\mathbf{B} + \Delta\mathbf{v}'\mathbf{B}^2 + \Delta\mathbf{v}'\mathbf{B}^3 + \ldots$. In this formula, provided that the output coefficients are stable or fixed, the same amount of output $\Delta\mathbf{v}'$ will first be induced with an increase in value added. Then the newly created output will be distributed to other sectors as intermediate input goods according to the fixed output coefficients, and will induce an increase in output by $\Delta\mathbf{v}'\mathbf{B}$. After this process is repeated infinitely, output will be increased as determined by the Ghosh matrix. As shown above, output changes of the downstream industry in the Ghosh model are induced by supply changes in intermediate goods from the upstream industry, and this process theoretically corresponds to the concept of forward linkage effects.[13]

Next, analogous to equation (2), let us consider a case in which a row vector of Sector *i* in Country *r* is hypothetically extracted from the international input–output table (i.e. all the output coefficients of Sector *i* in Country *r* are replaced with zero and assume the case in which intermediate outputs of the above sector are all exported to the non-endogenous countries). Then $\mathbf{x}(-ri)' = \mathbf{v}' [\mathbf{I} - \mathbf{B}(-ri)]^{-1}$, where $\mathbf{B}(-ri)$ is an output coefficient matrix in which a row vector of Sector *i* in Country *r* is hypothetically extracted, represents output induced in a hypothetical case, and hence the magnitude of forward linkage effects is measured by $FL(-ri) = [\mathbf{x}' - \mathbf{x}(-ri)']/x_j^r$, which is equal to output in each sector induced by one unit of output in an inducing sector, x_j^r.

Finally, the spatial linkages are represented by cells in $BL(-sj)$ column vector and $FL(-ri)$ row vector that correspond to the linkages with industries in the other endogenous countries. For example, a cell of Sector *k* in Country *t* in Vector $BL(-sj)$ represents the strength of spatial backward linkage effects of Sector *j* in Country *s* on Sector *k* in Country *t*.

Notes

1. Although the US is not a part of East Asia, all the endogenous countries covered in the Asian international input–output tables – China, Korea, Taiwan, Singapore, Malaysia, Thailand, the Philippines, Indonesia, Japan and the US – will be treated as one region in this study. Also, it should be noted that the Asian tables are the Isard-type international input–output tables which register entire flows of goods (and services) between the sectors in origin and destination countries in this region.
2. It is, of course, possible to use trade statistics and classify the traded goods according to the purpose of usage. However, there is a problem with the reliability of such data, because they are not necessarily consistent with the national accounts of the trading countries.
3. As shown below, the eight East Asian countries were highly dependent on import for procurement of intermediate goods. This is partly because these countries had relatively high intermediate input ratios but low self-sufficiency of such intermediate goods.
4. Looking at the subtotal of the eight East Asian countries (East Asia 8) and the total in Table 3.2, it is also seen that regional input and overseas dependency ratios as a whole increased in this period not only in intermediate goods but also in capital and consumption goods.
5. Over the period 1985–95, the regional input ratio of capital goods in the eight East Asian countries increased by 26 percent (from 9.4 percent to

11.8 percent), while that of consumption goods were extremely low and grew by 29 percent (from 2.1 percent to 2.7 percent). In any rate, regional input ratios of intermediate goods had grown faster than these figures at 38 percent.

6. The basic sector classifications of the Asian international input–output tables are as follows; 56 sectors for the 1975 table, 24 sectors for the 1985 table, and 78 sectors for the 1990 and 1995 tables. Among them, the sector classification for manufacturing industries in the 1985 table was not detailed enough so the 1985 table was excluded from the analyses of the Grubel–Lloyd index (in 56 sectors) and the spatial linkages (in 23 sectors). Also there is a difference in the coverage of countries in these tables; China and Taiwan were only incorporated into the international input–output tables after 1985.
7. Hoen (2002) calculated the Grubel–Lloyd index, using the EC input–output tables from 1975 to 1985. As a result, he found that (i) intra-industry trade had increased its share of trade within the EC, (ii) countries such as France, Germany and Belgium had relatively high GL indexes, (iii) manufacturing industries had high indexes. However, unlike this study, traded goods are not classified by the purpose of usage in Hoen's analysis, so the trend of intermediate goods cannot be seen.
8. Van der Linden (1998) computed the magnitude of spatial linkages, using the EC input–output table by applying the same methodology as this study. He found that among the seven countries (i.e. Germany, France, Italy, the Netherlands, Belgium, the UK, Denmark), Germany and France held a combined share of 71 percent in the number of strong spatial linkages, which is close to the 79.3 percent combined share of the US and Japan in this study. As shown above, this structure, which results in small economies having one-sided dependency on large economies, will not change even after the former's economies develop.
9. Characteristics of the Leontief model, such as price rigidity, stability of input coefficients and quantitative adjustment to derived demand, theoretically correspond to the Keynesian model under underemployment (Morishima 1955).
10 The number of sectors in the intermediate transaction matrix of the Asian international input–output table is [number of the endogenous countries] x [number of the sectors in each country].
11. Because of the characteristics of the Leontief model, such as perfect (price) inelasticity of demand, perfect elasticity of supply, and homogeneity of product in each sector (Oosterhave, Eding and Stedler 2001), the output is induced by a shift of the demand curve without affecting any price. Further, an assumption on the stability of input coefficients is supported by the Substitution Theorem (Samuelson 1951).
12. For $\mathbf{x} - \mathbf{x}(-sj)$ and $\mathbf{x}' - \mathbf{x}(-ri)'$, further mathematical development is possible by using the linear algebraic techniques. For details, see Milller and Lahr (2001).
13. As a precondition for the Ghosh model, inputs must be non-essential and must be perfectly substitutable with any other inputs, including primary

inputs (Gruver 1989). Further, as the output is delivered to each sector according to the fixed output coefficients, input coefficients of these sectors are changed accordingly. This is obviously not consistent with an assumption of fixed input coefficients in the Leontief model. Hence, in order to justify the usage of the Ghosh model, the new concept of "relative joint stability" was developed by Chen and Rose (1986, 1991); Rose and Allison (1989). Further, Dietzenbacher (1997) presented a proposal to reinterpret the Ghosh model as a price model to avoid the inconsistency with the Leontief model.

References

Balassa, B. (1966) "Tariff Reduction and Trade in Manufactures among the Industrial Countries," *American Economic Review*, 56, 3: 466–73.

Chen, C. Y. and Rose, A. (1986) "The Joint Stability of Input–Output Production and Allocation Coefficient," *Modeling and Simulation*, 17: 251–5.

Chen, C. Y. and Rose, A. (1991) "The Absolute and Relative Joint Stability of Input–Output Production and Allocation Coefficients," in W. Peterson, ed., *Advances in Input–Output Analysis, Technology, Planning and Development*, New York: Oxford University Press.

Chenery, H. B. and T. Watanabe (1958) "International Comparison of the Structure of Production," *Econometrica*, 26: 487–521.

Dietzenbacher, E. (1997) "In Vindication of the Ghosh Model: a Reinterpretation as a Price Model," *Journal of Regional Science*, 37, 4: 629–51.

Dietzenbacher, E. and Van der Linden, J. A. (1997) "Sectoral and Spatial Linkages in the EC Production Structure," *Journal of Regional Science*, 37, 2: 235–57.

Grubel, H. G. (1967) "Intra-Industry Specialization and the Pattern of Trade," *Canadian Journal of Economics and Political Science*, 33, 3: 374–88.

Grubel, H. G. and Lloyd, P. J. (1975) *Intra-Industry Trade: the Theory and Measurement of International Trade in Differentiated Products*, Basingstoke: Macmillan.

Gruver, G. W. (1989) "On the Plausibility of the Supply-Driven Input–Output Model: a Theoretical Basis for Input–Output Coefficients Change," *Journal of Regional Science*, 29: 441–50.

Hirschman, A. O. (1958) *The Strategy of Economic Development*, New Haven: Yale University Press.

Hoen, A. R. (2002) *An Input–Output Analysis of European Integration*, Amsterdam: North-Holland.

Miller, R. E. (1966) "International Feedback Effects in Input–Output Models: Some Preliminary Results," *Papers, Regional Science Association*, 17: 105–25.

Miller, R. E. and Lahr, M. L. (2001) "A Taxonomy of Extractions," in M. L. Lahr and R. E. Miller, eds, *Regional Science Perspectives in Economic Analysis: a Festschrift in Memory of Benjamin H. Stevens*, Amsterdam: North-Holland.

Morishima, M. (1955) *Introduction to Input–Output Analyisis* (in Japanese, *Sangyo Renkanron Nyumon*), Tokyo: Sobunsha.

Oosterhaven, J., Eding, G. J. and Stelder, D. (2001) "Clusters, Linkages and Interregional Spillover: Methodology and Policy Implications for the Two Dutch Mainports and the Rural North," *Regional Studies*, 35, 9: 809–22.

Ozaki, I. (2004) *Industrial Structure of Japan* (in Japanese, *Nihon no Sangyo Kozo*), Tokyo: Keio University Press.

Ozaki, I. and Ishida, K. (1970) "The Determination of Economic Basic Structure (1)" (in Japanese, "Keizai no Kihonteki Kozo no Kettei" (1)), *Mita Gakkai Zasshi*, 63: 15–35.

Rose, A. and Allison, T. (1989) "On the Plausibility of the Supply-Driven Input–Output Model: Empirical Evidence on Joint Stability," *Journal of Regional Science*, 29: 451–8.

Rasmussen, P. N. (1956) *Studies in Inter-Sectoral Relations*, Amsterdam: North-Holland.

Samuelson, P. A. (1951) "Abstract of a Theorem Concerning Substitutability in Open Leontief Models," in T. C. Koopmans, ed., *Activity Analysis of Production and Allocation*, New York: John Wiley & Sons.

Van der Linden, J. A. (1998) *Interdependence and Specialization in the European Union: Intercountry Input–Output Analysis and Economic Integration*, Capelle aan de IJssel: Labyrinth Publications.

4
Catching Up of Manufacturing Cum De Facto Economic Integration in East Asia

Daisuke Hiratsuka

1 Introduction

Several factors, including the tariff reduction inherent in WTO commitments, recent advancements in telecommunication, and large improvement of infrastructure, have led to a significant reduction in East Asian transportation costs, in the broad sense of the term. The reduction of transportation costs has expanded the cross-border economic activities by multinational corporations (MNCs) within the region. This has formed the production/distribution networks, discussed in Chapter 1, on the one hand, and catalyzed the catching up in manufacturing by the latecomers with the earlier starters on the other. Overall this phenomenon has advanced East Asia's de facto integration.

There have been some theoretical arguments on the issue of location of industry between North and South. Krugman (1979) advocated that international trade patterns were determined by a continuing process of innovation and technology transfer as seen in the world of an innovating North and a non-innovating South. Each product is initially produced in and exported by the North. When the technology involved in the production becomes available to the South, that is, when Southern labor substitutes for Northern labor, manufacturers in the North then move the industry to the South. Such relocation of manufacturing activities, led by technology transfer through FDI, can take place on a continuous basis. This may lead to a narrowing of the income gap between the North and the South. Because of the diminishing rents from new products, the North must continuously innovate. Otherwise, manufacturing in the North disappears as industries hollow out and migrate to the South. Continuous introduction of new products in the North generates a global innovation cycle in which the North and South can develop together.

This argument was further extended by Krugman and Venables (1995) who incorporated the concept of transportation costs. They argue that since the North offers a large market for intermediate goods and is therefore a more attractive place to locate production of intermediate goods (e.g. backward linkages), it is a better place to produce final goods for greater variation of intermediate goods. When transportation costs start to fall, the world economy organizes itself into an industrialized "core" and a deindustrialized "periphery,"[1] because manufacturers in the North locate production in this area. Initially, global economic integration leads to uneven development. However, if transportation costs continue to fall, the importance of being close to markets and suppliers, akin to the importance of forward and backward linkages, will decline. At that point, the advantage of low wages in the "periphery" offsets disadvantages in being remote from markets and suppliers. At this stage, manufacturing in the North moves out from the "core" to the "periphery." In consequence, an agricultural "periphery" becomes gradually industrialized.

These studies lead to the conclusion that manufacturing in the North moves to the South.[2] This leads to the agglomeration of manufacturing in the South, and finally the South, a latecomer to manufacturing, achieves catch up with the North, the forerunner or earlier starter in manufacturing activities. The agglomeration in the South, which therefore represents the catching up by the South with the North, advances when products are standardized and when transportation costs in the broad sense of the term fall enough to offset the Southern disadvantage of being far from markets and suppliers.

What kind of products are moved to the latecoming South? Krugman (1991b, 1991c: 1–34)[3] propounded an argument that the location of manufacturing is determined by three main factors: demand; the cost of fixed investment; and transportation costs. The interaction of market size marked by increasing returns with transportation costs plays an important role in location of production (Krugman 2004). This location theory accounts for the fact that manufactured products with low transportation costs and low fixed costs are moved to the latecomers when the world markets grow large. For example, a post-process plant for electronic parts, which are lightweight, can be easily moved to the latecomer. However, a pre-processing plant remains in the North, because such plants have relatively higher fixed costs.

This chapter aims to examine the catching up process of manufacturing activities in East Asia, using the North and South location framework, which has taken place in the formation of the regional production/distribution networks. To put it differently, without the catching up by the latecomers with the earlier starters and the resulting severe competition within the region, fragmentation would not have advanced in East Asia. This study helps to explain in what sectors the intra-industry trade has developed.

The real world is more complicated than the simple North (forerunner) and South (latecomer) structure. In examining the actual catching up in East Asia, three groups are identified: Japan as a front-runner, Asian NIEs (Hong Kong, Singapore, South Korea and Taiwan) as second-runners, and the ASEAN 4 (Indonesia, Malaysia, the Philippines and Thailand) and China as latecomers.

The concept of catching up is defined as the situation where a latecomer becomes the main producer of a good, replacing the forerunner or earlier starter, and increasingly resembles the earlier starter in its manufacturing activities (Akamatsu 1962). In the following sections, we first discuss the catching up development process, and then define "catching up" in the analytical framework used here. Finally, we examine to what extent the catching up process has actually occurred in East Asia. The analysis was carried out at the product and country group level over 1990–2001, in order to clearly understand the ongoing catching up of manufacturing activities in the region.

2 Development stages of the "catching up" process

"Catching up" is the situation in which a latecomer becomes a supplier in the world market, replacing a forerunner. To examine catching up in East Asia we first calculate for each product group the international competitive coefficient (ICC) index, which is one measurement of competitiveness (Watanabe and Kajiwara 1983; Hiratsuka 2005). The ICC index makes it possible to capture catching up in conjunction with the North and South framework. The ICC index is defined as net export (exports minus imports) over total trade (exports plus imports), and can be expressed as follows:

$$\text{ICC} = (\text{exports} - \text{imports}) / (\text{exports} + \text{imports})$$

The ICC index considers implicitly the demand and supply sides, since the numerator, "exports minus imports" is identical to "domestic supply minus domestic demand."[4] In fact, by observing the simple ICC index by product or industry over time, the domestic demand and supply gap can be discussed (Hiratsuka 2003, 2005). The ICC index takes a value between minus one and plus one. When the ICC index becomes positive (>0), domestic supply exceeds domestic demand. Conversely, when the ICC index becomes negative (<0), domestic supply is less than domestic demand. In cases where the ICC index is rising, domestic supply is increasing against domestic demand, and vice versa. This characteristic of the ICC value makes it possible to examine the stage at which each economy falls in terms of product development, as discussed below.

The graphic presentation of the ICC index reflects five development stages of a product in conjunction with import and export relations, that is, domestic supply and demand. It indicates which development stage manufacturing activities are in. Here, the five development stage terms defined by Yamazawa (1990) are used. These stages were used in the study of the catching up process in Japan. Figure 4.1 depicts the "ICC curve" tracing various values between minus one and plus one. The combination of the ICC index and the development stage can describe the five stages as follows:

(1) At the "introductory stage," when a forerunner exports new products and a latecomer imports them, the ICC index of the latecomer takes the value of minus 1.

(2) The stage in which the ICC index is increasing between minus one and zero is defined as the "import substitution stage." At this stage, industry in the latecomer shows weak competitiveness since the production level is not large enough in scale. The latecomer exports inferior-quality products to some extent, and yet domestic production is still less than domestic demand (the country is a net importer).

(3) At the "export stage," in which the ICC index is rising between zero and plus one, the latecomer produces at a large scale and expands exports rapidly. Eventually, domestic production exceeds domestic demand. It should be noted that the latecomer exports low-end products but imports high-end products from the forerunner.

(4) At the "mature stage," the ICC index declines to a level between plus one and zero. The product has "ripened" and the associated technology standardized. The forerunner slowly decreases exports, because it gradually fails to compete with the latecomer in its

Figure 4.1: The ICC curve according to the catching up product cycle

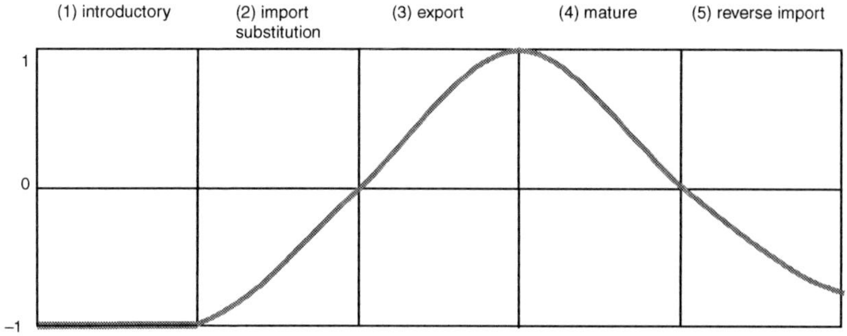

Source: author.

export markets. However, domestic production still exceeds domestic demand. The forerunner at the "mature stage" exports high-end products and imports low-end products.

(5) The stage at which the ICC index decreases to a level between zero and minus one is defined as the "reverse-import stage." At this stage, the forerunner fails to compete with the latecomer in the latecomer's domestic market, and domestic supply is less than domestic demand.

Thus, "catching up" can be defined as the latecomer moving up to the "export stage" from the "import substitution stage," while the forerunner moves down to more advanced stages, including the "mature stage" and finally the "reverse import stage." It is also theorized that in catching up, a so-called "leapfrogging" occurs, which refers to latecomers jumping in capabilities towards equality with both the second-runner and front-runner groups. This might happen because the latecomer implements new technology through FDI that creates the opportunity to be competitive. A flying geese pattern also occurs in which a front-runner is followed by a second-runner, and then by a latecomer. The second-runner, being followed by latecomers, may disappear for some product groups but will still exist within production seen as a whole.

3 The inter-industry catching up cycle

How much has the catching up diffused in East Asia? There are two catching up product cycles (Kojima 2000).[5] One is an inter-industry catching up cycle where new industries are developed; for example, a country might move from textile to light machinery production, and then to heavy machine production, or it might move from non-durable goods to durable goods, then to capital goods. The other type of cycle is intra-industry catching up. This catching up may occur from a downstream industry where factor endowments play a significant role, to a midstream industry that requires engineering elements, and then to an upstream industry that requires sizeable capital and technology. In the textile industry, catching up may go from apparel to yarn and fabric, and then to synthetic fiber. In the machinery industry, it may go from simple assembly to parts production, and then to other supporting industries such as molds.

This section examines how inter-industry catching up has diffused in finished goods in East Asia. Here, catching up is expected to occur sequentially as follows. First, catching up may take place in non-durable consumer goods, e.g. apparel, footwear and leather articles. Second, catching up may occur in durable consumer goods, e.g. furniture, home electrical appliances, personal computers and peripheral equipment, office and communication apparatus. Third, catching up may happen in transportation goods such as motorcycles, commercial vehicles and passenger cars. Lastly, catching up may occur in capital goods, e.g. machine tools and industrial machinery. Of primary concern is the catching up process of latecomers including the ASEAN 4 and China.

3.1 Non-durable consumer goods

Figure 4.2 exhibits the ICC values of apparel from 1990 to 2001. We apply a three-year moving average to the original ICC value series except for the initial year (1990) and the last year (2001). The latecomer group of the ASEAN 4 and China shows an ICC value of apparel close to one, while the second-runner group of Asian NIEs shows a decrease between one and zero. The frontrunner, Japan, shows an ICC value between zero and minus one. These tell us that the ASEAN 4 and China were in the "export stage" where domestic supply exceeded domestic demand. Meanwhile, the Asian NIEs (the second-runners) were at the "mature stage" where domestic supply exceeded domestic demand. However, domestic supply was decreasing against domestic demand in the range where the former still exceeded the latter. Japan was at the "reverse import stage" in which domestic demand exceeded domestic supply to a large extent. This indicates that Japan failed to remain at the "mature stage" within the apparel industry, and was forced to move to the final stage. Japanese apparel manufacturers currently produce niche products mainly for domestic consumers.

Footwear and leather articles are another example of non-durable consumer goods which have exhibited a similar catching up process to apparel (see Figure 4.3). China, Indonesia, Malaysia and Thailand were at the "export stage," while South Korea and Taiwan were at the "mutual stage," and Hong Kong and Singapore, as well as Japan, were at the "reverse import stage." The Philippines was at the "reverse import stage" as the ICC value for the country was between zero and minus one.

The above observations indicate that in non-durable consumer goods production, the latecoming ASEAN 4 and China passed the advanced economies of Asian NIEs and Japan. Manufacturing activities in non-durable consumer goods moved to the latecomer group of the ASEAN 4 and China. However, it should be noted that apparel and footwear and leather articles are subject to high tariffs in the ASEAN 4 and China. Perhaps more importantly, the ASEAN 4 and China have participated in the low value chain activity of manufacturing, while the higher value of economic activities such as design, distribution and marketing are handled by MNCs in the Asian NIEs, the US, Japan and the EU.

3.2 Light machinery assembly

Light machinery includes home electrical appliances, office and communication apparatus, personal computers and peripheral equipment, and precision apparatus. In the past, Japan was a major world supplier in East Asia. However, in the 1980s, it was faced with a shortage of labor, especially unskilled, as Japanese manufacturers expanded their world market share. This labor market situation pushed Japanese manufacturers to transfer manufacturing sites to the ASEAN 4 and China. When China further promoted the open door policy in 1992 that allowed foreign capital to operate for export purposes, it was chosen as a new export base by MNCs.

Personal computer and peripheral equipment is a typical product for which MNCs have chosen the ASEAN 4 and China as assembly sites. Figure 4.4 presents the ICC values of personal computer and peripheral equipment, and shows that the ICC value of the ASEAN 4 and China crossed the zero line in the 1990s. This indicates that the ASEAN 4 and China moved up to the "export stage" in the 1990s. It is noteworthy that the Philippines showed the highest value, very close to one. In 1995 and 1996, Japanese hard disc drive (HDD) makers, namely Hitachi, Toshiba and Fujitsu, relocated their 3.5 inch HDD manufactur-

Competitive Coefficient (ICC) Index

Figure 4.2: Apparel

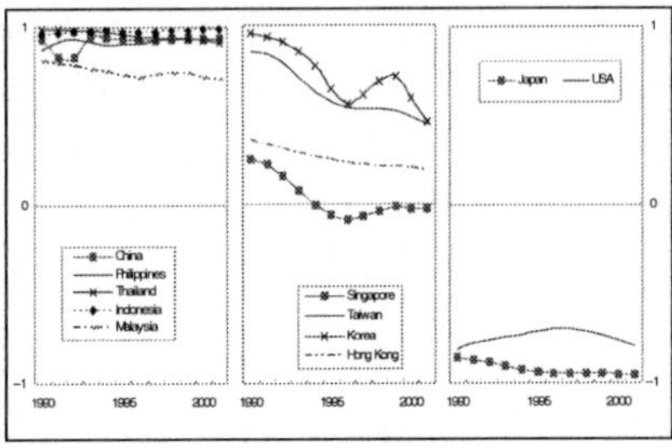

Figure 4.3: Footwear and leather articles

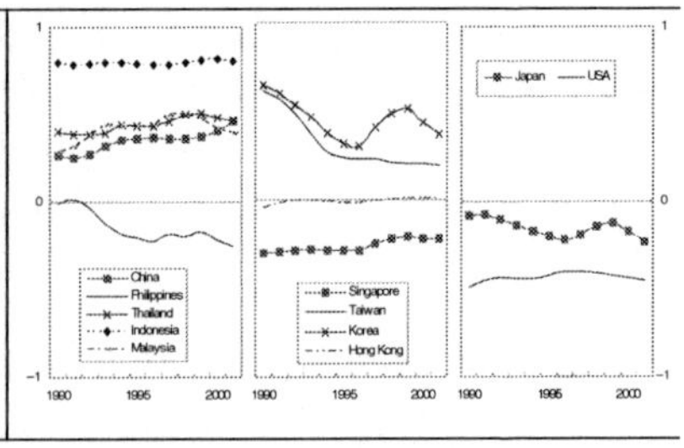

Figure 4.4: Personal computer and peripheral equipment

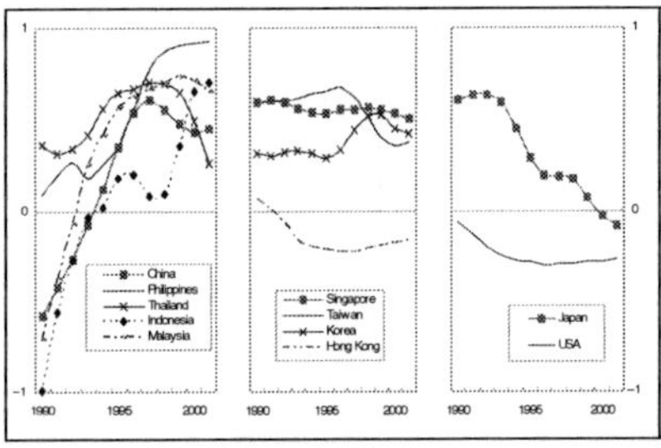

Figure 4.5: Office and communication apparatus

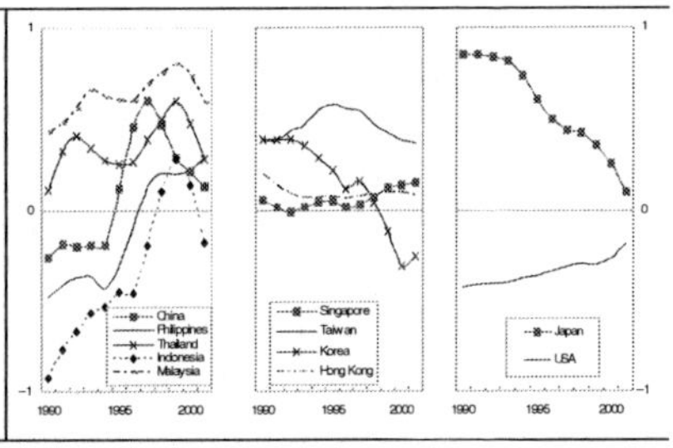

Figure 4.6: Home electrical appliances

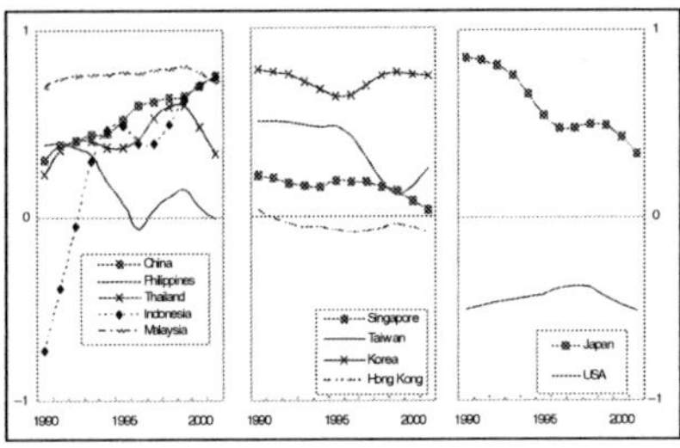

Figure 4.7: Precision apparatus

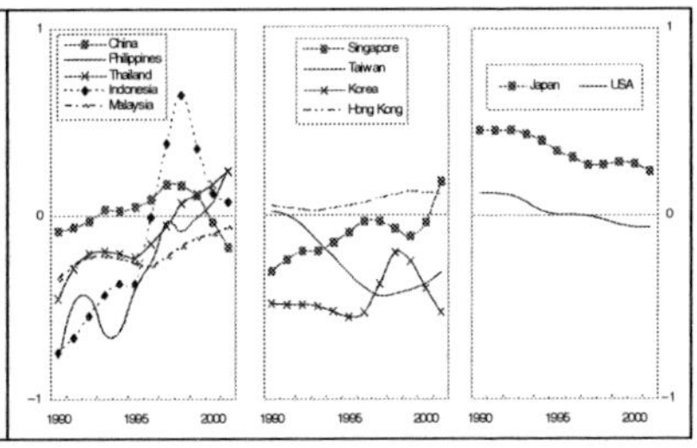

ing factories to the Philippines, where a large number of English-speaking engineers were available. They assembled laptop computers either by own brand manufacturing (OBM) or by own equipment manufacturing (OEM) since the key components of 3.5 inch HDDs are supplied. Meanwhile, South Korea, Singapore and Taiwan, earlier

Figure 4.8: Motorcycles

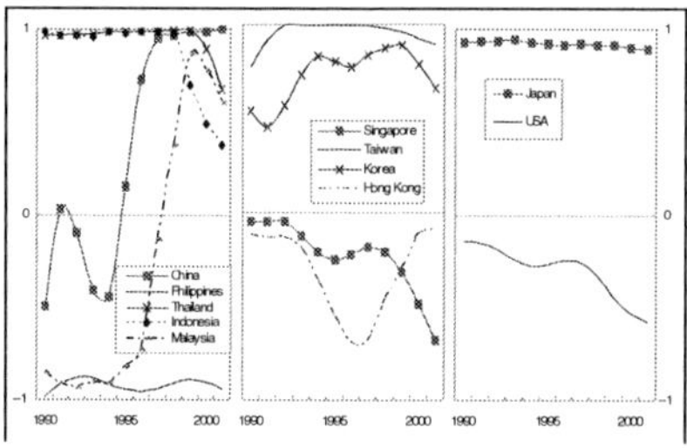

Figure 4.9: Commercial vehicles

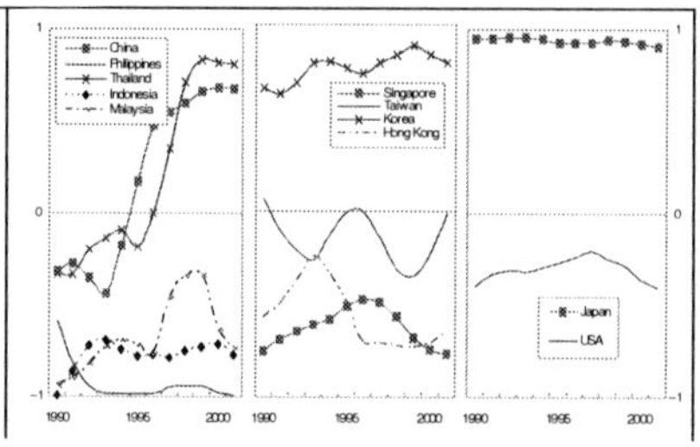

Figure 4.10: Passenger cars

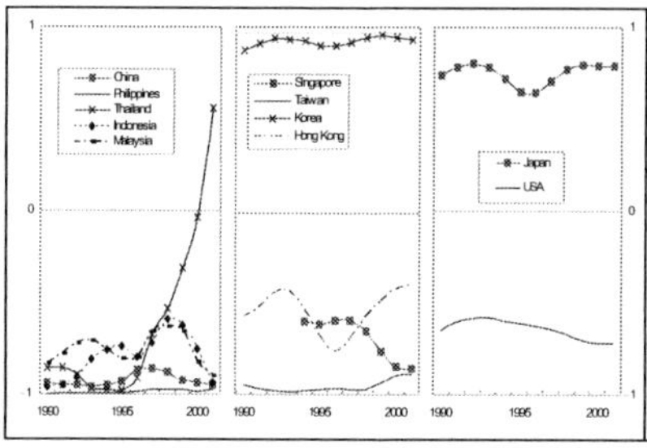

Figure 4.11: Machine tool

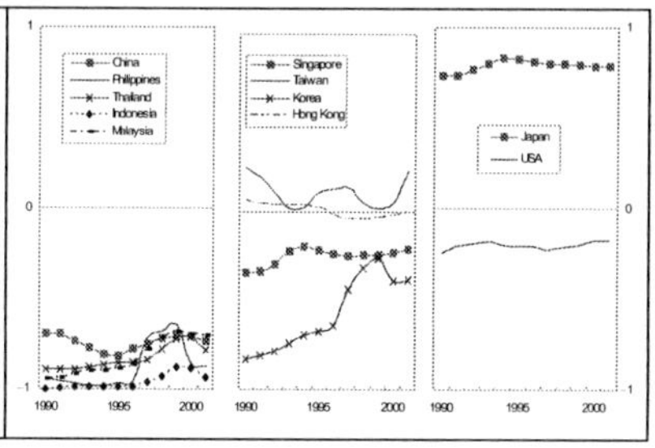

Figure 4.12: Industrial machinery

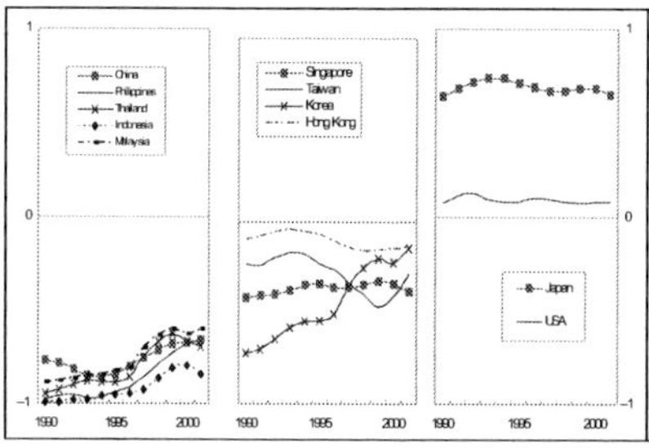

Figure 4.13: Yarn and fabric

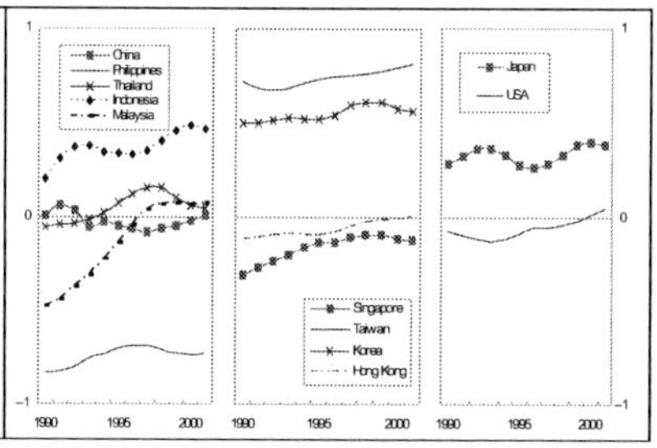

starters in the personal computer and peripheral equipment industry, also maintained high ICC value in the 1990s in the "mature stage". This indicates that initial advantages were locked in (Krugman 1991c); for example, Singapore continues to export high performance PC servers despite the competition from the latecomers. In contrast, Japan's ICC value decreased to below zero in 2000, moving down from the "mature stage" to the "reverse import stage." The personal computer and peripheral equipment market has exhibited tremendous growth, and

Figure 4.14: Synthetic fiber textile

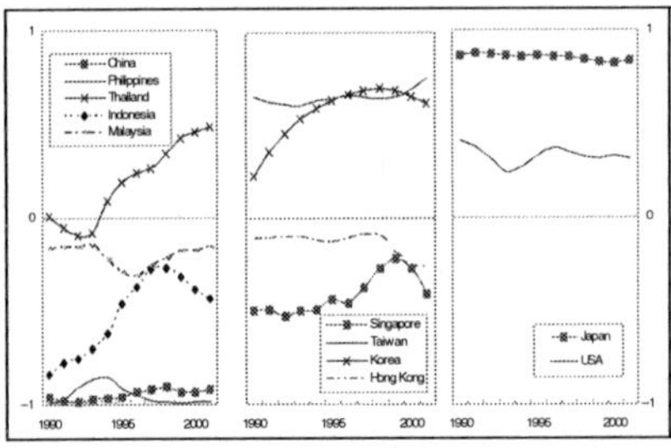

Figure 4.15: Home electrical appliance parts

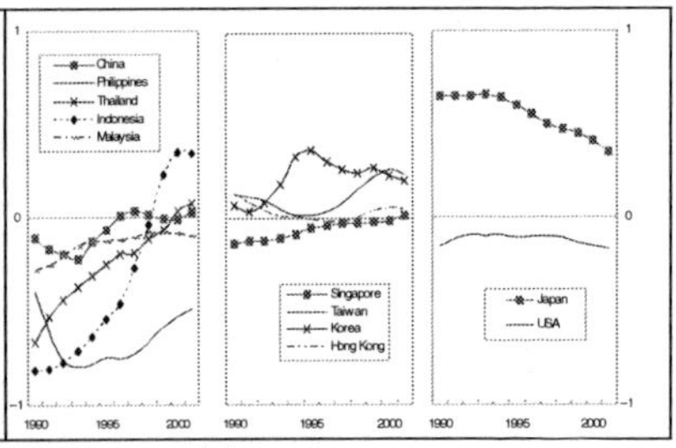

Figure 4.16: Electronic parts

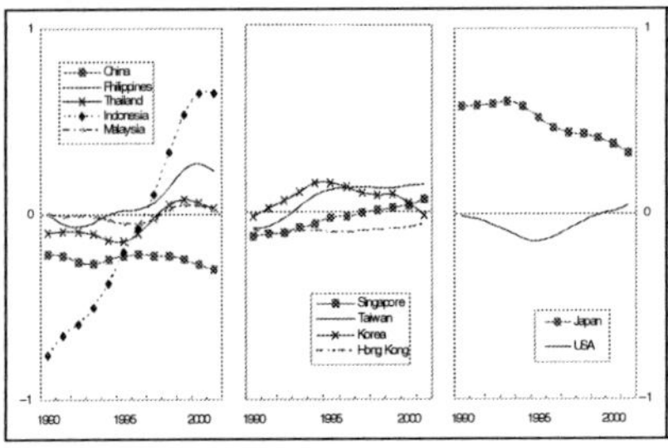

Figure 4.17: Office and communication apparatus parts

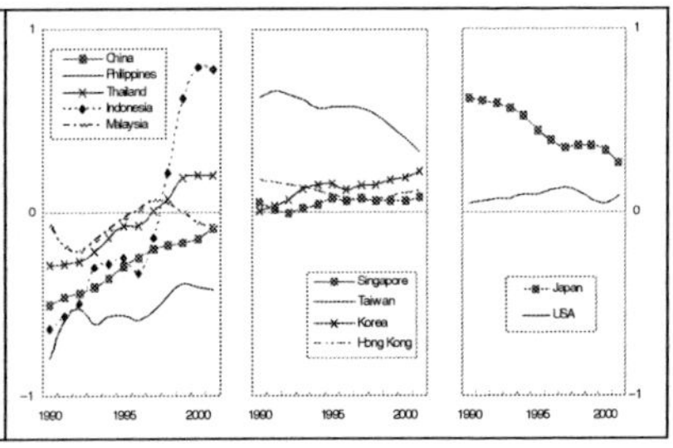

Figure 4.18: Molds

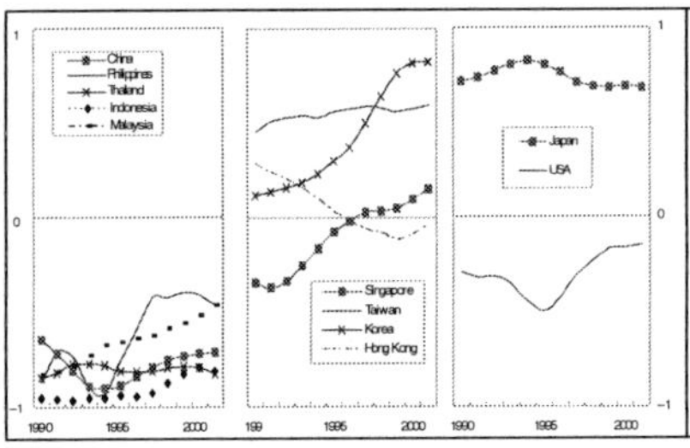

Figure 4.19: Motorcycle parts

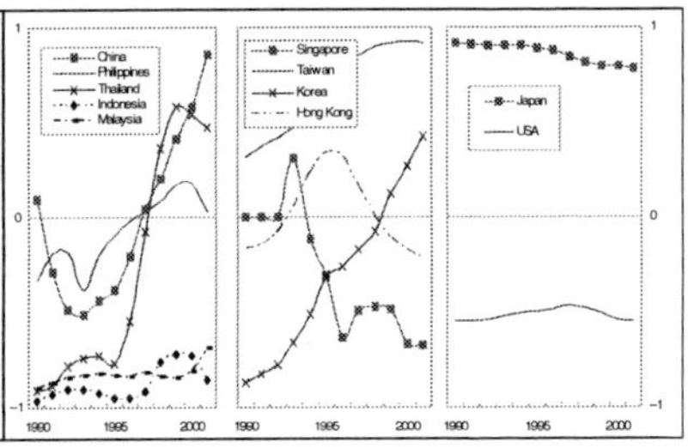

production processes that assemble parts into a unit are standardized. High performance units are assembled by Singapore, medium performance units by Malaysian and Thailand, and low-end products by China.

Office and communication apparatus including copying machines, printers and facsimile modems are similar to personal computer and peripheral equipment, as far as the catching up is concerned. The

Figure 4.20: Automobile parts

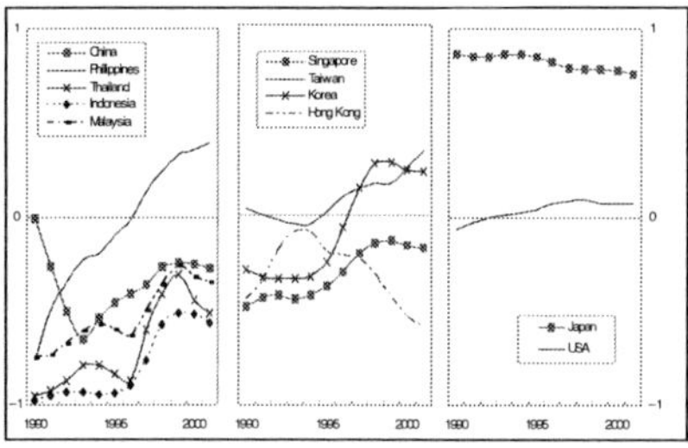

Figure 4.21: Machine tool parts

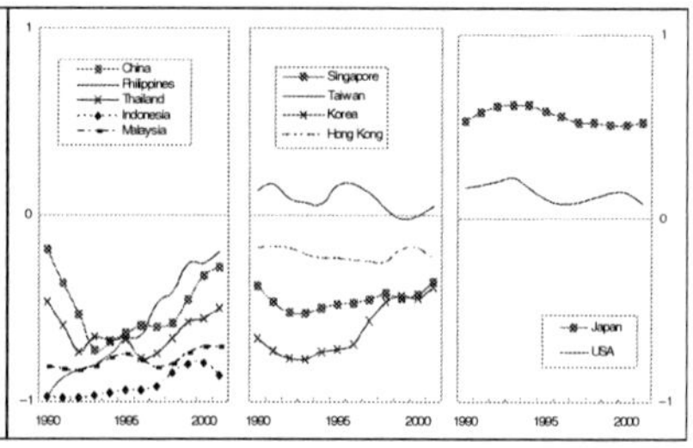

Figure 4.22: Industrial machinery parts

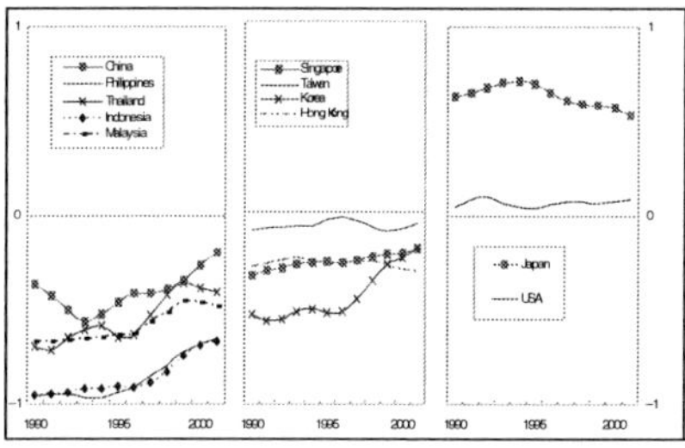

Figure 4.23: Basic petrochemical products

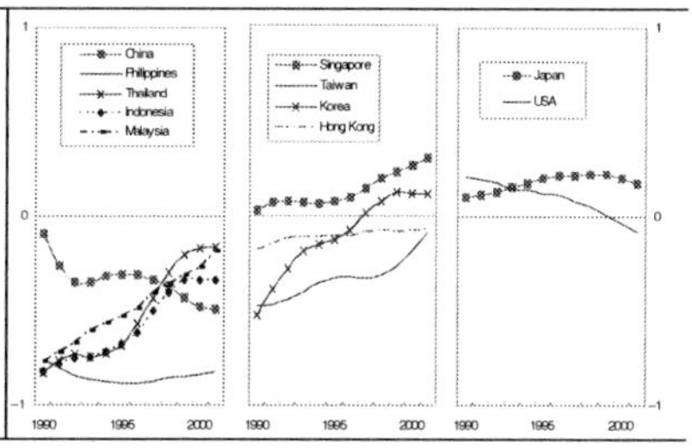

Figure 4.24: Petrochemical products

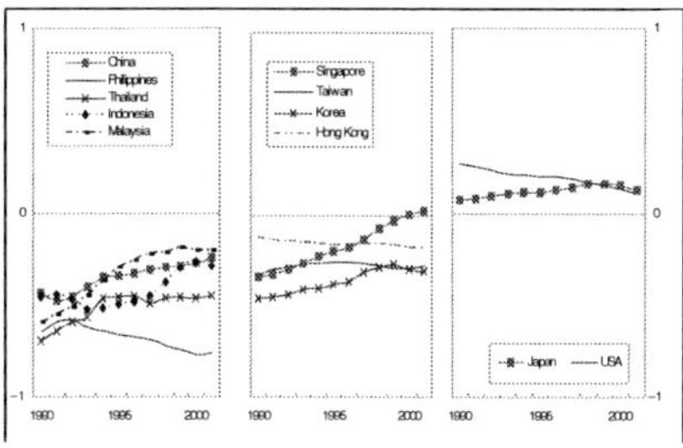

Figure 4.25: Iron and steel

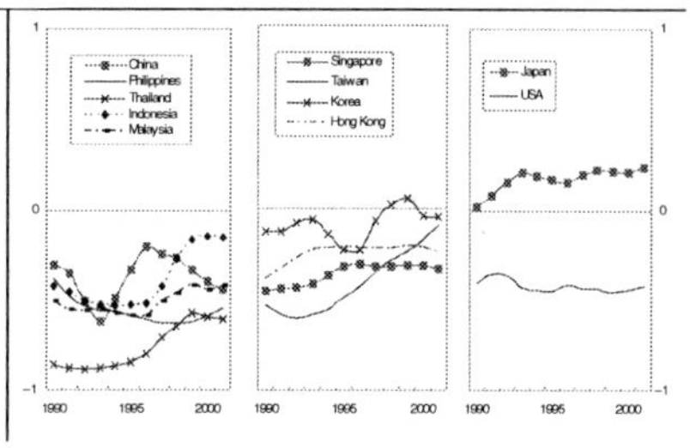

Note: The three years moving average procedure is applied to the original series except the starting year, 1990, and the ending year, 2001.
Source: Ajiken Indicators on Developing Economies: Extended for Trade Statistics (IDE-AIDXT).

ASEAN 4 and China saw enhanced ICC values in the 1990s, reaching the "export stage." It is noteworthy that South Korea's ICC value decreased to the "mature stage" in the 1990s (see Figure 4.5).

Home electrical appliances developed in the ASEAN 4, in particular in Malaysia, where parts are easily procured since the electronics parts were easily procured from Penang and the neighboring country of Singapore. Due to the spatial linkage effect, Malaysia became a production center of home electrical appliances in the early 1980s. Given this historical background, Malaysia's home electrical appliance industry shows very strong competitiveness as the ICC values are close to one throughout the 1990s. Figure 4.6 indicates that a great change occurred in the 1990s, as the ICC values of China, Indonesia and Thailand increased to the "export stage." Meanwhile the values of Taiwan, Singapore and Japan decreased to the "mature stage." It should be noted that the ASEAN 4 and China group divided into two camps. The winners were Malaysia, China, Indonesia and Thailand; the loser was the Philippines. The Philippines failed to maintain its competitiveness because of its remoteness from intermediate parts and its high wages. It is noteworthy that South Korea and Japan have maintained their competitiveness in home electrical appliances, compared to the personal computer and peripheral equipment, and office and communication industries. This is because home electrical appliances contain a higher variety of products; the production of low-end products has moved, but production of high-end products has remained at the home country of MNCs.

Nevertheless, as far as precision apparatus goes, catching up has not yet advanced. Not only the ASEAN 4 and China but also the Asian NIEs have remained at the "import substitution stage" although they have increased their competitiveness (see Figure 4.7). On the other hand, Japan continues to maintain strong competitiveness. This might be due to the fact that MNCs have not undertaken FDI for precision apparatus, because the market has not been large enough against fixed investment costs, and the industry requires very sophisticated process engineering.

3.3 Transportation machinery

Motorcycles, commercial vehicles and passenger cars are quite different from light machinery assembly goods in both regional international trade patterns and in production history. For instance, in Thailand, light machinery and assembly started mainly for export purposes, while transportation machinery was initially produced for the domestic market, and due to the home market effect, transportation machinery has developed to the export industry. This different production history has affected the international trade pattern within the region.

Within this industry, motorcycles is a base industry for transportation machinery in the ASEAN 4 and China. The motorcycle industry initially developed in Thailand and then in Indonesia as a domestic market-oriented industry. Due to the so-called "home market effect" that countries and/or regions tend to export products subject to increasing returns for which they have a large domestic market (Krugman 2004), the motorcycle industry has become an export industry for these countries in recent years. Japanese motorcycle manufacturers such as Honda and Suzuki have their main Asian factories in Thailand. Initially, a new model for the Asian market was introduced in Thailand, and then it was expanded to Indonesia and Vietnam. In contrast, China has a large number of indigenous motorcycle manufacturers. Chinese motorcycle manufacturers, faced with an oversupply problem as in other industries, have begun to export to neighboring countries.

Unlike light machinery, in motorcycles, Japan, South Korea and Taiwan still remain competitive in the "export stage" (Figure 4.8). Perhaps the wide division of labor in East Asia, in accordance with different product quality, allows the coexistence of the latecomers (the ASEAN 4 and China), the second-runners (South Korea and Taiwan), and the frontrunner (Japan). Japan and the ASEAN 4 produce different quality products. Japan, the world's largest motorcycle supplier, produces high and medium price models (US$3087 per unit in 2003), largely to the US and EU markets. Japanese subsidiaries in Thailand and Indonesia produce low quality models. Honda, Suzuki and Yamaha have established an international division of labor whereby the ASEAN 4 produce low-end goods to neighboring countries such as Cambodia, Vietnam and so on. These Japanese firms compete with South Korean manufacturers. On the other hand, China has become the second largest supplier in the world, and exports very low-end products (US$162 per unit in 2003). Chinese motorcycle manufacturers, who are indigenous suppliers faced with the oversupply problem, have begun to export. Their main export market is the US.

Similarly, the commercial vehicle industry has developed in Thailand, China, South Korea and Japan. These industries initially developed with a domestic market orientation. For instance, Thailand is a significant manufacturer of commercial vehicles in its market because the government has imposed lower sales taxes for commercial vehicles compared to passenger cars. For this policy, Thailand has become the second-largest world market for one ton pickup trucks. This fairly huge domestic market has attracted foreign suppliers, including part suppliers. Isuzu-GM, Honda, Matsuda-Ford, Mitsubishi, Suzuki and Toyota have regarded Thailand as a base for one ton pickup commercial vehicle production, not only for the Thai domestic market but also for external ones. The home market effect explains why Thailand shows high ICC index values and has climbed to the "export stage" (see Figure 4.9). In addition, most motorcycle part suppliers have provided parts to vehicle industries including commercial vehicles. As a result, parts suppliers agglomerated in Thailand.

As for passenger cars, there are only a few export suppliers in East Asia: Japan, South Korea and Thailand. Japan, which is the second-largest exporter next to Germany, has maintained an ICC value at the "export stage." South Korea attained the highest ICC value (see Figure 4.10). It has grown to the ninth-largest exporter in the world. The US is the largest export market for South Korea. On the other hand, Korea is not a large importer because of its high tariffs. Thailand's ICC value increased to the "export stage" in the 1990s. Thailand exports to neighboring ASEAN countries such as Indonesia, the Philippines, Malaysia, Singapore, Cambodia, Brunei and Laos, which account for almost half of its market. Malaysia used to export a relatively modest amount of passenger cars, such as the Proton Saga to the UK, Iran and so on. This export behavior has decreased recently while imported vehicles have increased in number because of the rise of national income in Malaysia. Only South Korea is catching up with Japan, while Thailand is just a small exporter to neighboring countries. In the automobile industry, including commercial vehicles, economies of scale play a very important role. In addition, parts suppliers are critical to becoming an exporter, as demonstrated in the Thai case. If suppliers are located far from the assembling plant, transportation costs would be high. Because of these economies of scale and transportation cost issues, automobile makers tend to concentrate production in a few countries.

3.4 Heavy machinery

The heavy machinery industry contains machine tools (Figure 4.11) and industrial machinery (Figure 4.12). Machine tools and industrial machinery exhibit a similar catching up pattern with precision apparatus. Because of its small production, and because its integral products require sophisticated processing technology and huge capital, this industry has a limited number of players. Japan has been a major supplier of heavy machinery, and Japanese manufacturers have not undertaken FDI to the ASEAN 4 and China except in a few instances. For these reasons, Japan preserves high competitiveness and remains at the "export stage." Meanwhile, not only the latecomer group of the ASEAN 4 and China but also the second-runner groups of the Asian NIEs are still at the "import substitution stage." The only exception is Taiwan, which has started to achieve catching up in machine tools.

3.5 Inter-industry catching up

As expected, manufacturing for non-durable consumer goods such as apparel has moved to the latecomers of the ASEAN 4 and China. The ASEAN 4 and China have attained catching up with the frontrunner of Japan, and also with the second-runners of the Asian NIEs for non-durable consumer goods. However, Japan and the Asian NIEs produce advanced products. Catching up by the latecomers of the ASEAN 4 and China implies that the unindustrialized "periphery" of the ASEAN 4 and China have become an industrialized "core," and East Asia, as a whole, has transformed, from the simple model where production is concentrated in Japan and the Asian NIEs, to a model where the greater East Asian region produces varieties of light machinery and products of varying qualitiy, and exports them to the world. As for transportation machinery, catching up has partly advanced for motorcycles, but has not advanced for other industries, because economies of scale play such an important role. It is noteworthy that South Korea has attained catching up with Japan for passenger cars. However, catching up has not advanced at all for heavy machinery.

4 Intra-industry catching up cycle

It was observed in the previous section that the latecomers of the ASEAN 4 and China have advanced in catching up for various finished products. Catching up has tended to advance fastest in downstream industries and more slowly in midstream and upstream industries. This is because the downstream industries are relatively more labor intensive while mid and upstream industries are more technology and capital intensive. This section examines whether catching up has occurred from downstream to midstream and finally to upstream industries. This section specifically deals with the fabric and weaving, and synthetic fiber sub-industries of the textile industry; parts of the light machinery and transportation machinery industries; the heavy machinery industry; and the mold and die, and material sub-industries of steel and chemical products.

4.1 The textiles industry

The textiles industry is roughly composed of three streams: downstream apparel, midstream fabric and weaving, and upstream fiber.

As discussed in the previous section, the ASEAN 4 and China have finished catching up with the Asian NIEs and Japan in apparel manufacturing. Apparel is a labor intensive industry in which low wages play a more significant role than any other factor such as distance to market and suppliers. Actually, Bangladesh and China are the world's first- and second-largest exporters of apparel (garment; HS6113). However, the midstream textiles industry, and yarn and fabric are quite different from finished apparel.

The yarn and fabric industry has developed well in East Asia. Figure 4.13 shows that most East Asian economies including Japan are at the "export stage" for yarn and fabric. This demonstrates that East Asia as a whole has been very competitive for yarn and fabric. There are differences in export unit prices of yarn and fabric. For instance, there is a quality ladder for woven fabric of synthetic yarn (HS5407), as evidenced by market prices: Japan is highest (US$15741 per ton), followed by South Korea (US$6501 per ton), Taiwan (US$4267 per ton), Thailand (US$4190 per ton) and China (US$752 per ton), reflecting comparative advantage. Most of these exports are directed to the extra-regional area. The intra-regional trade of yarn and fabric amounted to only 35.9 percent of total trade in 2001.

In the upstream textile industry, synthetic fiber requires huge capital and advanced technology, and therefore exhibits different patterns in the catching up stages from the midstream of yarn and fabric (Figure 4.14). The latecomers of the ASEAN 4 and China are still at the "import substitution stage," with the exception of Thailand. South Korea and Taiwan have raised their competitiveness and have attained the catching up with Japan. Meanwhile, Japan shows the most competitive profile among East Asian countries.

4.2 Parts of light machinery

As discussed in the previous section, the ASEAN 4 and China have progressed in catching up with the Asian NIEs and Japan in light machinery assembly for home electrical appliances, office and communication apparatus, and personal computers and peripheral equipment. This development creates an opportunity for the parts industries of these countries to develop through the "backward linkage effect." The question therefore arises as to whether catching up has advanced for light machinery parts.

The ICC values for home electrical appliance parts show a kind of flying geese or catching up pattern. The frontrunner, Japan, has been ahead of other East Asian economies, followed by the second-runners of the Asian NIEs and then by the latecomer group of the ASEAN 4 and China (Figure 4.15).[6] Especially South Korea and Taiwan have chased Japan, and Singapore, Thailand and China followed them. In spite of this pursuit by the followers, Japan has stayed ahead of other East Asia economies. This flying geese pattern indicates that East Asia as a whole has agglomerated parts of home electrical appliances and is very competitive in the world.

In comparison with home electrical appliances parts, catching up in electronic parts (Figure 4.16) and office and communication apparatus parts (Figure 4.17) has been more advanced. Here, the ICC values of the latecomer group of the ASEAN 4 and China, and the second-runner group of the Asian NIEs, have reached levels close to that of Japan. The ASEAN 4 and China have been chasing the Asian NIEs, and the Asian NIEs have been chasing Japan. It should be noted that the Philippines shows a very competitive profile for electronic parts, corresponding to its downstream of personal computer and peripheral equipment strength. The Philippines case indicates that electronic parts and personal computer and peripheral equipment have developed strong upstream and downstream linkages.

In East Asia, light machinery parts largely converge in terms of their ICC values. This means that the international trade pattern in East Asia has changed from "one-way trade" to "intra-regional trade." At one time, Japan exported most parts to other countries and/or regions in the region, but today Japan exports the key and advanced parts only. For example, within electronics parts China produces a lot of fuse units while Japan produces large-scale integrated circuits (LSI). Furthermore, each East Asian country produces functionally equivalent products, but their quality, reliability and durability are different. For example, Japan produces code for portable devices, but the ASEAN 4 and China produce code for stationary devices. Portable devices require expensive compact and durable parts, but stationary devices accept inexpensive large and non-durable parts. According to locational advantage, parts of different processing and function, and different quality and reliability, are mutually traded within the region. This is done through the production network, which has contributed to the development of cross-border production sharing (or so-called fragmentation) as well as within-border production sharing.

4.3 Molds and dies

Molds and dies are essential capital goods for the casting of machinery and the assembly and parts industries. Catching up in molds and dies in East Asia developed as Japan moved ahead of other economies. Japan was followed by Taiwan, and then South Korea. In the 1990s, however, South Korea raised its competitiveness by a great margin, while Japan increased its imports of molds and dies from South Korea and Taiwan, which decreased its ICC value slightly. As a result, the ICC values of South Korea exceeded those of Japan (Figure 4.18). Taiwan and Singapore also enhanced their competitiveness in terms of ICC value. In contrast, the ASEAN 4 and China have remained at the "import substitution stage" for molds and dies in spite of the fact that their markets are growing due to the development of their light machinery industries. It will take many years until the molding industries in the ASEAN 4 and China become competitive, because molds and dies require high precision techniques with machine tools.

4.4 Transportation and heavy machinery parts

The motorcycle parts industry has developed in tandem with the motorcycle assembly industry in East Asia. China and Thailand, as well as South Korea and Taiwan, countries in which the motorcycle industry has developed, have enhanced their competitiveness to the "export stage" for motorcycle parts (Figure 4.19). The motorcycle assembly and parts industries are developing through mutual backward and forward linkages. An exception is the Philippines, where motorcycle parts have reached at the "export stage," in spite of the fact that motorcycle assembly has not.

As for automobile parts, Japan has been far ahead of other East Asian economies. South Korea and Taiwan have attained catching up in recent years. Also the Philippines is succeeding in catching up. Catching up, however, has not diffused into many countries for motorcycle parts or for automobile parts.

The motorcycle parts industry has offered a base for the automobile parts industry in East Asia, because motorcycle and automobile industries share similar engineering technology. Taiwan and the Philippines, where the motorcycle parts industry has developed, have raised their competitiveness for automobile parts (Figure 4.20).

Not only the ASEAN 4 and China group, but also the Asian NIEs have still remained at the "import substitution stage" (Figure 4.21, Figure 4.22) for the heavy industrial and industrial machinery portions of machine parts. Only Taiwan, which has attained catching up for machine tools, has raised its competitiveness to the "export stage."

4.5 Materials industry

The materials industries are basic petrochemicals, petrochemicals and steel. Their competitiveness is almost completely determined by production scale. In East Asia, these materials industries have developed under protection, largely by joint ventures between domestic and foreign capital. The materials industries that have developed for domestic market exhibit a typical flying geese catching up pattern (Figures 4.23, 4.24 and 4.25). Japan has remained ahead of other East Asian economies except in the case of basic petrochemicals in Singapore. However, the Asian NIEs raised their competitiveness in the 1990s, and the competitiveness gap between Japan and the Asian NIEs has become marginal. As for the basic petrochemical industry, Singapore is already ahead of Japan in terms of the ICC index. The latecomers of the ASEAN 4 and China raised their competitiveness, but have still remained at the "import substitution stage" where domestic demand exceeds domestic supply.

4.6 Inter-industry catching up

The latecomers of the ASEAN 4 and China have achieved catching up with the Asian NIEs and Japan in yarn and fabric, which is a midstream textile industry. This reflects the fact that the downstream apparel industry has developed in the ASEAN 4 and China. Similarly, the ASEAN 4 and China have attained catching up in light machinery parts due to the backward linkage effect. On the other hand, the frontrunner Japan and the group of second-runners retain strong competitiveness in those midstream industries. This demonstrates that the catching up in midstream industries by the ASEAN 4 and China with Japan and the Asian NIEs has expanded intra-industry trade within the East Asian region, and has enhanced competitiveness against other regions such as NAFTA and the EU.

However, the catching up by the ASEAN 4 and China has not appeared in molds and dies. The Asian NIEs, however, have achieved catching up in molds and dies. Even the Asian NIEs have not succeeded, however, in catching up with Japan in parts of the heavy machinery and transportation industries. Catching up by the Asian NIEs with Japan does not appear in materials industries except by Singapore in the case of the petrochemical industry.

5 Development of intra-regional trade

The previous two sections found that catching up by the ASEAN 4 and China group and the group of Asian NIEs has diffused into various industries, either by inter-industry or intra-industry linkages. This indicates that the manufacturing structure tends to converge over time among nations in East Asia. Actually, the convergence is clearly emerging in parts of the light machinery industry. As a consequence of catching up, what changes in international trade position have occurred? Do the ASEAN 4 and China occupy the major world export share in light machinery and their parts, replacing that of Japan? What position do the Asian NIEs occupy? To answer these questions, this section calculates the world export share by product group, which corresponds to the same product groups used in the previous sections.

East Asia shows remarkable changes in world export share (Table 4.1). First, Japan's share of world exports in finished goods decreased from 11.1 percent in 1990 to 6.6 percent in 2001. South Korea's and Taiwan's world export share in finished goods decreased as well. In contrast, China's world export share in finished goods increased from 2.8 percent to 7.6 percent, which is the largest world export share among East Asia. The ASEAN 4's share also increased from 3.9 percent to 5.2 percent.

The decline in world export share of Japan is more drastic for light machinery; Japan's share decreased from 18.4 percent to 7.0 percent in personal computers and peripheral equipment, from 31.3 percent to 6.4 percent in office and communication apparatus, and from 25.7 percent to 8.5 percent in home electrical appliances. Meanwhile, China attained the largest world export share in 2001, reaching 11.2 percent in home electrical appliances and 7.8 percent in office and communication apparatus, and attained the second-largest world export share of 7.2 percent in personal computer and peripheral equipment. In 2001, the ASEAN 4 reached the largest world export share of 8.2 percent in personal computer and peripheral equipment and the second-largest share of 7.9 percent in home electrical appliances.

The world export share in parts has been changing also. Japan's parts world export share decreased from 15.3 percent in 1990 to 11.1 percent in 2001. The share of the ASEAN 4 and Singapore increased from 2.4 percent to 6.6 percent, and Singapore's increased from 2.4 percent to 4.6 percent. The share of the combined ASEAN 5 reached 11.2 percent in 2001, which is slightly higher than that of Japan, and larger than that of China, which reached 3.8 percent in 2001. The ASEAN 5 has become a production center for parts, equivalent to Japan. Particularly in electronic parts, the ASEAN 4 and the ASEAN 5 in 2001 accounted for 11.3 percent and 19.3 percent, respectively, of world

Table 4.1: World export share by country/region and by product group (%)

	China		ASEAN 4		Singapore		ASEAN 5		Taiwan		South Korea		Hong Kong		East Asia		Japan		All East Asia		NAFTA		EU	
Product group	1990	2001	1990	2001	1990	2001	1990	2001	1990	2001	1990	2001	1990	2001	1990	2001	1990	2001	1990	2001	1990	2001	1990	2001
Finished goods (weighted average)	2.8	7.6	3.9	5.2	1.9	1.9	5.8	7.1	3.0	1.9	3.1	2.7	4.3	4.8	18.9	24.1	11.1	6.6	30.0	30.8	17.6	22.9	52.3	46.3
Agricultural products	3.8	5.2	8.6	6.9	1.3	0.4	9.9	7.3	0.6	0.4	0.7	0.5	0.9	0.8	15.9	14.1	0.3	1.2	16.2	15.3	36.9	39.4	46.9	45.3
Processed agricultural products	2.7	3.9	6.5	7.7	1.4	1.0	7.9	8.7	22.5	22.5	1.0	0.8	1.7	1.4	14.6	15.5	0.9	0.8	15.4	16.4	22.5	24.8	62.0	58.8
Apparel	12.0	24.5	7.0	7.9	1.8	1.1	8.8	9.0	4.3	1.7	7.0	3.0	17.3	15.2	49.4	53.3	0.7	0.3	50.1	53.7	3.5	12.2	46.5	34.1
Footwear & leather articles	2.9	9.6	4.9	6.5	0.6	0.5	5.6	7.0	4.3	1.5	5.9	2.6	4.2	6.2	22.8	26.8	4.2	3.1	27.0	30.0	14.1	18.3	58.9	51.8
Furniture	1.7	10.3	3.8	8.4	0.5	0.8	4.3	9.2	6.3	2.5	0.9	0.3	1.5	2.1	14.6	24.4	0.9	0.3	15.5	24.7	8.4	20.9	76.1	54.5
Miscellaneous manufactured goods	2.8	9.9	2.7	3.3	1.2	2.4	3.9	5.7	6.6	2.8	4.1	1.6	7.6	9.8	25.0	29.9	6.5	3.4	31.5	33.3	14.6	22.7	54.0	44.0
Bicycle	3.6	34.9	2.1	1.6	0.1	0.0	2.2	1.6	44.0	24.1	2.5	0.9	2.7	2.8	55.0	64.3	3.2	0.3	58.2	64.6	4.1	6.5	37.7	28.9
TV games	2.0	18.9	0.2	0.3	0.5	1.1	0.7	1.4	19.9	0.2	0.3	0.1	15.5	2.6	38.4	23.1	34.6	12.5	72.9	35.6	13.5	20.8	13.5	43.7
Personal computer & peripheral equipments	0.1	7.2	0.7	8.2	10.3	9.1	11.0	17.3	6.1	6.7	3.0	4.1	1.4	2.6	21.6	38.0	18.4	7.0	39.9	44.9	22.6	21.3	37.5	33.8
Office & communication apparatus	1.0	7.8	2.1	4.6	2.6	1.7	4.7	6.2	3.6	4.4	2.2	1.5	5.1	6.3	16.6	26.4	31.5	6.4	48.1	32.7	11.6	21.4	40.3	45.9
Home electrical appliances	3.0	11.2	3.8	7.9	5.2	2.4	9.0	10.4	4.4	1.9	6.2	7.1	6.7	6.1	29.3	36.6	25.7	8.5	55.0	45.1	8.6	18.7	36.4	36.2
Precision apparatus	1.5	3.2	0.8	2.5	1.4	2.4	2.3	4.9	1.9	1.4	1.2	0.8	6.6	5.7	13.4	16.0	17.4	9.9	30.8	25.8	22.6	30.9	46.6	43.2
Motorcycle	0.1	7.7	0.4	1.8	3.1	0.1	3.4	1.9	1.4	2.3	0.5	0.8	2.8	0.6	8.2	13.4	59.7	48.7	67.9	62.1	7.2	6.8	24.9	31.1
Commercial vehicle	0.4	3.5	0.3	1.8	0.2	0.1	0.5	1.9	0.8	0.2	2.4	1.7	0.2	0.1	4.2	7.4	20.1	8.6	24.3	16.0	23.4	35.1	52.3	48.9
Passenger cars	0.0	0.0	0.1	0.3	0.0	0.0	0.1	0.3	0.0	0.0	1.1	4.1	0.1	0.2	1.3	4.7	25.2	18.1	26.5	22.7	16.2	22.2	57.3	55.0
Material (weighted average)	2.7	4.7	3.6	4.5	2.1	1.9	5.7	6.4	2.1	2.7	2.1	3.5	2.3	2.6	14.9	20.0	6.6	5.9	21.4	25.9	17.9	20.8	60.6	53.3
Natural fiber textile	15.4	13.5	1.4	1.3	0.4	0.2	1.8	1.5	1.6	2.3	2.1	3.5	4.1	1.7	23.1	19.5	0.4	0.1	23.5	19.7	43.6	45.8	33.0	34.6
Yarn & fabric	6.2	11.2	2.9	5.1	1.1	0.6	4.0	5.7	7.5	8.5	7.2	9.3	9.0	10.3	33.9	45.1	7.3	5.4	41.1	50.5	6.1	10.7	52.8	38.8
Glass & cement	2.5	5.8	2.8	3.6	0.6	0.5	3.3	4.1	1.9	0.8	1.1	1.0	2.9	3.7	11.7	15.5	5.3	5.1	17.1	20.6	8.3	17.0	74.7	62.4
Mineral products	7.4	7.7	17.7	16.7	0.1	0.1	17.8	16.9	0.0	0.1	0.2	0.1	0.2	0.2	25.7	24.9	0.6	0.8	26.3	25.7	43.8	41.2	29.9	33.0
Petroleum products & gases	1.4	2.1	8.5	10.7	12.2	7.0	20.7	17.7	0.7	1.4	0.9	6.0	0.8	0.4	24.5	27.5	1.5	1.6	26.0	29.1	21.6	26.4	52.3	44.5
Synthetic fiber textile	0.4	1.0	1.9	6.3	0.1	0.1	2.0	6.4	8.5	11.8	5.6	12.0	1.8	1.9	18.4	33.2	12.7	15.3	31.1	48.5	18.0	20.0	51.0	31.5
Basic petrochemical products	1.6	3.3	0.5	2.9	1.5	2.6	2.0	5.5	1.2	2.5	1.2	4.1	1.8	2.5	7.9	17.8	7.8	7.8	15.7	25.6	20.0	20.6	64.3	53.8

Table 4.1: World export share by country/region and by product group (%) – *continued*

	China		ASEAN 4		Singapore		ASEAN 5		Taiwan		South Korea		Hong Kong		East Asia		Japan		All East Asia		NAFTA		EU	
Product group	1990	2001	1990	2001	1990	2001	1990	2001	1990	2001	1990	2001	1990	2001	1990	2001	1990	2001	1990	2001	1990	2001	1990	2001
Petrochemical products	1.3	2.1	0.9	1.4	1.2	1.5	2.1	2.9	0.9	1.1	0.7	1.1	1.8	1.4	6.7	8.7	6.3	5.7	13.1	14.3	18.0	20.3	68.9	65.4
Iron & steel	1.4	3.9	1.5	2.5	0.8	1.0	2.3	3.5	1.2	3.1	3.0	4.6	0.9	2.1	8.8	17.2	11.3	10.8	20.1	28.0	13.5	15.9	66.4	56.1
Metal processing	1.9	8.7	1.0	2.3	1.1	0.9	2.0	3.2	5.6	5.5	2.8	2.5	2.0	2.8	14.4	22.6	7.3	5.2	21.7	27.9	12.3	21.1	66.0	51.1
Parts (weighted average)	1.5	3.8	2.4	6.6	2.4	4.6	4.8	11.2	2.7	3.7	2.0	3.0	2.7	4.6	13.7	26.4	15.3	11.1	29.0	37.5	22.3	26.2	48.7	36.2
Electronic parts	0.5	4.0	5.2	11.3	4.2	8.0	9.4	19.3	2.8	6.0	3.7	4.0	3.3	6.2	19.8	39.5	18.4	11.7	38.1	51.2	22.6	22.7	39.3	26.1
Parts of office & communication apparatus	0.9	8.8	4.0	5.6	5.5	3.4	9.5	9.0	11.7	2.5	2.9	4.5	7.9	11.6	32.8	36.4	15.8	10.7	48.6	47.1	17.6	21.8	33.8	31.1
Parts of home electrical appliances	2.2	7.3	1.7	4.9	2.7	2.5	4.4	7.4	4.9	3.2	3.1	4.2	6.4	5.5	20.9	27.5	18.4	9.6	39.3	37.2	15.2	26.5	45.5	36.3
Parts of precision apparatus	4.2	2.1	1.7	2.9	1.4	3.6	3.0	6.5	2.0	1.4	0.6	0.5	9.9	6.7	19.8	17.2	12.0	10.0	31.8	27.2	23.8	30.8	44.3	42.0
Parts of bicycle	1.5	14.7	1.2	6.8	4.5	5.6	5.7	12.4	22.7	21.4	0.3	0.3	1.9	5.1	32.2	53.9	31.4	11.0	63.6	64.9	3.7	7.8	32.7	27.4
Parts of motorcycle	1.7	8.7	1.1	7.7	0.0	0.1	1.1	7.8	11.1	10.1	0.1	1.3	2.4	0.2	16.3	28.1	49.5	34.5	65.8	62.6	3.5	6.0	30.7	31.4
Parts of automobile	3.7	1.1	0.1	1.2	0.3	0.4	0.4	1.6	1.0	1.3	0.3	1.5	0.1	0.1	5.5	5.6	13.9	12.0	19.4	17.6	26.5	35.0	54.2	47.5
Parts of machine tool	7.1	2.6	0.2	0.7	0.7	1.5	0.9	2.3	1.5	2.7	0.5	1.2	0.7	1.3	10.8	10.1	8.6	12.4	19.3	22.5	19.3	24.1	61.4	53.4
Parts of industrial machinery	0.7	1.9	0.4	1.0	1.1	1.4	1.5	2.4	0.8	0.9	0.7	1.2	0.5	0.8	4.0	7.2	11.3	10.1	15.4	17.4	23.5	30.3	61.1	52.3
Capital goods (weighted average)	0.5	1.7	0.4	0.7	0.8	0.9	1.2	1.6	1.4	1.7	1.7	3.9	1.7	3.9	6.0	9.7	12.4	11.4	18.4	21.1	23.0	26.9	58.6	37.5
Mold	1.2	2.1	0.6	2.0	1.1	1.8	1.7	3.8	2.9	6.2	2.6	6.6	6.4	3.3	14.8	22.0	15.3	18.8	30.2	40.8	14.4	20.2	55.5	39.0
Machine tool	1.3	1.7	0.2	0.7	0.8	1.0	1.0	1.7	3.4	5.6	0.6	1.8	1.8	1.9	8.1	12.6	22.5	23.6	30.6	36.2	10.1	16.3	59.3	47.5
Industrial machinery	0.4	1.7	0.2	0.8	0.6	0.8	0.8	1.6	1.7	2.0	0.8	1.9	1.0	1.2	4.7	8.4	14.1	12.7	18.7	21.1	14.0	19.8	67.2	59.1
Parts of rail locomotive	0.5	1.7	0.0	0.1	0.1	0.0	0.1	0.2	0.5	0.0	0.6	0.3	0.0	0.1	1.8	2.2	4.9	7.2	6.7	9.4	28.9	35.9	64.4	54.8
Rail locomotive	0.0	0.5	0.0	0.1	0.0	0.0	0.1	0.1	0.0	0.0	2.9	2.0	0.0	0.0	3.0	2.5	6.7	7.1	9.8	9.6	40.1	38.5	50.2	51.9
Parts of aircraft	0.9	0.9	0.6	0.9	1.5	1.2	2.2	2.1	0.0	0.2	0.9	0.6	3.7	0.3	7.6	4.1	2.3	4.3	9.9	8.4	58.1	45.6	32.0	46.0
Vessel	1.0	5.3	1.7	0.4	1.6	1.8	3.3	2.2	1.5	1.2	12.1	26.6	0.1	0.1	17.9	35.3	24.0	23.1	41.9	58.5	6.3	6.7	51.7	34.8
Aircraft	0.0	0.1	0.5	0.1	0.4	0.5	0.8	0.6	0.0	0.0	0.1	0.3	0.1	0.0	1.1	1.0	0.1	0.0	1.1	1.1	52.3	50.9	46.5	48.0
Unclassified items	0.2	7.0	0.0	0.0	0.0	0.0	0.0	0.0	0.0	0.0	0.0	0.0	2.2	1.0	2.4	8.0	0.0	0.0	2.4	8.0	22.7	35.6	74.9	56.4
Total Products	2.3	5.4	3.2	4.9	2.0	2.5	5.2	7.4	2.5	2.5	2.4	3.1	3.1	3.9	15.4	22.4	10.6	8.2	26.1	30.6	19.2	23.5	54.7	45.9

Source: by the author based on Ajiken Indicators on Developing Economies: Extended for Trade Statistics (IDE AID-XT).

Notes: The world is composed of East Asia, NAFTA, and EU15. ASEAN Four (Indonesia, Malaysia, the Philippines, and Thailand), ASEAN Five (ASEAN Four and Singapore), East Asia (ASEAN Five, South Korea, Hong Kong, and Taiwan), All East Asia (East Asia and Japan).

exports. Meanwhile, Japan's share decreased from 18.4 percent in 1990 to 11.7 percent in 2001.

The world export positions in office and communication apparatus parts and home electrical appliance parts are different from that of electronics parts. China occupies the large export share, at 8.8 percent in office and communication apparatus parts and 7.3 percent in home electrical appliances parts.

Japan still remains a major exporting country of capital goods. Its world export share of capital goods registered 11.4 percent in 2001, although its share decreased slightly from 12.4 percent in 1990. Japan dominated the world export share in molds, reaching an 18.8 percent share, machine tools (23.6 percent), and industrial machinery (12.7 percent). Meanwhile, the presence of the ASEAN 4, China and Asian NIEs is marginal in capital goods.

These observations indicate that, along with the development of catching up, the international trade structure in East Asia has transformed from the traditional pattern where Japan exports most intermediate goods and the ASEAN 4 and China assemble them and re-export, to the "diversified trade pattern" where Japan exports key parts and capital goods, the ASEAN countries and China are engaged in the production of specific parts for which they have a comparative advantage, and finally the ASEAN 4 and China assemble.

This has contributed to an expansion of intra-industry and intra-regional trade in East Asia, which has enhanced the competitiveness of East Asia as a whole. Table 4.2 shows the intra-regional export share by product group. The intra-industry regional export in parts in 2001 amounted to 38.9 percent for East Asia (excluding Japan) and 46.1 percent when Japan is included. However, intra-regional trade in finished goods is 17.1 percent for East Asia excluding Japan and 27.9 percent for East Asia including Japan. This figure is quite low compared to other regions; the intra-regional export ratio in finished goods was 61.2 percent for NAFTA and 66.0 percent for the EU in 2001. As an example, East Asia (excluding Japan) is the largest exporting area for home electrical appliances in the world, yet, in 2001 intra-regional exports amounted to only 19.0 percent. More than 80 percent of home electrical appliances are exported outside of the region.

East Asia has succeeded in catching up in manufacturing. Catching up has raised East Asia to the status of a global manufacturing center, accompanying the development of intra-industry and intra-regional trade in parts. However, the intra-regional trade in finished goods has not developed successfully. This may be related to the fact that East

Table 4.2: Intra-regional export share of East Asia, NAFTA and EU (%)

	East Asia		All East Asia		NAFTA		EU15	
Product group	1990	2001	1990	2001	1990	2001	1990	2001
Finished goods (weighted average)	18.6	17.1	25.1	27.9	43.0	61.2	71.3	66.0
Agricultural products	32.1	28.3	54.9	46.3	19.9	38.1	82.1	78.2
Processed agricultural products	24.8	23.0	52.8	48.7	33.9	48.9	72.2	70.4
Apparel	14.0	13.0	26.1	33.5	31.8	73.0	74.3	66.7
Footwear & leather articles	19.5	16.8	30.8	28.5	61.9	74.1	72.6	66.3
Furniture	11.3	11.0	30.8	29.3	66.2	75.6	70.5	60.4
Miscellaneous manufactured goods	17.3	15.9	26.2	27.6	36.5	53.8	61.7	56.6
Bicycle	5.1	8.9	8.5	27.6	31.2	62.6	83.7	85.0
TV games	22.6	64.6	32.3	58.7	64.6	81.8	76.2	85.2
Personal computer and peripheral equipments	9.5	17.0	12.1	27.2	21.7	47.3	79.1	76.3
Office and communication apparatus	14.5	14.0	16.0	24.2	33.8	54.0	60.6	56.5
Home electrical appliances	18.3	19.0	20.4	26.2	44.5	71.8	73.2	67.8
Precision apparatus	24.0	21.0	29.7	36.1	20.6	41.5	52.4	48.9
Motorcycle	40.4	10.6	17.7	7.1	13.1	25.5	76.7	75.6
Commercial vehicle	16.5	26.4	21.3	21.7	86.5	91.8	76.2	71.6
Passenger cars	5.4	3.7	3.8	3.8	84.5	89.0	72.4	68.5
Material (weighted average)	35.6	32.8	54.2	45.0	41.6	56.7	67.1	60.3
Natural fiber textile	30.7	24.8	58.0	44.9	7.6	27.5	71.7	56.9
Yarn & fabric	43.2	33.5	47.6	35.9	36.7	63.2	69.6	53.8
Glass & cement	27.2	22.2	44.9	37.1	54.5	45.3	58.0	46.9
Mineral products	28.9	36.5	76.3	63.7	45.5	70.0	70.5	71.2
Petroleum products & gases	35.1	39.2	78.3	68.1	51.9	81.4	71.0	64.8
Synthetic fiber textile	40.3	26.1	48.9	29.2	21.7	30.6	62.3	57.2
Basic petrochemical products	41.2	30.7	51.5	39.2	28.2	40.5	66.8	62.3
Petrochemical products	41.1	34.7	42.0	43.1	30.0	37.7	63.2	56.7

Table 4.2: Intra-regional export share of East Asia, NAFTA and EU (%) – *continued*

	East Asia		All East Asia		NAFTA		EU15	
Product group	1990	2001	1990	2001	1990	2001	1990	2001
Iron & steel	37.2	40.3	55.0	50.9	58.2	71.0	71.6	68.7
Metal processing	19.0	19.1	30.1	30.9	60.3	74.4	68.5	62.5
Parts (weighted average)	37.0	38.9	40.0	46.1	48.5	53.4	62.7	54.5
Electronic parts	36.5	42.9	42.1	52.6	36.1	43.3	65.4	56.0
Parts of office & communication apparatus	32.1	30.2	38.5	40.0	35.1	49.6	56.1	46.3
Parts of home electrical appliances	31.0	34.9	40.7	42.5	53.5	72.5	62.6	55.6
Parts of precision apparatus	33.0	23.9	41.4	34.4	29.3	42.4	51.0	44.5
Parts of bicycle	25.1	23.4	35.4	28.9	38.7	36.3	74.9	66.9
Parts of motorcycle	29.8	22.3	48.1	30.6	26.5	36.5	72.8	77.6
Parts of automobile	65.6	19.1	37.3	23.4	84.5	82.1	73.7	68.7
Parts of machine tool	71.4	32.5	63.4	41.2	31.6	39.9	58.1	46.3
Parts of Industrial machinery	36.0	29.3	34.9	30.8	42.2	47.7	56.6	48.5
Capital goods (weighted average)	31.6	24.3	36.0	29.9	22.3	31.9	50.2	50.2
Mold	32.9	39.9	48.5	52.4	76.1	77.7	68.1	50.7
Machine tool	31.7	31.9	34.4	31.3	33.0	38.6	53.5	48.6
Industrial machinery	43.9	29.2	45.8	36.7	35.8	43.2	53.4	48.1
Parts of rail locomotive	15.0	23.7	20.9	22.5	68.1	70.5	51.7	56.9
Rail locomotive	7.4	87.3	37.4	61.7	79.7	85.2	47.2	47.8
Parts of aircraft	20.6	25.8	18.5	18.8	19.1	16.4	68.6	34.8
Vessel	18.4	13.5	14.5	14.4	20.0	46.0	19.3	33.4
Aircraft	18.4	12.7	19.4	12.3	7.3	19.8	44.5	41.1
Unclassified items	0.0	84.8	0.0	84.8	100.0	100.0	78.2	65.8
Total products	26.6	27.1	35.6	37.1	41.4	55.4	66.1	60.3

Source: by the author based on Ajiken Indicators on Developing Economies: Extended for Trade Statistics (IDE AID-XT).

Notes: East Asia consists of Indonesia, Malaysia, the Philippines, Thailand, Singapore, South Korea, Hong Kong, and Taiwan. Japan is included in All East Asia (East Asia and Japan).

Asia has taken a dual export-oriented and protectionist policy for domestic industries. East Asia must liberalize its domestic markets to expand its intra-regional trade in finished goods. This implies that East Asia's de facto economic integration has been biased. It will take many years before East Asia can establish a real natural economic activity space.

6 Summary and conclusion

This study examined the extent of catching up advancement by latecomers with respect to forerunners in East Asia. For this purpose, the international competitiveness coefficient (ICC), which is one measurement of competitiveness, was calculated and applied by product group from 1990 to 2001.

The study found that in various manufactured product groups, the latecomers of the ASEAN 4 and China rapidly increased their competitiveness in the 1990s in terms of the ICC value, and their ICC values exceeded those of Asian NIEs and Japan. In other words, the ASEAN 4 and China have achieved catching up with the second-runners of Asian NIEs, and the frontrunner Japan. Meanwhile, the Asian NIEs have achieved more extensive catching up with Japan, in particular for light machinery parts, molds and dies, and for some transportation machinery. Surprisingly, most of the catching up was realized in a very short period in the 1990s. Catching up progressed in an inter-industry fashion (from industry to industry): from apparel; to light machinery assembling industries such as electrical appliances; to personal computer material and peripheral equipment; and to office and communication apparatus. Catching up has appeared partially in motorcycles, commercial vehicles and passenger cars. However, catching up has not yet advanced in heavy machinery industries such as industrial machinery and machine tools.

The catching up process also has advanced in intra-industry fashion (within industry). It is extending from the downstream industry to the midstream industries, e.g. fabric and yarn and synthetic fiber in textile industry, and parts in the light machinery industry. The advancement of intra-industry catching up indicates that finished and intermediate products have closely developed forward and backward linkages. The Asian NIEs have succeeded in advancing intra-industry catching up, compared to the latecomers group of the ASEAN 4 and China.

The study found that Japan is decreasing its world export share, while the ASEAN 4 and China are increasing remarkably in finished goods and parts. However, Japan still dominates the world export share in high capital goods, although Singapore, South Korea and Taiwan are raising their world shares in molds and dies.

This study observes that the old-fashioned flying geese development patterns can be applied to East Asia. What theoretical implication can be derived from this study? The observed pattern in non-durable consumer goods such as apparel agrees with the conventional trade theory in which changes in factor endowments and factor prices affect the trade pattern. On the other hand, the catching up in the light machinery industry but not in parts of light machinery suggests the production process-wise division of labor advanced in East Asia. The study results show that the intra-industry trade has developed in light machinery, in which the earlier starters export the advanced parts to the second-runner, and the latecomers assemble the final goods and components. This in turn supports the fragmentation theory discussed in Chapter 1.

Notes

The author wishes to express thanks to Françoise Nicolas (French Institute for Foreign Relations), Michel Fouquin (CEPII), and Kiichiro Fukasaku (OECD Development Center) for their helpful comments at the seminar held on October 15, 2004, the Centre d'Etudes Prospectives et d'Informations Internationales (CEPII). Special thanks go to Shigehisa Kasahara (UNCTAD) who has made careful comments and a lot of editorial suggestions. However, the author is solely responsible for all remaining errors and shortcomings.

1. Krugman (1991a) uses an industrialized "core" and an agricultural "periphery" model.
2. It is supposed that the North has the advantage in producing new products including a more skilled labor force, external economies, and simple differences in social atmosphere.
3. The original idea was presented in "Core and Periphery." See Krugman (1991b).
4. This is because domestic demand + export = domestic supply + import, and then export – import = domestic supply – domestic demand.
5. Kasahara (2004) gives a good survey on flying geese theory.
6. Indonesia has moved above China and Thailand. This may be because Indonesia has not imported enough due to the shortage of foreign reserves.

References

Akamatsu, Kaname (1962) "A Historical Pattern of Economic Growth in Developing Countries," *Developing Economies*, 1, 5: 3–25.

Hiratsuka, Daisuke (2003) "Competitiveness of ASEAN, China, and Japan," in *ASEAN-Japan Competitive Strategy*, ed. Yamazawa Ippei and Daisuke Hiratsuka, Chiba: Institute of Developing Economies-JETRO.

Hiratsuka, Daisuke (2005) "Catching up Process of Manufacturing in East Asia," *Discussion Paper*, no. 22: Institute of Developing Economies-JETRO.

Kasahara, Shigehisa (2004) "The Flying Geese Paradigm: a Critical Study of its Application to East Asian Regional Development," *Discussion Paper*, no. 169: United Nations Conference on Trade and Development (UNCTAD).

Kojima, Kiyoshi (2000) "Towards a Theory Specialization: the Economics of Integration," in *Induction, Growth, and Trade*, Essays in Honor of Sir Roy Harrod, ed. Walter Eltis, Maurice FitzGerald Scott and James Nathaniel Wolfe, Oxford: Clarendon Press, 305–24.

Krugman, Paul (1979) "A Model of Innovation, Technology Transfer, and the World Distribution of Income," *Journal of Political Economy*, 187, 2 (April): 253–66.

Krugman, Paul (1991a) "History and Industry Location: the Case of the Manufacturing Belt," *American Economic Review*, 81, 2 (May): 80–3.

Krugman, Paul (1991b) "Increasing Returns and Economic Geography," *Journal of Political Economy*, 99, 3 (June): 483–99.

Krugman, Paul (1991c) *Geography and Trade*, Leuven, Belgium: Leuven University Press and Cambridge, Massachusetts: MIT Press.

Krugman, Paul (2004) "The New Economic Geography: Where Are We?" International Symposium on "Globalization and Regional Integration-from the Viewpoint of Spatial Economics," December 2, organized by Institute of Developing Economies, IDE-JETRO (http://www.ide.go.jp/Japanese/Inter/Sympo/pdf/krug_summary.pdf., January 12, 2005).

Krugman, Paul and Venables, Anthony (1995) "Globalization and the Inequity of Nations," *Quarterly Journal of Economics*, 110, 4 (November): 857–80.

Vernon, Raymond (1966) "International Investment and International Trade in the Product Cycle," *Quarterly Journal of Economics*, 80, 2 (1966): 190–207.

Watanabe, Toshio and Kajiwara, Hirokazu (1983) *Ajia Suihei Bungyou no Jidai* (Japanese): JETRO.

Yamazawa, Ippei (1990) *Economic Development and International Trade: the Japanese Model*, Honolulu, Hawaii: Resource Systems Institute, East–West Center.

5
China's Specialization in East Asian Production Sharing

Guillaume Gaulier, Françoise Lemoine and Deniz Ünal-Kesenci

1 Introduction

Since 1980, China's economy has grown at the rate of 9 percent a year and its foreign trade has expanded at the pace of almost 15 percent a year. Its share of world trade rose from less than 1 percent to about 5 percent in 2002.[1] The emergence of China as a great economic and trade power is bringing far-reaching changes in the world economy and in international economic relations. China now holds a large share of the world market in traditional industries (accounting for about one-third of world exports in leather and shoes and one-fifth in clothing), but is also rapidly enlarging its shares in electrical and electronic exports, the fastest growing segments of world trade. In 2002 China recorded one-fifth of world exports of consumer electronics and of domestic appliances. For East Asian countries, China has become a major partner, often their first partner in the region. In 2003, China was Japan's second-largest export market, behind the US, and its first-largest supplier. For South Korea, China was the largest export market and its second-largest supplier behind the US. In 2003 and 2004, the accelerated increase of China's import demand (+40 percent and 37 percent respectively) has been the engine of economic growth in East Asia.

The aim of the chapter is to explain how China has achieved such outstanding trade performance. The study adds an original contribution to existing analysis of China's foreign trade, as it makes use of a very detailed database coming from China's Customs Statistics.[2] This database has made it possible to analyse China's trade flows depending on the type of exporting and importing firms (Chinese firms, firms with foreign capital, wholly foreign firms), and on the customs regime (assembly trade or "ordinary" trade). Moreover, the study examines the composition of trade flows by stage of production and by technological level.

Putting together these different classifications, the chapter presents a quite precise image of China's position in the international division of labor, and puts forward its strong involvement in the international segmentation of production processes and its integration in Asian production networks. The chapter shows that processing trade (assembly) is at the core of China's trade performance and especially of the rapid diversification of its manufactured exports from textiles to electronics. The bulk of processing trade is carried out by foreign affiliates, is based on inputs imported mainly from Asian countries and is responsible for China's overall trade surplus with the US and Europe. Most of China's imports from East Asian advanced economies are for processing, meaning that these flows are driven by the transfer of production facilities from East Asia to China. Foreign affiliates importing Asian inputs for processing generally have their parent firms in East Asia but may also include affiliates of US and European firms operating in Asia. The technology content of China's trade has increased rapidly. China's high-tech trade is concentrated in parts and components and takes place mainly with Asian countries. The overwhelming share of high-tech trade is handled by foreign affiliates, which casts some doubt on the dissemination of imported technology into the domestic sector.

The first section of the chapter points out how globalization provides new opportunities for latecomers to enter international trade through production sharing, a phenomenon which has been especially widespread in East Asia. The second section provides an in-depth analysis of China's trade flows. Based on the detailed data available from China's customs statistics, it assesses the role that international processing activities and foreign affiliates play in China's foreign trade, and the impact production sharing with Asian countries has on China's geographic and commodity trade patterns. The third section examines how assembly operations have been an important channel for technology transfer but have not favored the diffusion of technology in the domestic industries. The fourth section focuses on the changes which have occurred over the last twenty years in the trade patterns of East Asian countries both within the region and with the rest of the world, as a result of China's emergence as a major trading partner.

2 International production sharing in East Asia

2.1 The international segmentation of production processes

A segment of production is defined as the operations which produce a "finished" good used as an input for the following segment (Fontagné 1991); when the different segments take place in separate production units (subcontractors or affiliates) located in different countries, we witness international segmentation of a production process. The international segmentation of production processes, which has been observed for a long time, was not taken into account in the traditional theories of international trade. In the Ricardo and Hecksher–Ohlin trade models, countries specialize in final goods in which they have a comparative advantage. They export these goods and import products for which they have a comparative disadvantage and which they cease to produce. Foreign trade makes it possible to economize factors of production and thus leads to gains relative to a situation of autarky. In this traditional approach, domestic production processes are not interrupted by international trade.

The globalization process, which can be thought of as the reorganization of production on a worldwide basis, has existed for a long time, but has deepened since the 1980s, and has justified a rewriting of international trade theory. Production processes have become internationally fragmented, as firms located in different countries take part in the production of a commodity but at different stages of the value-added chain. The value-added chain is thus split up across different countries and firms. The international segmentation of production processes is driven by the search for cost minimization and economies of scale which arise through expanding markets. This international segmentation of production processes is enhanced by two factors: the evolution of technology and the strategy of multinational firms.

The evolution of technology determines the possibility of breaking up production processes in industries. The segmentation of production takes place in industries in which production processes can be broken down into technologically separate and independent operations providing intermediate inputs to be assembled in the final product (Lassudrie-Duchêne 1985). As manufactured products are becoming more and more technologically sophisticated, the number of stages of production increases and the productivity at the different stages changes rapidly; in this context a country tends to specialize only in individual segments.

Multinational firms have developed sourcing policies which rely on foreign, and even distant, suppliers; they have also localized the production of components in different countries, with the aim of a better utilization of different countries' comparative advantages. Outsourcing, defined as the import of intermediate inputs (from low-wage countries) by domestic firms (in developed countries) has increased and can be interpreted as a response to import competition (Feenstra and Hanson 1995, 1996). Such strategies are often associated with the rise of intra-firm trade, but this is not always the case; reorganization of production across country boundaries often takes place within processing trade operations. Subcontracting activities, associated with inter-firm trade, do not necessarily imply equity relationship between firms involved in the same production process (Fukasaku and Kimura 2001).

The international segmentation of production processes has led to changes in the structure of international trade and in countries' specialization patterns. First, it has given rise to rapid growth in trade of intermediate goods, which results from the interruption of the domestic production processes. International trade involves increasing flows of goods belonging to a single industry but at different stages of production. "A limited number of standardised semi-assembled goods are produced on a large scale and then combined to produce a large variety of final products" (Fontagné et al. 1996: 11). Second, this splitting up of the value-added chain allows for an increasingly deep specialization. The different stages of production correspond to different production functions so that a country may have a comparative advantage in one stage of production and a comparative disadvantage in other stages. It is thus useful to distinguish two types of specialization. When a country has a comparative advantage in the whole process of production of a given product, from upstream to downstream stages of production, we are in the presence of a so-called "horizontal" specialization. If comparative advantages can be found only in some stages of production, whereas others are disadvantaged, this is referred to as "vertical" specialization.[3]

This specialization along the production chain implies specific gains. Recent theoretical and empirical studies suggest that trade in intermediate goods is an important channel of the transmission of technology (Coe and Helpman 1995; Coe et al. 1997; Keller 2001). For emerging economies, imports of components for assembly may become the easiest way to acquire high-technology and benefit from technological spillovers which allow for an increase in total factor productivity.

Assembly trade, either for finished or intermediate products, is a crucial element in the international segmentation of production processes. Assembly may be a rather complex operation or on the contrary a simple operation, depending on the industry in question. Its characteristics are likely to change more rapidly than those of other stages of production. A country's involvement in the international fragmentation of production processes is influenced by the structure of its customs tariffs which favor (or inhibit) assembly trade. It has been shown that tariff exemptions or reductions on imported inputs increase the effective protection enjoyed by assembling activities as it reduces its costs of production. On the contrary a rise in tariffs on intermediate goods reduces the protection of the downstream segments of production, as it appears as a duty applied to assembling activities (Grubel and Johnson 1971).

2.2 Asian production networks

An international production network can be defined as "the organization, across national borders, of the relationships (intra and increasingly inter-firm) through which firms conduct research, development, product definition and design, procurement, manufacturing, distribution and support services" (Borrus 1996: 9). Firms located in East Asia (Asian firms as well as affiliates of US or European multinational companies) have shifted from exports to international production and reorganized their business activities across different countries in order to reduce costs and improve their capacities to react to technological changes and market requirements. They have built up cross-border production and trade networks which have underlain the progress of economic integration in East Asia.

These cross-border production and trade networks explain the rapid increase of both trade and foreign direct investment (FDI) flows between East Asian countries, and the far-reaching changes in the pattern of product trade and specialization across countries. Several factors have contributed to the expansion of Asian production networks. Besides geographic proximity, the heterogeneity of the Asian economies has stimulated the international segmentation of production processes since the different countries had different comparative advantages (Zysman et al. 1996). In the latter half of the 1980s, currency revaluations, which have affected the competitiveness of manufacturing industries in most developed countries of the region, have played a catalytic role in accelerating the relocation of their labor-intensive production to the low-wage countries of the region (Naughton

1997). Finally, the changes in the development strategies and trade policies implemented from the mid-1980s in countries such as Thailand, Malaysia, Indonesia and the Philippines, have also decisively contributed to the expansion of international production networks, as these countries have facilitated FDI in export-oriented businesses (Ando and Kimura 2003).

Although there are no comprehensive relevant statistics which allow precise measurement of the role of international production and trade networks, indirect evidence can be drawn from the analysis of trade flows on the one hand, and from the investigation of the investment strategies of firms on the other. Empirical studies of international trade flows have shown the growing importance of intermediate goods, and especially of "parts and components" in intra-Asian trade flows, indicating an increased vertical specialization (the splitting up of the value-added chain). As the possibility (and costs) of splitting up production processes into two or more steps depends on the technique of production, the forces driving to vertical specialization have been stronger in some industries, such as machinery and electrical machinery (Ando and Kimura 2003; Ng and Yeats 2003; Masuyama 2004; Fukao et al. 2003). The analysis of the investment strategy of Asian firms has found that international production networks are an important factor determining trade patterns in the region, that they are spread over a large number of countries, and involve both intra-firm and arm's-length trade. Surveys of East Asian firms generally show that their investment in the region is more efficiency-seeking and export-oriented than their investment in other parts of the world (Ando and Kimura 2003; Masuyama 2004; Fukao et al. 2003). Foreign affiliates account for a significant share of trade flows for most countries in East Asia.

Recent analysis points out that Japanese firms follow a specific strategy in East Asia, compared to their strategies in other parts of the world and compared to the strategies of US firms in the region (Ando and Kimura 2003; Masuyama 2004). Japanese investment abroad is more oriented towards East Asia than US FDI; Japanese affiliates in East Asia are more concentrated in manufacturing industries and more export-oriented than Japanese affiliates in North America and in Europe. They concentrate their exports in the region (Asian countries and Japan), which confirms the existence of strong intra-regional production networks, but contradicts the view that Japanese firms use export platforms in the region to sell to the US. Japanese firms investing in East Asia include a relatively large number of small and medium enterprises (SMEs), have less capital-intensive technology and less R&D expenditure, compared to Japanese firms investing in North America or in Europe.

2.3 The emergence of China

China appears as a latecomer in the international division of labor in East Asia and its case further illustrates how the splitting up of the value-added chain between different locations (countries) and the development of firms' cross-border production networks are driving the process of industrial growth and integration in East Asia (UNCTAD 1996, 2002; Borrus et al. 2000). China's case also highlights how a latecomer can enter globalization and carve out its place in the international division of labor. Since the mid-1980s, China has been involved in international production sharing with Asian economies, as labor-intensive stages of production have moved from advanced Asian economies to the mainland (Naughton 1996, 1997).

FDI in China has ballooned since the early 1990s. It is concentrated in manufacturing industries, as the service sectors were not opened to FDI before China's entry into the WTO. According to China's statistics, from 1991 to 2002, 60 percent of FDI came from the advanced East Asian economies: Hong Kong (45 percent), Japan (8 percent), Taiwan (8 percent), Singapore (5 percent) and South-Korea (4 percent). East Asian countries direct a larger share of their investment abroad to China than the US and Europe do.[4] Surveys have shown that East Asian investment in China has been mainly motivated by cost considerations and tend to concentrate more than others in export-oriented activities (Masuyama 2004; Fukao et al. 2003). East Asian FDI in China, as in other developing Asian economies thus differs from American and European investment which is mainly driven by market expansion strategies rather than by cost considerations (Zhang 1995; Tso 1998; Wei and Liu 2001). However, recent evolution indicates that East Asian investment in China has become more oriented towards the domestic market.

The first motivation of Japanese FDI in China (as ASEAN countries) is cost reduction, and Japanese foreign affiliates in China export more than half of their production (Fung et al. 2004; Masuyama 2004). The strategy of Japanese firms has evolved as their affiliates have strengthened their links with local firms and increased local procurements (vs. imports). However, Japanese firms tend to lag behind other foreign investors and face strong competition both from other foreign affiliates and from the local producers in the domestic market.

For South Korean firms, China has overtaken the US as the first host country for FDI in 2001. In an initial phase, South Korean investment in China was driven by cost considerations and was mostly export-oriented. However, in the late 1990s, a new wave of FDI was driven by large corporations (chaebols) and aimed at China's domestic market. This has been accompanied by the rise of South Korean FDI in relatively capital- and technology-intensive industries and in capital goods, which has raised the fear that the South Korean manufacturing industry may be facing the risk of hollowing out, as has happened in Taiwan (Lee and Kim 2004).

Taiwanese investment in China has been export-oriented, concentrated in labor-intensive industries, and led by SMEs. However, recent trends show an evolution towards larger and more technology- and capital-intensive projects. In the electronics industry, Taiwanese firms have extensively relocated their production in China. In 2002, almost half of Taiwan's information technology goods were produced on the mainland (Fung et al. 2003).

The rapid expansion of China's foreign trade has thus been closely associated with an ongoing reorganization of production in East Asia, driven by export-oriented investment on the mainland (Lemoine and Ünal-Kesenci 2002, 2004).

2.4 Dependence or catch-up?

The development of international production networks has contributed to the rise of successive waves of "new industrialised economies" (NIEs)[5] in Asia, especially the emergence of the latest tiers of new industrialized economies (Thailand, Malaysia, Philippines, then China and Vietnam). Since the 1980s, firms located in Asian industrialized economies (Hong Kong, Japan, Singapore, South Korea, Taiwan) have gradually moved the labor-intensive stages of their manufacturing industries to overseas export platforms located in low-wage countries, through foreign direct investment and out-processing of operations. This migration has helped Southeast Asian countries, and then China, to develop their comparative advantages in manufacturing industries and to progressively upgrade their industrial export capacities. East Asian production networks have thus contributed to the "recycling of comparative advantages" which has thus been at the core of East Asian industrialization.

The evolution of the specialization patterns of East Asian countries thus confirms the "flying geese model" developed by Akamatsu (1961: 205), who observed that "diffusion of new techniques to rising industrial nations proceeds rapidly, and these nations approach the technological level of advanced nations" and that "the underdeveloped nations are aligned successively behind the advanced industrial nations in the order of their different stages of growth in a wild-flying geese pattern."

However, the changes in the global economy, together with the development in technology and production techniques, have precluded homogeneous trajectories. Although latecomers may export similar products as the leaders did in earlier stages, their structures of production are quite different (ESCAP 1991; Bernard and Ravenhill 1995; OECD 1999; Guerrieri 2000; UNCTAD 1996). In fact, while Japan developed a strong indigenous innovative base prior to the increase of its global economic presence in the 1950s, Taiwan and Korea have remained dependent on imported technology, components and equipment from industrialized economies (mainly Japan). The latecomers, primarily Southeast Asian countries, have industrial structures which are characterized by the lack of a domestic manufacturing tradition, a high dependence on foreign controlled firms, a high import content of exports and limited backward linkages with local component suppliers.

The benefits that low-wage countries derive from their participation in international production sharing may be smaller than suggested by trade figures. The gains may be unequally spread between the firms involved in the value-added chain. Also, taking part in the labor-intensive stages of production does not automatically lead to the technological spillovers needed to move up the production chain and to ensure a sustainable trajectory of economic development (UNCTAD 1999, 2002; Kaplinsky et al. 2002; OECD 1999).

In the case of China, the benefits include large capital inflows and a rapid rise of exports which have contributed to its outstanding economic growth, the modernization of its industrial capacities and the building up of new industries (particularly the electrical and electronics industries) (Lardy 2002; Lemoine 2000; Wu 1999; Naughton 1997; Huchet 1997).

However, like other latecomers (such as Malaysia, the Philippines and Thailand) China has developed a specialization in low value-added production, based on its almost unlimited supply of low-cost labor. The following sections will show that its rise in international trade is heavily dependent on foreign affiliates which have developed limited backward and forward linkages (Zhang 1999; Sung 2000; Wu 1999; Lemoine and Ünal-Kesenci 2004).

3 China in the international division of labor in East Asia

3.1 China's selective trade policy

Trade policy is an important factor determining a country's involvement in the international splitting up of the value-added chain. Tariff structures may affect the degree of effective protection of the different sectors as tariff exemptions and reductions on imported inputs increase the effective protection enjoyed by the assembly activities using these inputs, as it reduces their costs of production (Grubel and Johnson 1971).

Most Asian economies have followed a "dual track" trade policy, which combined protection of the domestic industries through relatively high customs tariffs, and export promotion, through tariff exemptions on imported inputs for export production (Ando and Kimura 2003).

China provides an outstanding example of the use of such policy. Since the mid-1980s, the Chinese authorities have used different instruments to promote exports (Lardy 2002; Lemoine and Ünal-Kesenci 2002; Ianchovichina et al. 2000; Naughton 1996). Duty exemptions have been granted to selected categories of imports in order to promote export-oriented industries and to stimulate inflows of capital and technology through foreign direct investment. Intermediate products imported to be used in production of exports (processing activities) have been the most important category benefiting from tariff exemptions. Concessionary import duties have also been granted to equipment imported by foreign firms as a contribution to initial investment in affiliates in China.

Although China reduced its average customs tariff from 41 percent in 1992 to 16.8 percent by 1998–2001, the advantage derived from tariff exemptions has remained significant and this selective trade policy has proved very successful in creating export-oriented industries based on imported inputs. The large gap between nominal and collected tariff rates provides evidence of the extensive use of tariff exemptions (Lemoine and Ünal-Kesenci, 2004).

The following analysis shows that China's selective trade liberalization has led to an accelerated expansion of international processing activities, which have been the engine of the rapid diversification of its manufactured exports. The effective protection enjoyed by processing activities has favored strong productive links between China and its East Asian partners. China's integration in the production and trade networks of firms located in East Asia has been at the core of its foreign trade expansion. China's selective trade policy has thus strongly determined the commodity and geographic pattern of China's trade in the 1990s.

3.2 China's specialization in assembly operations

China's dual track policy has resulted in a highly fragmented trade sector. Four broad segments can be distinguished in China's foreign trade:

(1) "Ordinary trade" encompasses imports which are subjected to general tariff rates, that is imports aimed at the domestic market (for investment or consumption) and exports mainly based on local inputs.
(2) "Processing trade" encompasses imports of goods to be assembled or transformed in China and re-exported. This corresponds to the international practice of "inward processing" which is defined by the World Customs Organization as "the Customs procedure under which certain goods can be brought into a Customs territory conditionally relieved from payment of import duties and taxes, on the basis that such goods are intended for manufacturing, processing or repair and subsequent exportation."[6] China's customs statistics distinguish two types of inward processing. "Processing and assembling" refers to the type of inward processing in which foreign suppliers provide raw materials, parts or components under a contractual arrangement for the subsequent re-export of the processed products. Under this type of transaction the imported inputs and the finished outputs remain the property of the foreign supplier. "Processing with imported materials" refers to the type of inward processing in which raw materials or components are imported for the manufacture of the export-oriented products. In both cases the imported inputs (raw materials, semi-finished goods, parts and components) are exempted from customs tariffs. Neither these imported inputs, nor the output, normally enter China's domestic market.
(3) Imports of goods by foreign invested firms as part of their initial investment. These imports are exempted from customs duties and are mainly made up of equipment and machinery.
(4) Other exports and imports, which are not subject to the general tariff regime (compensation trade, international aid, warehousing and entrepot trade).

Trade figures corresponding to these different trade segments have been available only since 1992. Within each category it is possible to identify the respective contributions of domestic (wholly Chinese) firms and of foreign firm affiliates since 1994.

China's foreign trade expansion has relied mainly on operations taking place within the regime of processing trade. As early as 1992, processed exports made up 46 percent of total exports. This share rose to 55 percent in 1996 and has since represented more than half of China's exports (Figure 5.1). During the Asian crisis (1997–8), processed exports performed better than other categories of exports, and this resilience can be explained by their high import content which makes them less vulnerable to the effects of a real appreciation of the exchange rate (Dées and Lemoine 1999).

Correspondingly, imports under the regime of processing trade (imports for processing) have increased rapidly since 1992 and their share in total imports rose from less than 40 percent to almost 50 percent in 1997–8 (Figure 5.1). Since 1998 they have lagged behind ordinary imports which registered a strong rise partly due to the anti-smuggling measures implemented by the government but also, more

Figure 5.1: Breakdown of China's trade by customs regimes, 1992–2003

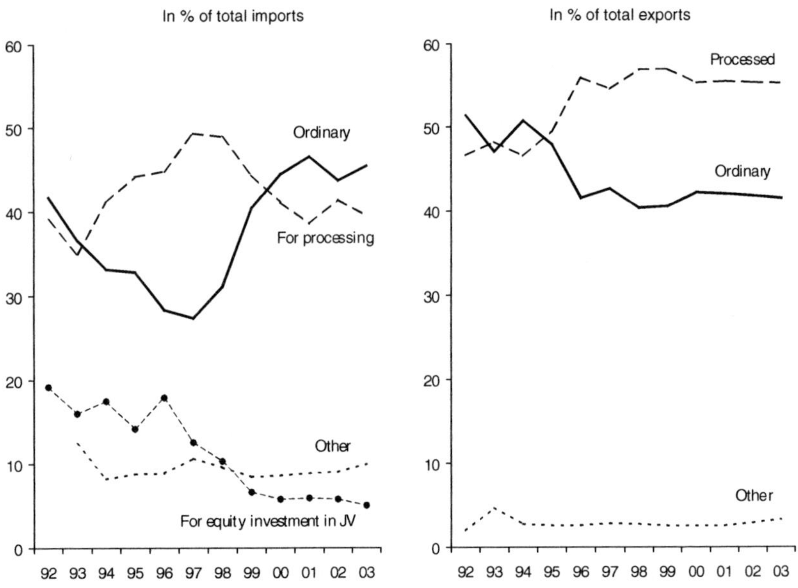

Source: China's Customs Statistics, authors' calculations.

substantially, to a rapid decline in the level of tariff rates in the late 1990s. Imports for processing accounted for about 40 percent of total imports in 2003. Ordinary imports still accounted for less than half of total imports.

3.3 The reorganization of production in Asia

The positions of major trade partners in China's different trade regimes reflect the reorganization of industrial production within East Asia (Table 5.1).

Table 5.1: Breakdown of China's trade by main partner and customs regimes (in % of total trade and US$ bn)

Imports	*World*	*3 Dragons**	*Japan*	*EU 15*	*USA*	*ROW*
1993						
Imports by all customs regimes	100	28	22	15	10	25
Ordinary imports	37	3	8	8	5	13
Imports for processing	35	18	8	2	2	6
Other customs regimes	28	7	7	6	3	6
2002						
Imports by all customs regimes	100	26	18	13	9	33
Ordinary imports	44	7	6	8	5	17
Imports for processing	41	16	8	2	2	12
Other customs regimes	15	3	3	3	2	4

Exports	*World*	*3 Dragons*	*Japan*	*EU 15*	*USA*	*ROW*
1993						
Exports by all customs regimes	100	29	17	13	18	22
Ordinary exports	47	12	10	7	6	13
Processed exports	48	16	7	7	13	6
Other customs regimes	5	0	0	0	0	4
2002						
Exports by all customs regimes	100	25	15	15	21	24
Ordinary exports	42	8	6	7	7	15
Processed exports	55	16	9	8	14	8
Other customs regimes	3	1	0	0	1	1

* Hong Kong, South Korea, Taiwan

The pattern of China's imports by partners and by customs regimes shows that the weight of East Asian countries in China's total imports results from their strong involvement in the processing trade. In 2002, almost 60 percent of China's imports from the Three Dragons (Hong Kong, South Korea, Taiwan) and 40 percent of its imports from Japan (against 35 percent in 1993) were aimed at supplying inputs for processing industries. The strong intensity of East Asian exports to China can thus be explained by the international splitting up of the value-added chain within the region. As a result, Japan and the Three Dragons were by far the major source of inputs for China's processing activities, providing almost 60 percent of these imports. Forty percent of China's imports for processing came from the Three Dragons, and one-fifth from Japan.

By contrast, European and American firms contributed only marginally to the supply of goods for processing; taken together, the imports from the US and the EU accounted for less than 10 percent of China's total imports for processing in 2002. Their weak presence in this segment of China's imports, compared to the East Asian countries, partly explains their relatively low export intensity to China compared to Asian countries (Lemoine and Ünal-Kesenci 2002). Supplies of inputs for processing accounted for a relatively small fraction of their exports; 15 percent and 22 percent of China's imports are from the EU and the US, respectively, in 2002. A comparison with 1993 does not show major changes.

Processed exports also account for a large share of Chinese exports to East Asia (up to 60 percent in 2002, against 50 percent in 1993), as the East Asian countries reimport a growing part of the production they relocated to the mainland. However, China's processed exports are much less concentrated in East Asia than corresponding imports. Less than half of exports after processing was directed to the Dragons and Japan in 2002 (as in 1993), a share which is still overstated since the largest part of processed exports recorded as going to Hong Kong is in fact aimed at the US and the European markets (EC 1997).

The US and the EU account for a much larger share in China's processed exports (40 percent in 2002) than in its imports for processing (10 percent). Moreover, their share in China's exports would be even larger if exports transiting through Hong Kong were reallocated to their final destination.

China's processing trade therefore has a built-in geographical asymmetry, as exports and imports follow different geographical patterns. East Asia is the main source of imports for processing as multinational firms (from Asia, the US or Europe) have moved their production facilities from East Asia to China in order to improve their cost competitiveness. As a result, Chinese processed exports have a high content of imported Asian goods; ten dollars of processed exports incorporate four dollars of intermediate goods supplied from Japan and the Dragons.

Regional trade balances show that China records its largest processing trade surplus with its Western partners. Processing activities are responsible for China's large trade surpluses with Europe and the US. Excluding processing trade, China records a trade deficit with the EU and its trade with the US is almost balanced. In 2002, processing trade with Japan and the Three Dragons has also become an important source of trade surplus, while it was a source of deficit in 1993, and even in 1997. This indicates that since the end of the 1990s, firms located in East Asia have more extensively used China as a production base not only to sell in world markets but also for supplying their own domestic markets.

3.4 Commodity changes in processing trade[7]

The rapid expansion of China's processing trade has been associated with clear structural changes (Table 5.2).

Table 5.2: Processing trade: sectoral breakdown in 1993 and 2002

*Sectors**	*Imports for processing (%)*			*Processed exports (%)*	
	1993	2002		1993	2002
Electrical machinery	17	39	Electrical machinery	18	30
Chemical products	17	15	Machinery	6	22
Fiber and cloth	23	11	Wearing apparel	20	8
Machinery	3	9	Toys & misc. manuf. prod.	12	7
Metallurgy	11	8	Leather and shoes	15	6
Precision instruments	4	5	Chemical products	5	5
Wood and paper products	5	3	Precision instruments	5	4
Leather and shoes	6	3	Wood and paper products	4	4
Toys & misc. manuf. prod.	4	2	Fiber and cloth	5	3
Raw agricultural products	1	1	Metallurgy	4	3
Raw materials & fuels	3	1	Other transport equipment	1	2
Wearing apparel	1	1	Motor vehicles	1	1
Building materials	1	1	Food products	1	1
Metal products	1	0	Metal products	1	1
Food products	1	0	Raw agricultural products	1	1
Motor vehicles	1	0	Raw materials & fuels	1	1
Other transport equipment	0	0	Building materials	1	1
Total	100	100	Total	100	100

* See Appendix 1 for sector classification.

Source: China's Customs Statistics, authors' calculations.

(1) There was a relative decline of processing trade in the most traditional industries (textile and garments, leather and shoes). The share of these sectors declined both on the export and import sides; taken together they accounted for more than 40 percent of total processed exports in 1993 and for only 15 percent in 2002. On the import side the corresponding shares were 30 percent and 17 percent.
(2) The product composition of international processing operations shifted towards machinery and electrical machinery; the share of these two sectors taken together rose from 24 percent to 53 percent of imports for processing and from 29 percent to 56 percent of total processed exports.
(3) Chemical products accounted for an important part of imported inputs (15 percent) but for a small part of exports, indicating that most imported chemical materials are incorporated in the production of goods belonging to other sectors.

3.5 Foreign affiliates[8]: the engine of China's trade expansion

Foreign affiliates play an important and growing part in China's foreign trade and their rise in China's foreign trade is based on assembly activities. Figure 5.2 shows that foreign affiliates accounted for more than 55 percent of exports in 2003 (against 20 percent in 1993), their processing operations for 45 percent. These activities thus represented 80 percent of overall foreign affiliates' exports and, conversely, foreign affiliates handled almost 80 percent of overall processed exports. On the import side, processing activities played a less prominent part but nevertheless accounted for more than half of foreign affiliates' imports in 2003. It is worth noting that between 1992 and 2003, foreign affiliates also rapidly increased their imports not aimed at processing activities; in 2003 imports for domestic use (i.e. excluding those for processing) represented 45 percent of their total imports. This means that foreign affiliates were responsible for about one-quarter of China's total imports for the domestic market.

Foreign affiliates play an especially important part in China's trade with the East Asian countries (Table 5.3). In 2002 they accounted for between 60 percent and 67 percent of China's imports from Japan and the NIEs, and for more than 60 percent of China's exports to Japan, Hong Kong and Singapore. Interestingly, the rise of foreign affiliates in China's trade with the East Asian countries between 1993 and 2002 is due to wholly foreign firms which, in 2002, carried

Figure 5.2: Share of foreign affiliates firms (FA) in total China's trade, 1992–2003

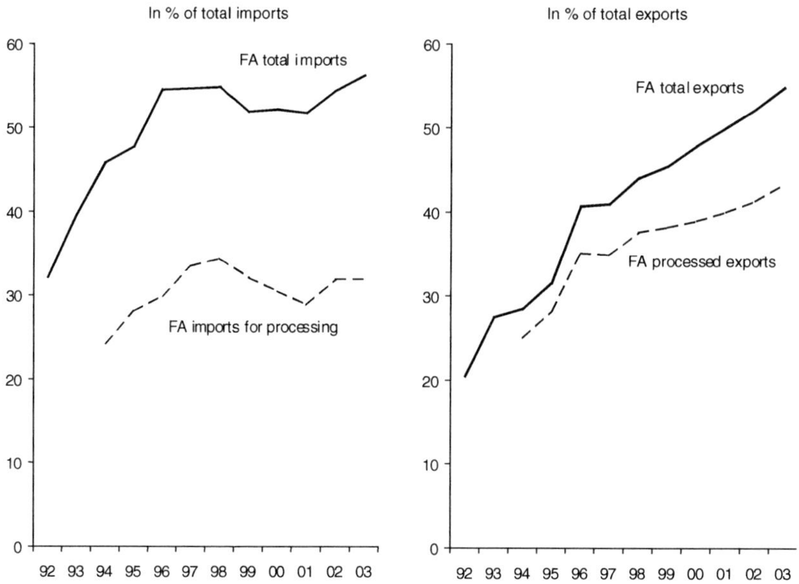

Source: China's Customs Statistics, authors' calculations.

out more trade activities than joint ventures. The importance taken by foreign affiliates suggests that China's bilateral trade with these countries is likely to include a significant amount of intra-firm trade.

In contrast, foreign affiliates represent less than half of China's imports from Europe and the US. However, their share is considerably higher in China's exports to the US, reflecting both the increased competitiveness of international production bases in China and the outsourcing strategies of American firms.

In 2002, foreign affiliates were responsible for about one-third of China's trade surplus. They make their surpluses on the "Western" markets (with the US and to a lesser extent with Europe) while they record large deficits with most East Asian partners. In fact, their surplus with Hong Kong should be eventually attributed to their trade with Europe and the US.

Table 5.3: Foreign affiliates in China's trade with major partners, 1997 and 2002

1997	*World*	*EU 15*	*USA*	*Japan*	*Hong Kong*	*Singapore*	*Korea*	*Taiwan*
All export flows (% total flows)	100	100	100	100	100	100	100	100
FA total exports	41	38	52	50	42	45	34	47
JV	*24*	*21*	*25*	*31*	*28*	*25*	*17*	*22*
WFOF	*17*	*18*	*27*	*20*	*13*	*20*	*17*	*25*
FA processed exports	35	33	47	40	37	40	28	39
JV	*19*	*16*	*21*	*24*	*24*	*21*	*12*	*17*
WFOF	*16*	*17*	*26*	*17*	*12*	*18*	*16*	*22*
All import flows (% total flows)	100	100	100	100	100	100	100	100
FA total imports	55	55	47	67	63	63	64	69
JV	*35*	*45*	*33*	*41*	*38*	*40*	*36*	*30*
WFOF	*20*	*10*	*14*	*27*	*25*	*23*	*28*	*39*
FA imports for processing	33	12	21	44	52	37	48	53
JV	*19*	*8*	*12*	*25*	*30*	*20*	*24*	*23*
WFOF	*15*	*4*	*9*	*19*	*22*	*17*	*24*	*30*
Overall trade balance (US$bn)	40.4	4.6	16.4	2.8	36.8	–0.1	–5.8	–13.0
FA total trade balance	–2.8	–1.5	9.3	–3.5	13.9	–0.9	–6.4	–9.7
JV	*–5.7*	*–3.8*	*2.7*	*–2.0*	*9.8*	*–0.7*	*–3.8*	*–4.2*
WFOF	*2.9*	*2.3*	*6.6*	*–1.5*	*4.1*	*–0.2*	*–2.6*	*–5.6*
FA processing trade balance	16.2	5.5	11.9	0.2	12.5	0.1	–4.6	–7.4
JV	*8.4*	*2.3*	*4.9*	*0.4*	*8.5*	*0.1*	*–2.5*	*–3.2*
WFOF	*7.8*	*3.2*	*7.1*	*–0.2*	*4.0*	*0.0*	*–2.1*	*–4.2*

Table 5.3: Foreign affiliates in China's trade with major partners, 1997 and 2002 – *continued*

2002	*World*	*EU 15*	*USA*	*Japan*	*Hong Kong*	*Singapore*	*Korea*	*Taiwan*
All export flows (% total flows)	100	100	100	100	100	100	100	100
FA total exports	52	50	58	62	63	65	49	57
JV	*23*	*21*	*21*	*30*	*27*	*34*	*21*	*15*
WFOF	*30*	*28*	*37*	*32*	*36*	*31*	*27*	*42*
FA processed exports	41	40	48	47	54	54	35	45
JV	*16*	*15*	*15*	*21*	*21*	*28*	*14*	*10*
WFOF	*25*	*25*	*33*	*26*	*33*	*26*	*21*	*35*
All import flows (% total flows)	100	100	100	100	100	100	100	100
FA total imports	54	49	48	67	63	61	63	67
JV	*23*	*31*	*21*	*30*	*28*	*20*	*28*	*16*
WFOF	*31*	*18*	*27*	*37*	*36*	*41*	*36*	*52*
FA imports for processing	32	12	21	39	53	36	41	49
JV	*11*	*6*	*6*	*16*	*23*	*11*	*15*	*11*
WFOF	*21*	*7*	*15*	*23*	*30*	*25*	*26*	*39*
Overall trade balance (US$bn)	30.4	9.7	42.7	–5.0	47.7	–0.1	–13.0	-31.5
FA total trade balance	9.7	5.0	27.4	–6.0	30.2	0.2	–10.5	–21.9
JV	*4.6*	*–1.8*	*8.8*	*–1.5*	*12.7*	*0.9*	*–4.6*	*–5.0*
WFOF	*5.2*	*6.8*	*18.5*	*–4.5*	*17.5*	*–0.7*	*–5.9*	*–16.9*
FA processing trade balance	40.5	14.5	27.8	2.2	26.0	1.2	–6.2	–15.8
JV	*19.0*	*4.9*	*8.7*	*1.8*	*10.1*	*1.2*	*–2.1*	*–3.4*
WFOF	*21.5*	*9.6*	*19.1*	*0.4*	*15.9*	*0.1*	*–4.1*	*–12.4*

FA: foreign affiliates; JV: joint venture; WFOF: wholly foreign owned firm.
Source: China's Customs Statistics, authors' calculations.

4 Vertical specialization, high-tech trade and regional integration[9]

4.1 China's trade by stage of production

In order to identify more precisely China's position in the international segmentation of the production process, it is useful to analyze export and import flows according to the stage of production of traded goods. The following analysis is based on the BEC (Broad Economic Categories) classification which distinguishes five stages of production (see Appendix 2): (1) primary products, including fuels; intermediate goods which encompass two categories, (2) semi-finished goods and (3) parts and components; and final goods which encompass two categories, (4) capital goods and (5) consumption goods.

China's imports are heavily dominated by intermediate products which amounted to 63.3 percent of its total imports in 2002 (Table 5.4). Within the category of intermediate goods, parts and components constitute by far the most dynamic imports (27.5 percent in 2002), although imports of semi-finished products are still more important (35.9 percent).

On the export side, final goods are by far the most important category (60.0 percent in 2002), within which consumer goods take an overwhelming share (40.3 percent), but capital goods are rising more rapidly (from 12.6 percent in 1997 to 19.7 percent in 2002). In final goods exports, a shift has occurred away from consumption goods towards capital goods, indicating that China is upgrading its export capacity towards more technology-intensive products. Moreover, parts and components make up an increasing share of exports (15.5 percent in 2002).

The rapid increase in exports and imports of parts and components indicates a deepening in the international division of production processes. This finding is in line with the conclusions of research into production sharing in East Asia (Ng and Yeats 1999, 2003), which show that trade in components has been the most dynamic part of East Asian trade in the 1990s. Following the distinction proposed by the authors between producers of components (countries having a positive trade balance in components) and assembly countries (countries having a negative trade balance in components), China clearly stands as an assembly country, a position similar to that of other low-wage Asian countries such as Indonesia, Thailand and Malaysia.

Table 5.4 confirms that China's position in the international division of labor is characterized by strong comparative advantage (structural

Table 5.4: China's trade pattern and comparative advantage* by stage of production, 1997–2002

	Breakdown of imports		Breakdown of exports		Contribution to trade balance*	
	1997	*2002*	*1997*	*2002*	*1997*	*2002*
Primary goods	10.6	10.3	5.1	2.9	–27	–37
Intermediate goods	65.9	63.3	33.4	37.1	–160	–131
Semi-finished goods	47.0	35.9	25.3	21.6	–107	–71
Parts & components	18.9	27.5	8.2	15.5	–53	–60
Final goods	23.5	26.3	61.5	60.0	187	168
Consumption goods	4.4	5.1	48.9	40.3	219	176
Capital goods	19.1	21.2	12.6	19.7	–32	–8
Total	100.0	100.0	100.0	100.0	0	0

* See Appendix 4 for the indicator of contribution to trade balance.
Source: China's Customs Statistics, authors' calculations.

surpluses) in consumption goods, associated with large disadvantages (structural deficits) in intermediate goods, and small structural deficits in capital goods and in primary goods.

China's trade in intermediate goods is heavily concentrated in Asia-Oceania, confirming that production sharing is above all a regional process (Table 5.5). More than 80 percent of intermediate imports (semi-finished products and parts and components) come from Asia-Oceania and more than 60 percent of exports of parts and components are directed to this area. Within Asia-Oceania, China records its largest structural deficit[10] in intermediate goods, a smaller deficit in capital goods, and a large surplus in consumption goods. With the rest of the world, China's trade surpluses stem from consumption goods, and with North America also from capital goods, due to a rapid rise in exports of computer equipment.

4.2 Production sharing and technological catch-up

How has production sharing with Asian countries enhanced China's technological catch-up? This point is investigated by looking at the technological content of China's exports and imports. This analysis uses the CEPII high-tech product classification based on OECD and Eurostat studies which make a distinction between products with high technology content and other products, at a detailed level of classification (the HS 6-digit level).[11]

Table 5.5: China's trade pattern by region and stage of production, 2002

	Primary goods	Semi-finished goods	Parts & components	Capital goods	Consumption goods	Total
Contribution to trade balance* (in thousands of total trade)						
WORLD	–37	–71	–60	–8	176	0
Asia-Oceania	–5	–62	–53	–16	72	–64
Western Europe	–2	–2	–9	–6	25	6
America	–9	–1	1	11	60	62
Others	–21	–6	1	4	18	–4
Export breakdown (% of world total)						
WORLD	3	22	16	20	40	100
Asia-Oceania	2	12	10	9	17	51
Western Europe	0	3	2	4	6	15
America	0	4	3	6	13	26
Others	0	2	1	1	4	9
Import breakdown (% of world total)						
WORLD	10	36	27	21	5	100
Asia-Oceania	3	25	20	12	3	63
Western Europe	1	3	4	5	1	14
America	2	4	3	3	1	13
Others	4	3	1	0	0	9

* See Appendix 5.

Source: China's Customs Statistics, authors' calculations.

Table 5.6 presents the pattern of China's trade by technology content and stages of production. It shows first that the high-technology content of China's trade rapidly increased in recent years; second, that high-tech exports increased more rapidly than high-tech imports, and that China's trade deficit in this category of products narrowed significantly between 1997 and 2002. In 2002, imports of high-technology products accounted

Table 5.6: The pattern of China's high-tech trade by stage of production (% of total flows)

	Imports		*Exports*		*Balance*	
	1997	*2002*	*1997*	*2002*	*1997*	*2002*
Semi-finished products	1	1	1	1	1,7	1,7
Parts & components	6	8	2	6	–3,6	–3,7
Capital goods	4	6	2	5	–2,1	–1,5
Consumption goods	0	0	0	0	0,5	0,9
Total	11	15	7	12	–3,5	–2,6

Source: China's Customs Statistics, authors' calculations.

for 15 percent of China's imports and for 12 percent of its exports, against 11 percent and 7 percent respectively in 1997. High-tech products hold an unexpectedly large share in China's trade, compared with other developing economies (Lemoine and Ünal-Kesenci 2004).

The high-tech content of China's exports can be explained by its high-tech import content; more than half of China's imports of high-tech products consist of parts and components, which, to a large extent, are incorporated in exports. Interestingly, most exports of high-tech products also take place in parts and components, illustrating the deepening of the international division of labor.

The technological upgrading of China's trade is thus intrinsically linked to its position in the international segmentation processes and to its specialization in assembly operations based on imported inputs.

4.3 China's high-tech trade and regional integration

The largest share of China's high-tech imports originates from East Asia[12] (Table 5.7). This share reached 70 percent in 2002, compared

Table 5.7: Breakdown of China's trade in high technology products by production stages and major zones, 2002 (in %)

	Imports				
	Asia-Oceania	*Western Europe*	*America*	*Others*	*World*
Semi-finished products	3	1	1	0	5
Parts & components	40	5	6	1	52
Capital goods	27	5	8	1	42
Consumption goods	0	0	0	0	1
Total	70	11	15	3	100
	Exports				
	Asia-Oceania	*Western Europe*	*America*	*Others*	*World*
Semi-finished products	5	2	2	1	9
Parts & components	33	5	8	1	47
Capital goods	17	8	14	2	41
Consumption goods	1	1	1	0	3
Total	56	15	25	5	100

Source: China's Customs Statistics, authors' calculations.

with 56 percent in 1997. Since 1997, the US and Western Europe have lost ground in the supply of high-tech products to China. The pattern of China's high-tech exports is stable; more than half is going to East Asia, one-quarter to America and one-sixth to Europe.

High-technology trade between China and East Asia is concentrated in parts and components, which account for almost 60 percent of both China's high-tech exports and imports to and from the region.

Production sharing with Asian countries has thus been an important factor stimulating technological transfer to China and favoring the upgrading of its export capacity. However, looking in more depth into the channels of technology transfer raises questions about the broad impact on the diffusion and assimilation of foreign technology by Chinese industry. Two observations cast some doubt on the progress of indigenous technological level. First, four-fifths of high-tech exports in 2002 come from processing activities. Second, China's high-tech trade is more and more heavily dominated by foreign affiliates.

4.4 The dependence of China's high-tech trade on foreign affiliates

In 2002 foreign affiliates were responsible for two-thirds of China's high-tech imports, and fully foreign alone for almost half of these imports (Table 5.8). High-tech imports from Asia were even more dependent on foreign affiliates, which took up to three-quarters of these imports, with fully foreign firms accounting for almost 60 percent. High-tech imports from the US and Europe were much less dependent on foreign affiliates and Chinese firms realize more than half of these imports, which consist mainly in capital goods.

Foreign affiliates play an even more dominant part in China's high-tech exports (Table 5.9). They are responsible for three-quarters of China's high-tech exports, with fully foreign firms accounting for almost half of the total. More than half of high-tech exports go to Asia and foreign affiliates are responsible of 80 percent of China's high-tech exports to Asia.

Of course, the multinational firms which are involved in China's trade with Asian countries are not only East Asian firms and also include lead firms from the US and Europe which have developed global production networks and have recently focused on manufacturing in China.

China has thus become an important base for global manufacturing, especially in the electronic industry, and this has decisively contributed to raise the technological level of China's exports and imports.

Table 5.8: China's high technology imports by region, firm type and production stage, 2002 (% of world total)

Production stage	*Firm type*			*Total*
	Chinese	*JV**	*FFOF**	
Asia-Oceania Total	**17**	**15**	**39**	**70**
Semi-finished products	1	1	1	3
Parts & components	7	9	24	40
Capital goods	8	5	14	27
Consumption goods	0	0	0	0
Western Europe Total	**6**	**4**	**2**	**11**
Semi-finished products	0	0	0	1
Parts & components	2	2	1	5
Capital goods	4	1	1	5
Consumption goods	0	0	0	0
America Total	**8**	**3**	**4**	**15**
Semi-finished products	0	0	0	1
Parts & components	2	2	3	6
Capital goods	6	1	1	8
Consumption goods	0	0	0	0
Other Total	**2**	**0**	**0**	**3**
Semi-finished products	0	0	0	0
Parts & components	1	0	0	1
Capital goods	1	0	0	1
Consumption goods	0	0	0	0
World Total	**33**	**22**	**45**	**100**
Semi-finished products	2	1	1	5
Parts & components	12	13	28	52
Capital goods	19	8	16	42
Consumption goods	0	0	0	1

**JV*: joint venture; FFOF: fully foreign-owned firms.
Source: China's Customs Statistics, authors' calculations.

But this upgrading seems to have remained strictly circumscribed to the production and export bases created by foreign firms in the mainland.

5 The impact of China's emergence on Asian trade

China's integration in the East Asian production networks, described in the above section, has considerably affected both the distribution of intra-regional trade and the positions of the East Asian countries in their trade with the rest of the world.

Table 5.9: China's high technology exports by region, firm type and production stage, 2002 (% of world total)

Production stage	*Firm type*			*Total*
	Chinese	*JV**	*FFOF**	
Asia-Oceania Total	**11**	**16**	**28**	**56**
Semi-finished products	3	1	0	5
Parts & components	4	7	22	33
Capital goods	4	8	5	17
Consumption goods	0	0	0	1
Western Europe Total	**4**	**5**	**6**	**15**
Semi-finished products	1	1	0	2
Parts & components	1	1	3	5
Capital goods	2	4	2	8
Consumption goods	0	0	0	1
America Total	**8**	**5**	**12**	**25**
Semi-finished products	2	0	0	2
Parts & components	1	1	6	8
Capital goods	4	4	5	14
Consumption goods	0	0	0	1
Other Total	**2**	**2**	**1**	**5**
Semi-finished products	1	0	0	1
Parts & components	0	0	1	1
Capital goods	1	1	0	2
Consumption goods	0	0	0	0
World Total	**24**	**29**	**47**	**100**
Semi-finished products	7	2	1	9
Parts & components	6	9	32	47
Capital goods	11	17	13	41
Consumption goods	1	1	1	3

* JV: joint venture; FFOF: fully foreign owned firm.
Source: China's Customs Statistics, authors' calculations.

5.1 The rise of East Asia[13] in world trade

From 1980 to 2002, the contribution of East Asia to world trade increased considerably. The share of East Asia in world exports rose from 13.4 percent to 23.4 percent and in world imports from 13.2 percent to 18.9 percent (Table 5.10). Apart from Japan and Hong Kong, all East Asian economies contributed to this rise, but China alone accounted for half of the registered increase.

The distribution of East Asian exports (imports) by country of destination (origin) has dramatically changed since the beginning of the

Table 5.10: Share in world trade

	Exports			*Imports*		
	1980	*1990*	*2002*	*1980*	*1990*	*2002*
Japan	6.6	8.6	6.7	6.3	6.2	5.0
China	0.9	1.7	6.0	1.1	1.3	4.1
Asian NIEs	3.2	5.9	6.1	3.8	6.1	6.4
South Korea	0.9	1.9	2.6	0.8	1.2	1.1
Taiwan	1.0	2.0	2.1	1.1	1.5	1.3
Singapore	0.7	1.1	1.1	1.1	1.9	2.3
Hong Kong	0.7	0.9	0.3	0.8	1.5	1.7
ASEAN (without Singapore)	2.8	2.7	4.7	2.0	2.6	3.5
Malaysia	0.7	0.9	1.6	0.5	0.7	1.1
Thailand	0.3	0.6	1.1	0.4	0.9	0.9
Indonesia	1.2	0.8	1.0	0.6	0.6	0.6
Philippines	0.3	0.3	0.6	0.4	0.4	0.6
Vietnam, Cambodia, Laos	0.1	0.1	0.3	0.1	0.0	0.3
Brunei Darussalam	0.2	0.1	0.1	0.0	0.0	0.0
East Asia	13.4	18.8	23.4	13.2	16.2	18.9

Source: CEPII-CHELEM database, authors' calculations.

1980s (Figure 5.3). From 1980 to 2002, on the export side, trade patterns switched in favor of China, whose rise in East Asian exports (from 6 percent to 25 percent) almost completely compensated the relative fall of Japan (from 50 percent to 30 percent). The weight of the NIEs remained almost stable, at about one-quarter of regional exports. Exports from the ASEAN* registered a relative decline during the 1980s and a revival in the 1990s which put its share of regional exports in 2002 at the same level as in 1980 (20 percent).

On the import side, the major change also came from the contraction of Japan's share (from 48 percent to 27 percent of the regional total), which was compensated by the rise of China, whose share rose from 8 percent to 21 percent. The weight of the NIEs also increased. The gain recorded by the ASEAN* occurred in the 1990s (from 16 percent to 18 percent of regional imports).

Over the last two decades, there was thus a convergence in the positions of the different countries/groups of countries in the region's trade. On the export side, China with one-quarter of the region's trade in 2002, is catching up with Japan (29 percent), and with the NIEs (26 percent). ASEAN* is also on a catching up process, reaching 20 per-

Figure 5.3: Share of East Asian countries in regional trade (% of total East Asian trade)

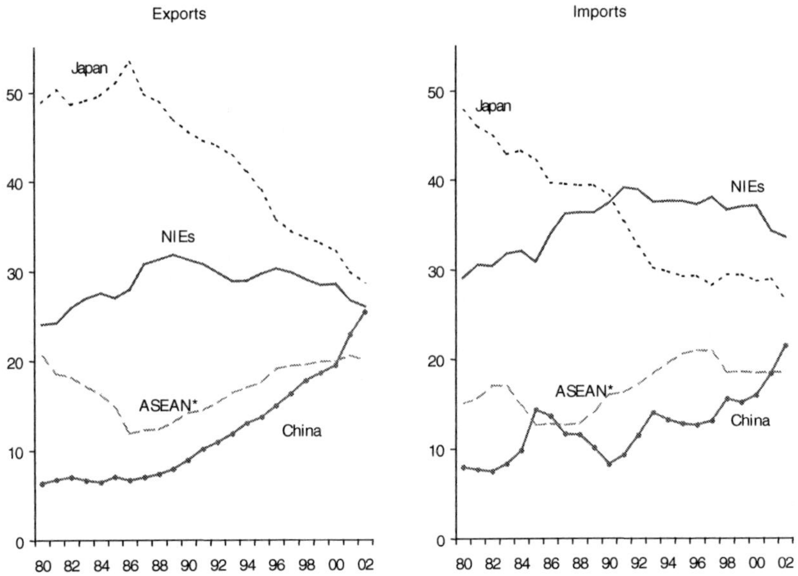

Note: NIEs: Hong Kong, Singapore, South Korea, Taiwan; ASEAN*: ASEAN countries excluding Singapore.
Source: CEPII-CHELEM database, authors' calculations.

cent of the regions's exports in 2002, although it is at a slower pace than China.

On the import side, a similar convergence of intra-regional trade powers is taking place. Since the beginning of the 1990s, the NIEs (34 percent of regional imports in 2002), have overtaken Japan (27 percent). In 2002, China (21 percent) overtook the ASEAN* (18 percent).

5.2 The rise of intra-regional trade

The segmentation of production processes between China and the other East Asian countries has led to an increased concentration of intra-regional trade within East Asia. In 2002 East Asian countries directed 42 percent of their exports to the region (against 36 percent in 1990) and had 50 percent of their imports coming from the region (against 42 percent in 1990). The increased concentration on intra-regional trade is to a large extent due to China's enlarged role in regional trade. China's share in intra-regional trade almost doubled, from 10 percent to 20 percent, as shown in Table 5.11.

Table 5.11: East Asia: distribution of intra-regional trade in 1990 and 2002 (%)

2002	*Imports*				
Exports	*Japan*	*NIEs**	*China*	*ASEAN***	*East Asia*
Japan		12	9	7	28
NIEs*	5	7	10	8	30
China	10	6		3	19
ASEAN**	7	9	3	4	23
East Asia	23	35	22	21	100

1990	*Imports*				
Exporters	*Japan*	*NIEs**	*China*	*ASEAN***	*East Asia*
Japan		23	4	10	37
NIEs*	11	9	5	8	32
China	5	4		1	10
ASEAN**	11	8	1	2	21
East Asia	27	43	10	21	100

* New industrialized economies: South Korea, Hong Kong, Singapore,Taiwan
** Without Singapore

Source: CEPI-CHELEM database.

5.3 Substitution and competition in world markets

China has become an export base for the firms located in Japan and the Asian NIEs, which used to export finished goods to the American and European markets, but now export intermediate goods to their affiliates in China. China's exports to the EU and the US have skyrocketed and have displaced exports from Japan and the NIEs at an accelerated pace.

The case of Asian exports of electrical and electronic goods to the US and Europe provides clear evidence of this substitution.

The tremendous rise of China's exports of electrical goods to the US since the mid-1980s has been accompanied by a relative stagnation of exports by Japan and the NIEs (Figure 5.4). As a result Chinese exports overtook NIEs and Japanese exports in the late 1990s; ASEAN* exports continued to rise up to the end of the 1990s and have declined since. In electronic goods, the differences in market shares of the different exporters to the US were much wider up to the early 1990s. NIE and Japanese exports have stagnated since the mid-1990s while China's and ASEAN* exports have continued their accelerated growth.

Figure 5.4: US imports from East Asia, 1980–2002 (US$ thousands)

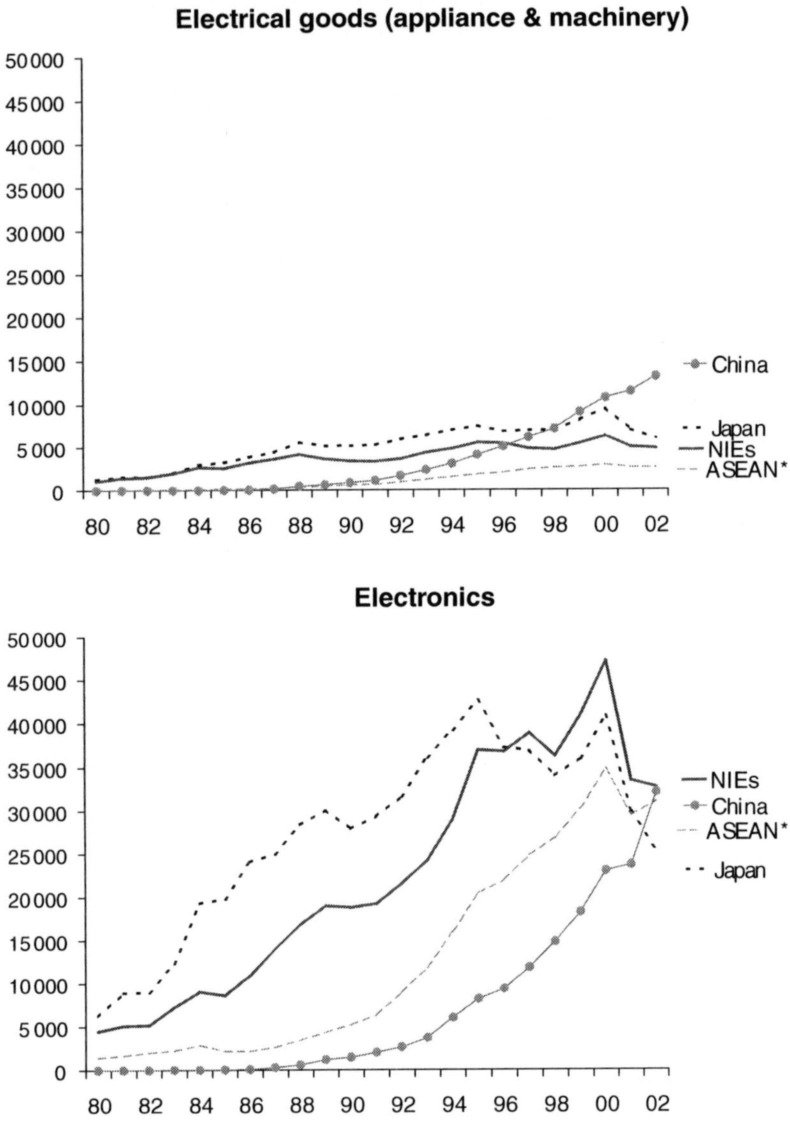

Note: NIEs: Hong Kong, Singapore, South Korea, Taiwan; ASEAN*: ASEAN countries excluding Singapore.
Source: CEPII-CHELEM database, authors' calculations.

Figure 5.5: EU 15 imports from East Asia, 1980–2002 (US$ thousands)

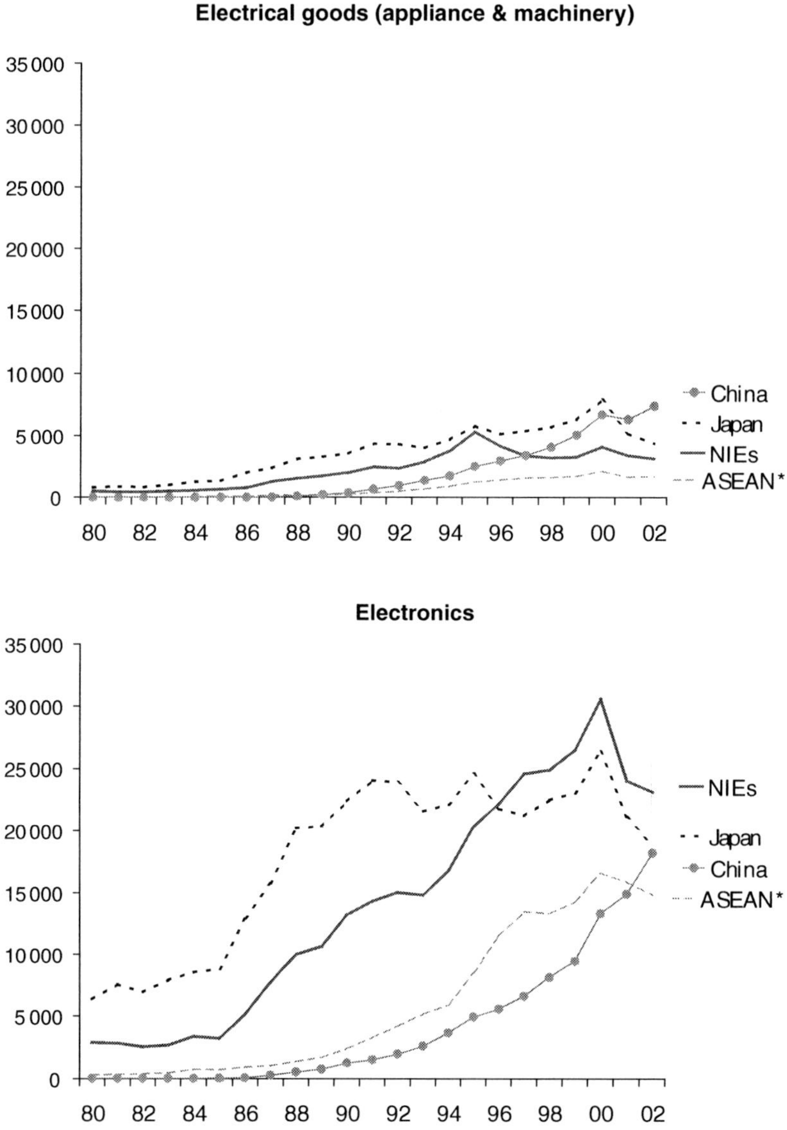

Note: NIEs: Hong Kong, Singapore, South Korea, Taiwan; ASEAN*: ASEAN countries excluding Singapore.
Source: CEPII-CHELEM database, authors' calculations.

Figure 5.6: The share of East Asia in total US trade deficit (% of US total trade balance)

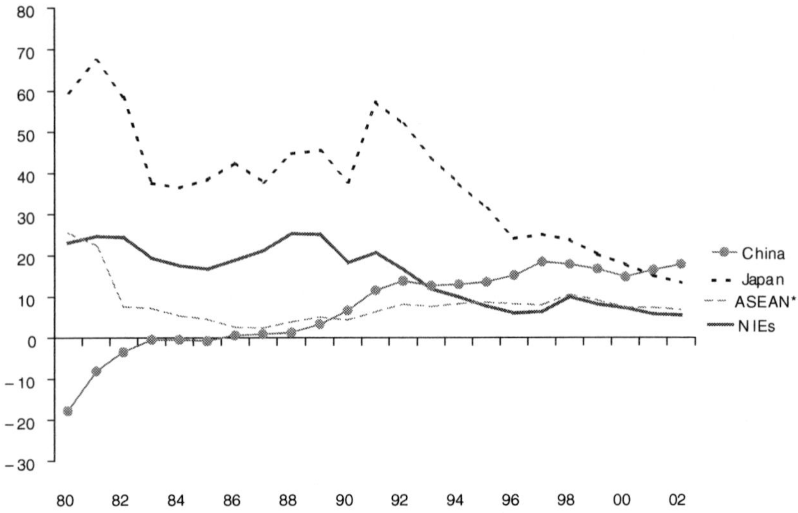

Note: NIEs: Hong Kong, Singapore, South Korea, Taiwan; ASEAN*: ASEAN countries excluding Singapore.
Source: CEPII-CHELEM database, authors' calculations.

Since 2001, following the drop of other Asian exporters, China has caught up with the NIEs as the largest exporter of electronic goods to the US.

Similar trends are observed in the East Asian exports to the EU (Figure 5.5). In electronic and electrical goods, the steady rise of China's exports was accompanied by the drop or the leveling of Japan and NIE exports in the late 1990s. As a result of this substitution effect, China has become the major Asian supplier of electrical goods to the EU, and has almost caught up with Japan. ASEAN* exports in both sectors continued to increase rapidly up to 2000 and have fallen since.

The contribution of the different Asian countries or group of countries to the US trade deficit reflects the displacement of Japan and NIE exports to China's exports. In the 1990s, the share of Japan and NIEs in the US trade deficit declined significantly, while China was responsible for an increasing share of this deficit (Figure 5.6).

5.4 Triangular trade

China's emergence has considerably accentuated the "triangular" trade pattern, already followed by ASEAN* countries, and characterized by deficits with East Asia in intermediate goods, and surpluses with Western countries in final goods. China's opening up has speeded up the withdrawal of the most advanced Asian economies from the production and export of labor-intensive products (consumption goods) and enlarged trade of sophisticated intermediate goods within East Asia. The structural factors underlying the triangular trade pattern will remain strong in the coming years.

China is likely to maintain a long-lasting specialization in labor-intensive products. Its huge labor supply, and the expected migration of its labor force from agriculture to industry in the coming years, will maintain the country's comparative advantage in this field. China's gains in market share, which have come primarily at the expense of the advanced economies of the region, will continue to be an incentive for the latter to move up the value-added chain. China will displace the NIEs in labor-intensive industries that they relinquish, just as in an earlier period the NIEs displaced Japan in these industries (Ahearne et al. 2003). The main threat is to the less advanced Asian economies which face China's competition in labor-intensive products. It is not clear whether they can move up the quality and technology ladder to keep a competitive edge over China (Lall and Albaladejo 2004).

The analysis of trade in high-technology products suggests complementarity rather than competition between China and the Asian advanced economies (Lall and Albaladejo 2004). The present study has shown that most of China's trade in high-tech products is handled by foreign firms and relies on supplies of high-tech components from East Asia. The technological upgrading of China's exports will remain dependent on FDI. The distribution of FDI between China and ASEAN* countries will be an important determinant of the evolution of their respective specialization in the future.

However, several factors are likely to work in favor of a reduction of trade imbalances associated with triangular trade. Recent trends in China's foreign trade indicate that the country is not only an export base but more and more an end market for foreign firms. China has considerably cut its tariff rates since the late 1990s and this has led to an accelerated growth of imports for the domestic market, or "ordinary imports." The further reductions in tariff rates which have been scheduled in China's agreement with the WTO, combined with the economic growth which has accelerated since 2002, resulted in an outstanding growth of imports for domestic use in 2002 and 2003. The opening of its potentially huge market should reduce China's global trade surplus in the long run. As European and US firms have relatively strong positions in this "domestic segment" of Chinese imports, and as their economies show strong complementarities with China's economy, they should benefit from the enlarged access to this market. Most studies on the consequences of China's accession to WTO conclude that developed countries will benefit most from the gains linked with China's opening up (Ianchovichina et al. 2001; Fan and Zheng 2000; Lejour 2000; Lemoine and Ünal-Kesenci 2002; Wang 1999). However as barriers to entry into this market are lowered, competition also increases, as more and more countries will be able to bear the costs of entry.

Moreover, as advanced Asian economies are increasing their imports from China, this will reduce the dependence of China's exports on Western markets. The positive balance that China has recently recorded in its processing trade with these economies indicates that production bases in China are more and more oriented towards supplying their East Asian domestic markets.

6 Conclusion

The emergence of China has had far-reaching implications for the East Asian economies. It has accelerated the reorganization of production in East Asia and the expansion of East Asian trade both within the region and with the rest of the world. The international division of labor within the region has expanded and intensified, as firms have developed production and export bases on the mainland. Production of labor-intensive goods has moved to China, which has expanded its share in Western markets at the expense of the advanced Asian countries. The latter have accelerated their exports of sophisticated intermediate goods to China. In this triangular trade pattern, the US and EU trade deficits with China have widened, while their deficits with Japan and the NIEs have narrowed.

China has become an important platform for manufacturing in East Asia. Trade data show that China's trade performance is highly dependent on the investment and outsourcing strategies of foreign firms which have decisively contributed both to the accelerated increase of China's exports and to their rapid technological upgrading over the last ten years. Foreign firms handle the bulk of China's trade in high-tech products, which raises the question of their dynamic impact on the upgrading of the domestic industrial capacities. The prospects of China's technological catch-up will depend on its ability to disseminate foreign technology into the local industrial sector and to develop its own innovative capacities.

The opening up of China's domestic market since its WTO accession, combined with its sustained economic growth rate, should lead to a reduction of trade imbalances, as strong domestic demand will boost imports of capital goods, and to a lesser extent of sophisticated consumption goods from industrialized countries. It will also raise imports of raw materials and agricultural commodities coming from developing or emerging countries.

Appendix 1: sector classification

SECTORS	HS2	HS2 TITLE
Raw agricultural products	01	Live animals.
	02	Meat and edible meat offal.
	03	Fish & crustacean, mollusc & other aquatic invertebrate.
	05	Products of animal origin, nes or included.
	06	Live tree & other plant; bulb, root; cut flowers etc.
	07	Edible vegetables and certain roots and tubers.
	08	Edible fruit and nuts; peel of citrus fruit or melons.
	10	Cereals.
	12	Oil seed, oleagi fruits; misc. grain, seed, fruit etc.
	13	Lac; gums, resins & other vegetable saps & extracts.
	14	Vegetable plaiting materials; vegetable products nes.
Food products	04	Dairy prod; birds' eggs; natural honey; edible prod nes.
	09	Coffee, tea, mat– and spices.
	11	Prod mill indust; malt; starches; inulin; wheat gluten.
	15	Animal/veg fats & oils & their cleavage products; etc.
	16	Prep of meat, fish or crustaceans, molluscs etc.
	17	Sugars and sugar confectionery.
	18	Cocoa and cocoa preparations.
	19	Prep of cereal, flour, starch/milk; pastrycooks' products.
	20	Prep of vegetable, fruit, nuts or other parts of plants.
	21	Misc. edible preparations.
	22	Beverages, spirits and vinegar.
	23	Residues & waste from the food industry; prepared animal fodder.
	24	Tobacco and manufactured tobacco substitutes.
Raw materials & fuels	25	Salt; sulphur; earth & stone; plastering materials; lime & cement.
	26	Ores, slag and ash.
	27	Mineral fuels, oils & products of their distillation etc.

Appendix 1: sector classification – *continued*

SECTORS	HS2	HS2 TITLE
Chemical products	28	Inorganic chemicals; compounds of precious metals, radioactive elements etc.
	29	Organic chemicals.
	30	Pharmaceutical products.
	31	Fertilizers.
	32	Tanning/dyeing extract; tannins & derivatives; pigments etc.
	33	Essential oils & resinoids; perfume, cosmetic/toilet preparations.
	34	Soap, organic surface-active agents, washing preparations, etc.
	35	Albuminoidal subs; modified starches; glues; enzymes.
	36	Explosives; pyrotechnic products; matches; pyrop alloy etc.
	37	Photographic or cinematographic goods.
	38	Misc. chemical products.
	39	Plastics and articles thereof.
	40	Rubber and articles thereof.
Wood and paper products	44	Wood and articles of wood; wood charcoal.
	45	Cork and articles of cork.
	46	Manufactures of straw, esparto/other plaiting materials etc.
	47	Pulp of wood/other fibrous cellulosic materials; waste etc.
	48	Paper & paperboard; articles of paper pulp, paper/paperboard.
	49	Printed books, newspapers, pictures & other products etc.
	94	Furniture; bedding, mattress, matt support, cushions etc.
Leather and shoes	41	Raw hides and skins (other than furskins) and leather.
	42	Articles of leather; saddlery/harness; travel goods etc.
	43	Furskins and artificial fur; manufactures thereof.
	64	Footwear, gaiters and the like; parts of such articles.

Appendix 1: sector classification – *continued*

SECTORS	HS2	HS2 TITLE
	43	Furskins and artificial fur; manufactures thereof.
	64	Footwear, gaiters and the like; parts of such articles.
Fiber and cloth	50	Silk.
	51	Wool, fine/coarse animal hair, horsehair yarn & fabric.
	52	Cotton.
	53	Other vegetable textile fibres; paper yarn & woven fabric.
	54	Man-made filaments.
	55	Man-made staple fibres.
	56	Wadding, felt & non-woven; yarns; twine, cordage, etc.
	57	Carpets and other textile floor coverings.
	58	Special woven fabric; tufted tex fabric; lace; tapestries etc.
	59	Impregnated, coated, cover/laminated textile fabric etc.
	60	Knitted or crocheted fabrics.
Wearing apparel	61	Articles of apparel & clothing, knitted or crocheted.
	62	Articles of apparel & clothing, not knitted/crocheted.
	63	Other made up textile articles; sets; worn clothing etc.
Building materials	68	Articles of stone, plaster, cement, asbestos, mica/similar materials.
	69	Ceramic products.
	70	Glass and glassware.
Metallurgy	72	Iron and steel.
	73	Articles of iron or steel.
	74	Copper and articles thereof.
	75	Nickel and articles thereof.
	76	Aluminium and articles thereof.
	78	Lead and articles thereof.
	79	Zinc and articles thereof.
	80	Tin and articles thereof.
	81	Other base metals; cermets; articles thereof.
Metal products	82	Tool, implement, cutlery, spoons & forks, of base metals etc.
	83	Miscellaneous articles of base metal.

Appendix 1: sector classification – *continued*

SECTORS	HS2	HS2 TITLE
Machinery	84	Nuclear reactors, boilers, machinery & mechanical appliances; parts.
	93	Arms and ammunition; parts and accessories thereof.
Electrical machinery	85	Electrical machinery equipinent, parts thereof; sound recorders etc.
Motor vehicles	87	Vehicles other than rail/tram roll-stock, parts & accessories.
Other transport equipment	86	Rail/tram locomotion, rolling-stock & parts thereof etc.
	88	Aircraft, spacecraft, and parts thereof.
	89	Ships, boats and floating structures.
Precision instruments	90	Optical, photographic, cinematic, measuring, checking, precision, etc.
	91	Clocks and watches and parts thereof.
	92	Musical instruments; parts and accessories of such articles.
Toys & misc. manufactured products	65	Headgear and parts thereof.
	66	Umbrellas, walking-sticks, seat-sticks, whips, etc.
	67	Prepared feathers & down; artificial flowers; articles human hair.
	71	Natural/cultured pearls, precious stones & metals, coins etc.
	95	Toys, games & sports requisites; parts & accessories thereof.
	96	Miscellaneous manufactured articles.
	97	Works of art, collectors' pieces and antiques.
	98	Special Classification Provisions.

Appendix 2: classification of production stages from BEC classification

In this study, the data from China's Customs Statistics, available at the 6-digit level of the Harmonized System, were aggregated according to the BEC classification of production stages. The classification by Broad Economic Categories of the United Nations reclassifies the Standard International Trade Classification (SITC, Rev. 3) headings on the basis of the principal use of the products. It converts foreign trade data into categories of final or intermediate use, such us capital goods, intermediate goods or consumer goods, following the usage in the System of National Accounts (SNA). We grouped BEC items in five stages as follows:

3 stages	5 stages	Code BEC	Title BEC
Primary goods		111	Food and beverages mainly for industry
		21	Industrial supplies, nes, primary
		31	Fuels and lubricants, primary
Intermediate goods	Semi-finished goods	121	Food and beverages, processed, mainly for industry
		22	Industrial supplies, nes, processed
		322	Fuels and lubricants, processed
	Parts & components	42	Of capital goods, except transport equipment
		53	Of transport equipment
Final goods	Capital goods	41	Capital goods except transport equipment
		521	Other industrial transport equipment
	Consumption goods	112	Food & beverages, primary, mainly for household consumption
		122	Food & beverages, primary, processed, for house. consumption
		51	Passenger motor cars
		522	Other non-industrial transport equipment
		53	Parts and accessories of transport equipment
		61	Durable consumer goods nes
		62	Semi-durable consumer goods nes
		63	Non-durable consumer goods nes

Appendix 3: the CEPII's list of high-tech products

The definition of high-tech products used in this CEPII study comes from Fontagné et al. (1999). The definition corresponds to a list of 252 products at the 6-digit level of the Harmonized System, derived from a joint list published by Eurostat and the OECD.

Since 1984 the OECD has published a classification of sectors according to their level of technology. It distinguished three levels (high, medium, low) based on the direct content in R&D for each sector. This classification identified six sectors of high-technology: aerospace, office machinery, pharmaceuticals, electronic and telecommunications, precision tools, and electric machinery. This classification has been extensively used in order to examine high-technology trade over 1970–80. More recently, the OECD (1995) issued a new classification, according to the direct and indirect technological content. This classification is based on the ISIC Rev. 2, and is articulated with trade data using the SITC Rev. 3.

Besides this classification of *sectors*, OECD and Eurostat has elaborated a classification at a *product* level. Within medium- and high-technology sectors (minus the automobile industry, plus weapons), it selected a list of products having a high content in R&D. The list includes 230 high-technology products at the 5-digit level of the SITC nomenclature (a list referred to here as OECD-1995-product). Hence, there is no correspondence between the high-technology sector (as referred to in OECD publications) and the list of high-technology products. It should be noted that this methodology introduces a slight selection bias, since it examines only the R&D content of the products which belong to sectors already classified as high-technology sectors. The high-technology products which do not belong to high-tech sectors are not identified and do not figure in the OECD-Eurostat list. They are thus implicitly considered as non-high-tech products.

Appendix 4: Indicator of contribution to trade balance

To measure China's revealed comparative advantages, we used the indicator of "contribution to the trade balance" (Lafay, 1994). The idea is to measure comparative advantages (*largo sensu*) under an assumption of balanced trade.

$$CTB_{ij}^{k} = 1000^{*}\left[(X_{ij}^{k} - M_{ij}^{k}) - \sum_{k}\sum_{j}(X_{ij}^{k} - M_{ij}^{k})\left(\frac{X_{ij}^{k} - M_{ij}^{k}}{\sum_{k}\sum_{j}(X_{ij}^{k} + M_{ij}^{k})}\right)\right]$$

with i for the declaring country (China), j for its partner and k for the products.

If there were no comparative advantage or disadvantage for any product k, then the country's total trade balance (surplus or deficit) should be distributed across all industries according to their share in total trade. The "contribution to the trade balance" is the difference between the observed and this theoretical balance. Here, these "contributions" are weighted by total trade of China.

A positive contribution is interpreted as a "revealed comparative advantage" for that industry. By definition, the sum over all industries and partners is zero. The indicator is additive: thus the values for products or industries can be aggregated to any desired level.

Contribution to the trade balance is a structural indicator which tries to eliminate business cycle variations (by comparing an industry's performance to overall performance) and, unlike many other indicators, is a symmetrical indicator in the sense that it focuses not only on exports, but also on imports.

Notes

1. Average of exports and imports (source CEPII-CHELEM).
2. This database has been provided to the authors by the International Trade Center (WTO), Geneva.
3. Note that the notions of "horizontal" and "vertical" specialization have a different meaning when they refer to product differentiation; the former concerns similar products of different varieties, the latter different qualities.
4. According to OECD statistics on international investment flows, China accounted for less than 1 percent of the stock of investment abroad of the US and of most European countries; 5 percent in the case of Japan and 15 percent in the case of South Korea
5. NIEs: Hong Kong, Singapore, South Korea and Taiwan. ASEAN* = ASEAN countries excluding Singapore.
6. http://www.wcoomd.org/.
7. For sector classification see Appendix 1.
8. "Foreign affiliate" in this chapter encompasses all firms with foreign capital, including joint ventures and firms in which foreign investors hold 100 percent of capital.
9. For the definition of the stages of production used in this section see Appendix 2.
10. Structural deficit (surplus) is measured by the indicator of contribution to trade balance, see Appendix 4.
11. For the classification of high-tech products, see Appendix 3.
12. As the overwhelming share of China's high-tech trade with Asia-Oceania takes place with East Asian countries, this section refers to "East Asia" when commenting on Tables 5.8 and 5.9.
13. East Asia is defined as Japan, NIEs (HK, Taiwan, Korea, Singapore), ASEAN* (Indonesia, Malaysia, Philippines, Thailand, Vietnam, Laos, Cambodia, Brunei).

References

Ahearne, Alan, Fernald, John, Loungani, Prakash and Schindler, John (2003) "Comrades or Competitors?" Federal Reserve Bank of Chicago, *Working Paper*, WP-03–27, March.

Akamatsu, Kanamae (1961) "A Theory of Unbalanced Growth in the World Economy," *Weltwirtschafliches Archiv*, 86: 196–215.

Ando, Mitsuyo and Kimura, Fukunari (2003) "The Formation of International Production and Distribution Networks in East Asia," *NBER Working Paper*, no. 10167, December.

Bernard, Mitchell and Ravenhill, John (1995). "Beyond Product Cycles and Flying Geese: Regionalization, Hierarchy, and the Industrialization of East Asia," *World Politics*, 47, 2: 171–9.

Borrus, Michael (1996) "Left for Dead: Asian Production Networks and the Revival of US Electronics," Berkeley Roundtable on the International Economy, University of California, Berkeley. http://www.ap.harvard.edu/mainsite/papers/recoop/borrus/borrus.html.

Borrus, Michael, Ernst, Dieter and Haggard, Stephan (2000) *International Production Networks in Asia: Rivalry or Riches?* London and New York: Routledge.

Coe, David T. and Helpman, Elhanan (1995) "International R&D Spillovers," *European Economic Review*, 39, 5: 859–87.

Coe, David T., Helpman, Elhanan and Hoffmaister, Alexander W. (1997) "North–South R&D Spillovers," *Economic Journal*, 107, 127: 134–49.

Dées, Stéphane and Lemoine, Françoise (1999) "The Devaluation of the Yuan: 'A Little Impatience May Ruin a Great Project' (Confucius)," *La Lettre du CEPII*, no. 178, April.

EC, European Commission and CESD, The Customs General Administration of the PRC and the International Trade Center UNCTAD/WTO (1997) *Comparison of Bilateral Trade Statistics of China and the European Union: Discrepancies and Underlying Factors*, Geneva, November 4.

ESCAP UN (1991) *Industrial Restructuring in Asia and the Pacific*, Bangkok: United Nations, March.

Fan, Mingtai and Zheng, Yuxin (2000) "The Impact of China's Trade Liberalisation for WTO Accession: a Computable General Equilibrium Analysis," paper presented at the Annual Conference of Global Economic Analysis, Melbourne, Australia, June 20–30.

Feenstra, Robert C. and Hanson, Gordon H. (1995) "Foreign Investment, Outsourcing and Relative Wages," *NBER Working Paper*, no. 5121, May.

Feenstra, Robert C. and Hanson, Gordon H. (1996) "Globalization, Outsourcing, and Wage Inequality," *NBER Working Paper*, no. 5424, January.

Fontagné, Lionel (1991) *Biens Intermédiaires et Division Internationale du Travail*, Paris: Economica.

Fontagné, Lionel, Freudenberg, Michael and Ünal-Kesenci, Deniz (1996) "Statistical Analysis of EC Trade in Intermediate Products," *External Trade Series – Studies and Research*, 6D, Eurostat.

Fontagné, Lionel, Freudenberg, Michael and Ünal-Kesenci, Deniz (1999) "Trade in Technology and Quality Ladders: Where Do EU Countries Stand?" *International Journal of Development Planning Literature*, 14, 4: 561–82.

Fukao, Kyozi, Ishido, Hikari and Ito, Keiko (2003) "Vertical Intra-Industry Trade and Foreign Direct Investment in East Asia," *Journal of Japanese and International Economies,* 17, 4: 468–506.

Fukasaku, Kiichiro and Kimura, Fukunari (2001) "Globalisation and Intra-Firm Trade: Further Evidence," Mimeo, May.

Fung, K. C., Iizaka, Hitomi, Kim, Hee-Kyung and Siu, Alan K. F. (2004) "Korean, Japanese and Taiwanese Direct Investment in China," *Proceedings on Rising China and the East Asian Economy,* Korean Institute of International Economic Policy. Korea, March 20.

Gaulier, Guillaume, Jean, Sébastien and Ünal-Kesenci, Deniz (2004) "Regionalism and the Regionalisation of International Trade," *CEPII Working Paper,* no. 2004–16, November.

Grubel, Herbert G. and Johnson, Harry G. (1971) "The Welfare Implications of Effective Protection," In *Effective Tariff Protection,* ed. H. G. Grubel and H. G. Johnson, pp. 85–107, Geneva: Graduate Institute of International Studies and General Agreement on Tariffs and Trade.

Guerrieri, Paolo (2000) "International Competitiveness, Regional Integration, and Corporate Strategies in the East Asian Electronic Industry," in *International Production Networks in Asia: Rivalry or Riches?* ed. M. Borrus, D. Ernst and S. Haggard, London and New York: Routledge.

Huchet, Jean-François (1997) "The China Circle and Technological Development in the Chinese Electronic Industry," in *The China Circle: Economic and Technology in the PRC, Taiwan and Hong Kong,* ed. B. Naughton, Washington, DC: Brookings Institution Press.

Ianchovichina, Elena, Martin, Will and Fukase, Emiko (2000) "Comparative Study of Trade Liberalization Regimes: the Case of China's Accession to the WTO," paper prepared for the Annual Conference of Global Economic Analysis, Melbourne, Australia, June 20–30.

Ianchovichina, Elena and Martin, Will (2001) "Trade Liberalization in China's Accession to WTO," *Journal of Economic Integration,* 16, 4: 421–45.

Kaplinsky, Raphael, Morris, Mike and Readman, Jeff (2002) "Globalization of Product Markets and Immisering Growth: Lessons from the South-African Furniture Industry," *World Development,* 30, 7: 1159–77.

Keller, Wolfgang (2001) "The Geography and Channels of Diffusion at the World's Technology Frontier," *NBER Working Paper,* no. 8150, March.

Lafay, Gérard (1994) "The Measurement of Revealed Comparative Advantages," in *International Trade Modelling,* ed. M.G. Dagenais and P. A. Muet, London: Chapman & Hall.

Lall, Sanjaya and Albaladejo, Manuel (2004) "China's Competitive Performance: a Threat to East Asian Manufactured Exports?" *World Development,* 32, 9: 1441–66.

Lardy Nicholas R. (2002) *Integrating China into the Global Economy,* Washington, DC: Brookings Institution Press.

Lassudrie-Duchêne, Bernard (1985) "L'échange International avec Segmentation des Produits," in *Le Protectionisme,* ed. B. Lassudrie-Duchêne and J. L. Reiffers, Paris: Economica.

Lee, Keun and Kim M. Mihnsoo (2004) "The Rise of China and the Korean Firms Looking for a New Division of Labor," *Proceedings on Rising China and the East Asian Economy*, Korean Institute of International Economic Policy, Korea, March 20.

Lejour, Arjan (2000) "China and the WTO: the Impact on China and the World Economy," paper prepared for the Annual Conference of Global Economic Analysis, Melbourne, Australia, June 20–30.

Lemoine, Françoise (2000) "FDI and the Opening up of China's Economy," *CEPII Working Paper*, no. 2000–11, June, www.cepii.fr.

Lemoine, Françoise and Ünal-Kesenci, Deniz (2002) "China in the International Segmentation of Production Processes," *CEPII Working Paper*, no. 2002–02. March, www.cepii.fr.

Lemoine, Françoise and Ünal-Kesenci, Deniz (2004) "Assembly Trade and Technology Transfer: the Case of China," *World Development*, 32, 5: 829–50.

Masuyama, Seiichi (2004) "The Asian Strategy of Japanese Multinationals: Focus on China," *Tokyo Club Research Meetings*, February 9.

Naughton, Barry (1996) "China's Emergence and Prospects as a Trading Nation," *Brookings Papers on Economic Activity*, Vol. 2: 273–344.

Naughton, Barry (1997) *The China Circle: Economic and Technology in the PRC, Taiwan and Hong Kong*, Washington, DC: Brookings Institution Press.

Ng, Francis and Yeats, Alexander (1999) "Production Sharing in East Asia: Who Does What, for Whom and Why?" *World Bank Policy Research Working Paper Series*, no. 2197.

Ng, Francis and Yeats, Alexander (2003) "Major Trade Trends in East Asia. What Are Their Implications for Regional Cooperation and Growth?" *World Bank Policy Research Working Paper Series*, no. 3084, June.

OECD (1980) "International Trade in High Research and Development-Intensive Products," SITC/80.48.

OECD (1983) "International Trade in High-Technology Products: an Empirical Approach," DSTI/SPR/83.13.

OECD (1984) "Specialization and Competitiveness in High, Medium and Low R&D-Intensity Manufacturing Industries: General Trends," DSTI/SPR/84.49.

OECD (1995) "Classification of High-Technology Products and Industries," DSTS/EAS/IND/STP(95)1.

OECD (1999) "Foreign Direct Investment and Recovery in South-East Asia."

Sung, Yun-Wing (2000) "Costs and Benefits of Exports-Oriented Foreign Investment: the Case of China," *Asian Economic Journal*, 14, 1: 55–70.

Tso, Allen Y. (1998) "Foreign Direct Investment and China's Economic Development," *Issues and Studies*, 34, 2: 1–34.

UNCTAD (1996) *Trade and Development Report*, New York and Geneva: United Nations.

UNCTAD (1999) *World Investment Report*, New York and Geneva: United Nations.

UNCTAD (2001) *Trade and Development Report*, New York and Geneva: United Nations.

UNCTAD (2002) *Trade and Development Report*, New York and Geneva: United Nations.

Wang, Zhi (1999) "The Impact of China's WTO Entry on the World Labor-Intensive Export Market: a Recursive Dynamic CGE Analysis," *The World Economy*, 22, 3: 379–406.

Wu, Yanrui (1999) "The Performance of FDI," in *Foreign Direct Investment and Economic Growth in China*, ed. Y. Wu, Cheltenham, UK and Northampton, MA, USA: Edward Elgar.

Wei, Yingqi and Liu, Xiaming (2001) *Foreign Direct Investment in China: Determinants and Impact*, Cheltenham, UK and Northampton, MA, USA: Edward Elgar.

Zhang, Xiaoguang (1999) "Foreign Investment Policy, Contribution and Performance," in *Foreign Direct Investment and Economic Growth in China*, ed. Y. Wu, Cheltenham, UK and Northampton, MA, USA: Edward Elgar.

Zhang, Zhaoyong (1995) "International Trade and Foreign Direct Investment: Further Evidence from China," *Asian Economic Journal*, 9, 2: 153–67.

Zysman John, Doherty, Eileen and Schwartz, Andrew (1996) "Tales from the Global Economy: Cross-National Production Networks and the Reorganisation of the European Economy," *Berkeley Rountable on the International Economy Working Paper*, WP-83, June.

6

Vertical Intra-Regional Production Networks in East Asia: a Case Study of the Hard Disc Drive Industry

Daisuke Hiratsuka

1 Introduction

Under global competition and oligopolisitic production, volume manufacturing production has prevailed, and has required much of engineers and workers, as well as huge capital resources. Due to the availability of human resources and suppliers, East Asia has become a leader of volume production. Indeed, multinational corporations (MNCs) have successively moved their manufacturing locations to the cheap labor countries of East Asia from Singapore, to Malaysia and Thailand, and finally to China. In the meantime, capital intensive processes have remained in Japan and the United States.

As discussed in Chapter 1, the manufacturing production process in East Asia, particularly in electronics, has been so fragmented across countries/regions that many countries have participated in production for the same final products. This production fragmentation is a new phenomenon that developed in the 1990s. In the past, Japan supplied almost all the material and parts to East Asia, but no longer does so. The industrialized ASEAN countries of Singapore, Malaysia, the Philippines, Indonesia, China, and recently even Vietnam have supplied most parts and components. Due to the development of logistic services and low transportation costs, many countries have begun participating in the manufacturing process, which has led to the formation of vertical intra-regional production networks and an expansion of intra-regional and intra-industry trade.

But why and how has the production fragmentation and the corresponding development of vertical intra-regional production networks evolved in East Asia? And what does the production fragmentation actually look like? This chapter aims to investigate the development process and features of vertical intra-regional production networks in East Asia at the industry level, as well as at the firm level, focusing on the hard disc drive (HDD) industry. In the HDD industry, East Asia dominates global manufacturing, and the manufacturing process has been fragmented across countries in the region.

The chapter is laid out as follows. Section 2 introduces the core–periphery and core firm–suppliers framework to explain the industrial clusters formed by movement of the production facilities by MNCs. Sections 3 and 4 review the development of the industry in East Asia in the context of this framework, showing how the HDD assembly industry initially clustered in Singapore, and then extended to other countries in East Asia. Sections 4 and 5 discuss international procurement of HDD and show that each production site is linked together systematically due to low transportation costs, and that intra-regional production networks have developed in the HDD industry across countries within the region.

2 Industrial clusters formed by core firms and suppliers

2.1 The core–periphery and core firm–suppliers framework

Krugman and Venables (1995) present the core and periphery model, with the incorporation of the concept of transportation costs, which provides an explanation of how manufacturing production moves from the core (industrialized and innovating countries) to the periphery (non-industrialized and non-innovating countries).[1] When transportation costs begin to fall, the world economy will organize itself into an industrialized core and a deindustrialized periphery. But if transportation costs fall enough so that low wages in periphery countries offset these countries' remoteness from markets and suppliers, manufacturing in the core will move from the core to the periphery.

But, what will happen to the periphery when a foreign supplier moves there? More concretely, how do the periphery countries become industrialized? Kuchiki (2005) incorporates the concept of a core firm in explaining industry clustering in the periphery.[2] According to Kuchiki (2005), core firms in the industrial zones, together with the combination of good infrastructure and human resources, play a crucial role in industrial agglomeration. The process of industry clustering can be interpreted as certain suppliers in the core country following the core firm when a core firm moves to the periphery. Such supplier movement improves the locational advantage of the periphery on the supply side, which catalyzes other core firm and supplier groups to move there. Eventually, with several groups of core firms and suppliers, an industry has clustered in the periphery, transforming the previously non-industrialized periphery into an industrialized one. However, the industrialized periphery is still non-innovative, and the key technology still remains in the innovative core country.

The above core firm and suppliers argument for industry clustering can be particularly applied to Japanese multinational corporations (MNCs) which have advanced to East Asia. Most of the Japanese MNCs operating in East Asia have outsourced to suppliers coming from Japan, either "keiretsu" or "non-keiretsu" since their head offices generally have not agreed to outsource to local suppliers.[3] In contrast, American MNCs have outsourced some engineering processes to local suppliers because American suppliers have not followed the core firms, probably due to large geographical distances. In consequence, the core American firms and the outsourced indigenous suppliers have formed industrial clusters in East Asia. Some indigenous suppliers have grown large and have started supplying parts for US and Japanese assemblers, and have followed their major customers when they moved expansively to new frontiers.

2.2 Sequential emergence of the industrialized periphery

The next logical question is why has the frontier of the industrialized periphery continually expanded in East Asia? In other words, why have MNCs extended their manufacturing production to the new frontiers from one place to the next, for example from Singapore and Penang, then to Thailand, then to the Philippines, Indonesia and China, and very recently to Vietnam?

Locational advantages are determined by the availability of suppliers and human resources, transportation costs and the presence of markets, and the investment facilitation measures provided by the governments concerned. All of these factors change occasionally. First, investment facilitation measures including tax incentive policies have moved from country to country in East Asia. For instance, when Thailand allowed foreign capital participation for export purposes in 1983, Malaysia and Indonesia followed to relax foreign capital participation in 1986, and the Philippines followed suit in 1991. Second, wages for skilled labor, especially engineers, increased elastically according to demand, and as a result, the advantage of cheap labor gradually diminished. Third, the suppliers following migration of a core firm improved the locational advantages of the frontier. This changes the locational advantages of countries/regions, which have forced core firms and suppliers to extend to new frontiers sequentially.

Why have some suppliers followed the assemblers and others not? Transportation and communication tools have greatly advanced: nevertheless, geographical proximity does matter. Assemblers prefer to employ suppliers who are located close to them, in order to reduce transportation costs, shorten the lead time from order to shipment, and lower communication costs. Transportation costs are declining due to the development of transportation technology and investment by freight forwarders, but are still relatively high. Transportation costs account for about 1 percent of total sales in the HDD industry although they have reduced greatly in recent years.[4] Shortening the lead time is a very important issue to assemblers, especially for electronic devices, since products' sale prices decline every month. In addition, communication costs are quite high if the geographical distance between customer and supplier is large.[5] Communication with customers is very important to suppliers, particularly for mechanical products with frequent specification changes, and where precision technology is required. Through frequent communications, suppliers can obtain advance information regarding prices, evaluation of products, delivery schedule, future production outlook, and occasionally the customer's new products and its corporate strategy.[6] Suppliers can respond quickly to the emergent situation when delivered products are rejected by customers.[7] Geographical proximity enables suppliers to respond speedily and correctly to the needs of their customers.[8]

2.3 Intra-regional production networks

Meanwhile, some suppliers have not always followed their customers. With low transportation costs, suppliers can ship parts over long distances. In this regard, tiny and valuable parts can be transported from long distances. Naturally, suppliers prefer to continue operations rather than move. To produce products of high quality, it is necessary to have skilled engineers and experienced operators; these are largely immovable. Workers do not move easily to a new manufacturing site even within a country. Furthermore, starting up a new operation facility requires large investments of money and time. Suppliers therefore prefer to continue their operations until they are forced to move, having considered all the transportation costs, fixed investment costs, and market conditions.[9]

In fact, the development of logistic services has reduced technological distance, lead time from order to shipment, and transportation costs, and has enabled suppliers to deliver parts speedily to their long-distance customers. Nowadays, logistic services have become very sophisticated: forwarders provide not only transportation services from supplier to customer but also inventory management, informing suppliers of their customer's inventory. In addition, big suppliers employ electric procurement systems in which customers, suppliers and forwarders are linked on a real time basis, which has reduced lead times and lowered labor costs. Furthermore, reduction of lead time generates profit because market prices, particularly for electrical devices, fall every month. Hence, if suppliers have two production sites, one in China and the other in Southeast Asia,[10] the delivery within East Asia would be very smooth.

Assemblers and suppliers exploit the different locational advantages that each country has in terms of supplier, market and factor endowments. Choice of location, however, differs by firm; for example, some prefer to locate in Thailand and some in Indonesia. Some suppliers have followed the core firms, but some not. Some assemblers, especially the American MNCs, have outsourced to local suppliers. The mixture of these different locational strategies has formed industrial clusters in country after country in East Asia. Thanks to the increasing development of logistic services and transportation and communication tools, industrial clusters located in different countries, according to the locational advantage, have been systematically linked, forming vertical intra-regional production networks in East Asia. The remaining sections of this chapter confirm these points, using the HDD industry as a case study.

3 Concentration and dispersion of hard disc drive (HDD) assembly in East Asia

3.1 Outline of HDD industry

Krugman (1991a, 2004) emphasizes the history (cumulative processes) which leads to the agglomeration of industry and the possibility of multiple equilibriums. The cumulative process of industrial clusters in the electronics industry has transformed Southeast Asia into an electronics industry belt. The sequential occurrence of concentration and dispersal of industry have gradually created East Asia's manufacturing belt where industrial clusters have been integrated systematically (Ernst 1999). How has the industrial cluster actually formed in East Asia? This section and the following sections will discuss the cumulative process of the HDD assembly industry and its parts and components industries in East Asia, specifically examining production fragmentation for the HDD industry. The HDD industry is a good example of fragmentation with respect to the manufacturing process, and of a vertical intra-regional production network.

Until the early 1980s, there were many HDD final assemblers, and almost all of them were concentrated in the United States. Today, only 1 percent of the final assembly of HDDs has remained in the United States, while Southeast Asia dominates with almost 70 percent of world production (Ernst 1997). Due to large economies of scale, the industry structure has become oligopolistic; the market is currently dominated by three American firms (Seagate, Maxtor and Western Digital) and three Japanese ones (Hitachi/IBM, Fujitsu and Toshiba). Research and development, including design of HDDs, and high-tech wafer fabrication processes, are operated in the United States and Japan, at the MNCs' home facilities. However, other manufacturing processes have been operating in East Asia, especially in Southeast Asia, but recently also in China.

The main components of an HDD are disk media, heads, integrated circuit boards, and precision motors; an HDD also has other small mechanical parts. The main components are assembled separately in different locations in East Asia by component assemblers. Most of them are Japanese affiliates. Then, the main components and other small parts are assembled at the high-tech facilities of American and Japanese HDD assemblers in East Asia. All of the six final assemblers operate in East Asia. The component production process has been sliced into many stages and the sliced processes have been outsourced to many suppliers. The HDD industry, hence, has a hierarchical tree structure composed of the final assemblers, the component suppliers and parts suppliers. This structure has enabled these players to attain scale economies for short life products, and has shared investment costs among assembler and suppliers.

3.2 Cluster of HDD assembly in Singapore

Seagate Technology, currently the world's leading HDD maker, was the pioneer in moving manufacturing of HDDs from the United States to Singapore. It did this in 1982, three years after the company was founded in California (Lobo 2000). Starting with manufactured components, Seagate's facility in Singapore quickly progressed to final assembly. By the end of 1984, Seagate had shifted almost all HDD assembly to Singapore.

Seagate attained low cost manufacturing in Singapore, which made up for high transportation costs and communication costs due to large geographical distance, and succeeded in expanding sales. The success of Seagate promoted the shift of HDD production by other firms from the United States (Silicon Valley) to Singapore. Thereafter, other American HDD assemblers followed Seagate, including Computer Memories (1983), Tandon (1983), Maxtor (1984), MiniScribe (1984), Microscien International (1985), Micropolis (1986), Corner Peripherals (1987), Control Data (1987), Cybernex (1987), Unysis (1988), Western Digital (1988), SyQuest (1989) (McKendrick et al. 2000: 98). By the end of the 1980s, Singapore had become the center of final assembly of HDDs.

Why did Seagate choose Singapore? What locational advantage did Singapore have? The Singapore government provided tax incentives in the form of a full tax exemption for a specific period, usually five years (Wong 1999). More importantly, at the time, local suppliers had been nurtured in Singapore and many engineers spoke English, since the American semiconductor firms had operated in Singapore for a long time since National Semiconductor (1968), Texas Instruments (1968), Tandon (1971) and Hewlett Packard (1972) had moved their production facilities to Singapore. The long operation by American semiconductor firms in Singapore had developed supporting industries and nurtured indigenous firms in precision engineering. Furthermore, the users of HDD started to concentrate in Singapore: these were Digital Equipment Corporation (1981) and Apple (1981). There were many suppliers and markets in Singapore. Singapore had large locational advantages in human resources, supplier and market availability, and the government investment facilitation measures.

3.3 Extension of HDD assembly from Singapore

The development of the HDD industry brought about the relocation of the HDD industry across East Asia, as well as the reorganization of production. The American HDD makers gradually shifted their lower-end factories out of Singapore to cheaper manufacturing countries, namely Thailand, Malaysia, and recently China (*Shanghai Star*, March 27, 2003).

In the mid-1980s, many MNCs moved their production facilities to Thailand. At that time, the currencies of Singapore, South Korea and Taiwan were appreciating against the US dollar. Furthermore, Thailand allowed foreign capital participation for export purposes in 1983, and announced a list of promoted areas for investment in 1985. In 1987, regulations on foreign capital participation were further relaxed so that 100 percent of foreign capital participation was allowed when business exports reached more than 80 percent of products, or for firms located in remote areas.[11] The promoted firms received a full tax exemption for three to eight years, according to the promoted industry and whether the firm was located in a rural area. For these reasons, a large number of the MNCs undertook foreign direct investment in Thailand. Firms operating in Singapore had extended manufacturing production to the new frontier of Thailand. Seagate was one of the pioneers.

The cumulative process of the HDD industry in Thailand started when Seagate shifted head-stack assembly from Singapore to Samutphrakarn, a suburb of Bangkok, in 1983. The assembled head stack was shipped from Thailand to Singapore. This event began the transformation of Thailand into one of the global HDD production bases. In 1987, Seagate started final assembly in Chokchai (Nakhon Ratchasima province) in the northeast of Thailand (McKendrick et al. 2000: 190). Seagate got a long tax holiday by locating in Zone 3, the remote area from Bangkok. But the company stopped final assembly in 1999 when the full tax holiday for Seagate expired. Seagate restarted a new final assembly plant in Chokchai in 2004, since the Thai government provided a full tax holiday for eight years in order to promote the HDD industry.

Fujitsu, a Japanese manufacturer which participated in the HDD business in the United States in 1986, started final assembly for desktop PCs in Bangkok in 1994.[12] In 2001, Fujitsu switched from 3.5 inch HDDs for desktop PCs to 2.5 inch HDDs for notebooks in the same area.

IBM began HDD assembly in 1991, at Union Technology Thailand (UTC) in Sriracha, Chonburi province, through a contract manufacturing agreement with Saha Union, an industrial conglomerate. IBM started its own facility in 1997 in Prachinburi province, and began expansion to a phase 2 plant in 1999. In 2003 the HDD operations of IBM were renamed Hitachi Global Storage Technologies after being acquired by Hitachi.[13]

In 2002, Western Digital Technologies began operating a manufacturing facility in Navanakorn in the Bangkok area, which had been owned by Fujitsu (Western Digital 2002 and 2003). Fujitsu had huge land and facilities. The company sold some of the land and facilities for the 3.5 inch HDD plant to Western Digital, and switched to the 2.5 inch HDD in the same area.

Four of the six assemblers, namely, Seagate, Fujitsu, IBM/Hitachi and Western Digital, have operated final assembly in Thailand. Thailand has formed a large cluster of HDD final assembly since the latter half of the 1980s.

Meanwhile, Japanese HDD assemblers have formed an HDD cluster in Manila, in the Philippines; Hitachi started operations in 1995. There were two reasons why Hitachi moved to the Philippines. One was the availability of English-speaking engineers. Japanese final assemblers had to start large-scale operations very quickly due to market competition. The Philippines, where many thousands of English-speaking engineers were available, met the requirements. Another reason was tax incentives. The Philippine government provided a full tax exemption for five years to projects that employed new technology. The Japanese assembler could substantially escape from income tax indefinitely under the tax exemption program, employing new technology continuously. In 1996, Fujitsu and Toshiba followed Hitachi.

The third largest American HDD assembler, Western Digital, has taken a different locational strategy. Western Digital closed two manufacturing facilities in Singapore during 1999 and 2000, and relocated its hard drive production lines to low-cost Kuala Lumpur, Malaysia in 2000 (Western Digital 2002). The new location is close in distance from both Singapore and Penang where there are many suppliers and markets. In Penang, Dell computers started operations in 1995, and the world's top five largest electric manufacturing services (EMS) operated there starting in the 1990s.

Locations with good market access tend to be relatively attractive for firms (Venables 2004). The HDD industry development in China is a typical case. Most PC assemblers, namely, Dell, Hewlett-Packard (HP), Apple and Toshiba, have assembled PCs in China. Due to this market access effect, China has started to form a large HDD industry cluster. Industry leader Seagate was a pioneer, moving the manufacture of its low-end drives to Shenzhen, China beginning in 1995. This became the third largest final assembly site for Seagate. In 1998, IBM/Hitachi (acquired by Hitachi in 2003) started HDD assembly in Shenzhen, through a contract manufacturing agreement with ExcelStor, a subsidiary of Great Wall. In 2005, Hitachi started its own factory in Shenzhen to produce the 3.5 inch HDDs. Maxtor set up a new factory in Suzhou, China in mid-2005, which took over the manufacturing of entry-level disk drives from the first Singaporean plant in 1984 and second plant in 1999, leaving the higher-end production (*Shanghai Star*, March 27, 2003). Seagate, IBM/Hitachi and Maxtor have transformed China into the largest HDD final assembly center in the world.

4 Clusters of HDD suppliers

Due to the core firm and suppliers effect mentioned earlier, the HDD components and parts industries have clustered in the assembling sites across countries within the region. The market access effect works not only in final products but also in intermediate goods; firms producing intermediate goods tend to locate close to their downstream customers, and the downstream customers want to locate close to intermediate suppliers (Venables 1999, 2004). The HDD industry provides a good example of these effects.

Initially, assembly of HDD heads and printed circuit boards concentrated in Singapore. Seagate moved head assembly to Singapore, and had to outsource the mechanical parts to local engineering suppliers, because only a few American suppliers followed Seagate. But at first, their technological level did not satisfy Seagate's requirements, since HDDs required quite high technology compared with other electronics industries. With technical support from Seagate, local suppliers finally supplied precision parts and components to Seagate (Wong 1999; McKendrick et al. 2000: 155–83). Other American suppliers also outsourced to local suppliers. Fourteen suppliers became listed at the Stock Exchange of Singapore. They are: Cheung Who Technology (1972), Amtek Technology (1980), Seksun (1981), and Brilliant Manufacturing (1984) for top cover; Beyonics Technology (1981), Venture Corpor-

Table 6.1: Singapore major suppliers of hard disc drives

Amtek Engineering (1980)	Top cover
Beyonics Technology (1981)	Base plates, PCBA
Brilliant Manufacturing (1984)	Top covers, base plates, spindle components
Cheung Who Technology (1972)	Top covers, disc clamps, VCM components
Elec & Eltek (1993)	PCB
First Engineering (1980)	Plastic components
Hi-P International (1980)	Plastic components
Jurong Technologies (1986)	PCB board assembly
Magnecomp International (1995)	Suspension heads
MMI (1989)	Base plates, suspension assembly
Norelco (2001)	HDD manufacturing equipment
Seksun (1981)	Top covers
Unisteel Technology (1988)	Fasteners
Venture Corporation (1984)	PCB board assembly

Source: Singapore Exchange Limited (SGX) of Stock Exchange of Singapore.

ation (1984), Jurong Technologies (1986), and Elec & Eltek (1993) for printed circuit boards; MMI (1989) and Magnecomp International (1995) for suspension; First Engineering (1980), Hi-P International (1980) for plastic components, Norelco (2001), and Unisteel Technology (1988) (see Table 6.1).

Disk media has also moved to Singapore. In 1995, Hoya Magnetics started production of glass disk media in Singapore. Hoya ships disk media not only to Singapore but also to Thailand, the Philippines and China.

Manufacture of HDD mechanical parts is clustered in Thailand where, in 1982, Minebea started manufacturing bearings, rotary parts and other machinery parts. Minebea moving to Thailand improved the infrastructure of supporting industry for the country. Coupled with the Thai government's corporate tax policy, the head assembly process moved from Singapore to Thailand. Seagate established a labor-intensive process facility for head-stack assembly (HSA) in Samutphrakarn, a suburb of Bangkok, in 1983. Seagate started head-disk assembly (HDA) in 1987 in Chokchai. These catalyzed the clustering of HDD head assembly in Thailand. Read-Rite, which specialized in thin film technology for heads, started a head assembly facility in Ayutthaya in 1991, which was eventually acquired by Western Digital in 2003. The assembly of actuators for heads was located in Thailand by Fujikura (1985), Minebea (1985), Thailand-based K. R. Precision (1988), Singapore-based Magnecomp (1992), and Eng Precision (1999), while voice coil magnet assembly was started by TDK (1992) and Hana (1993). Most of these facilities are located in Ayutthaya.

HDD spindle motor factories have also clustered in Thailand. In 1986, Seagate started the operation of motors in Chokchai in Nakhon Ratchasima province, followed by Minebea (1988) and Nidec (1989). Magnets for spindle motors have similarly clustered in Thailand; Minebea (1985), Seagate (1994) and Daido (1994) built facilities in Ayutthaya for magnets. The assembled head and spindle motors are shipped to Thailand, Singapore, Malaysia and Shenzhen via Hong Kong.

Printed circuit boards and disk media, on the other hand, have extended to Penang, Malaysia. The American semiconductor firms have operated there for a long time; they are Motorola (1967), National Semiconductor (1972), Texas Instruments (1972) and Intel (1972). For their forward linkage effect, printed circuit board industries have clustered in Penang, and the world's top five electronic manufacturing service (EMS) companies concentrated in Penang in the 1990s. They are Flectronics, Celestica, Sanmina-SCI, Solectron and Jabil, who are all users of printed circuit boards. Singapore printed circuit board manufacturers have also extended to Penang. Natsteel Electronics (1992) is one printed circuit board manufacturer from Singapore. Local printed circuit board manufacturers have grown, such as Trans Capital (1992). These industry developments attracted Komag, the largest American media disk supplier, to build a manufacturing plant in Penang in 1993. The media disk plant was the first to produce advanced thin-film disks outside of the United States and Japan. Komag expanded the first Penang plant in 1995, and built a second plant in Penang in 1997.[14] The EMS and Komag have transformed Penang into a printed circuit board and disk media center.

Mechanical parts have also clustered in Malaysia. The American semiconductor firms have outsourced engineering services to the local suppliers. Indeed, National Semiconductor in Penang outsourced eight local suppliers in precision engineering in the early 1970s.[15] Many local subcontractors were nourished by Intel in the 1980s, and have since participated in the HDD industry. These include Eng Teknology (1988) and LKT Technology (1978)[16] for actuators. In the late 1980s, Singapore-based American and Japanese firms first moved head assembly to Penang. Maxtor (1988), Control Data (1988), Hitachi Metal (1989), Seagate (1989) and Read Rite (1991) started head assembly operations in Penang. Singaporean firms, such as CAM Technology (1992) for base plates and MMI Industries (1992) for voice-coil motors and base plates, extended their operations to Penang from Singapore, in order to expand manufacturing. Consequently, mechanical parts of the HDD have clustered in Penang by the MNCs and local suppliers.

A small mechanical parts cluster has developed in the Philippines, where three Japanese final assemblers, namely Hitachi (known as Global Data Storage after buying IBM's HDD business in 2003), Toshiba and Fujitsu, concentrated in this country. As shown in Figure 6.1, there were only a few HDD parts suppliers in Manila before 1995: San Technology, Sumitomo for voice coil motors (VCM) (1988) and Shinetsu Magnetic for VCM (1993). However, when the three HDD final assemblers advanced to Manila, many parts suppliers followed them and started operations there. These were Japanese first-tier and second-tier suppliers, such as Nidec for spindle motors (1996), TDK for magnetic heads (1997), Nitkoshi for head storage (1999), and Touritsu for plastic filters (2001). Singapore- and Penang-based second-tier suppliers fol-

Figure 6.1: A hard disc drive cluster in the Philippines

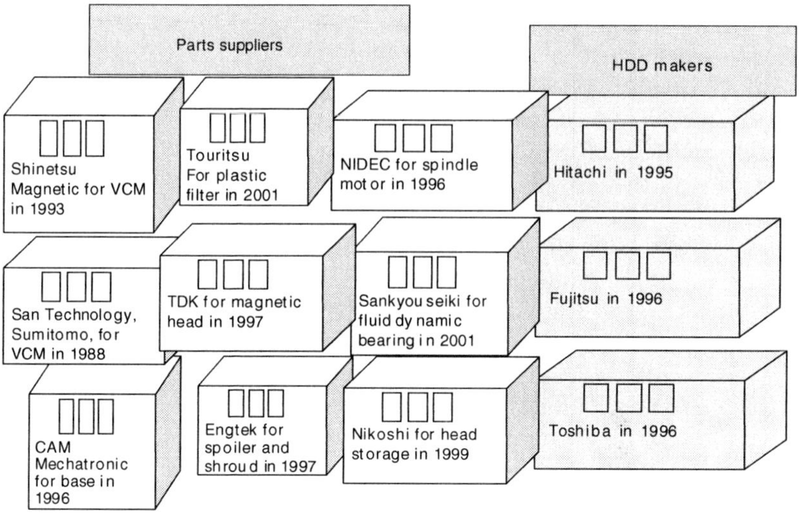

Source: author.

lowed, including Singapore-based CAM Mechatronic for bases (1996), and Malaysia-based Engtek for spoilers and shrouds (1997). By the end of the 1990s, Manila became a new HDD industry center next to Singapore and Thailand.

Most suppliers have been following final assemblers to Shenzhen, China. Belton Group, based in Hong Kong, was the pioneer to shift actuator production to Shenzhen in 1989.[17] TDK (1994) built a large electronics parts plant in Xiamen which produced head parts including carriage, and Penang-based Engtek established itself in Dongguan in 1996 for actuator manufacturing (Eng Teknology Holding 2000). IBM started head assembly in Shenzhen in 1996, and moved to head slider and disk media in 1999. In 1999, PCB maker Global Brands Manufacture (GBM), an affiliate of Taiwan-based Pou Chen Group, established a printed circuit board plan with CMK (Japan) in Huang Jiang, 35 kilometers from Shenzhen. Currently, most of the Japanese, Singapore and Malaysia HDD components manufacturers have established operations or plan to operate in China. Nihon Hatsujyou (NHK) and Brother Precision built plants in 2003 in Shenzhen, and NHK and Brother Precision ship suspension and bases, respectively.

5 Vertical intra-regional production networks

The HDD assembling industry has concentrated in only a few locations: Singapore, Thailand, the Philippines, China and Malaysia. Due to the core firm and suppliers effect, the HDD components and parts manufacturers have clustered in the countries within East Asia where the assemblers located. Some clusters seem to have peculiar features, but most of them are quite similar in nature. The core firm and supplier effect has formed almost the same make-up clusters across countries in East Asia. The production fragmentation argument assumes that locational advantages are different from country to country, and the MNCs explore the different locational advantages. This assumption leads to a natural question: do the HDD assemblers procure from overseas parts and components suppliers not available within a country? Exactly how fragmented is production?

Figure 6.2 shows the procurement of Hitachi Global Storage Technologies (HGST) in Prachinburi, Thailand. HGST Thailand procures

Figure 6.2: Parts procurement of a hard disc drive assembler located in Thailand

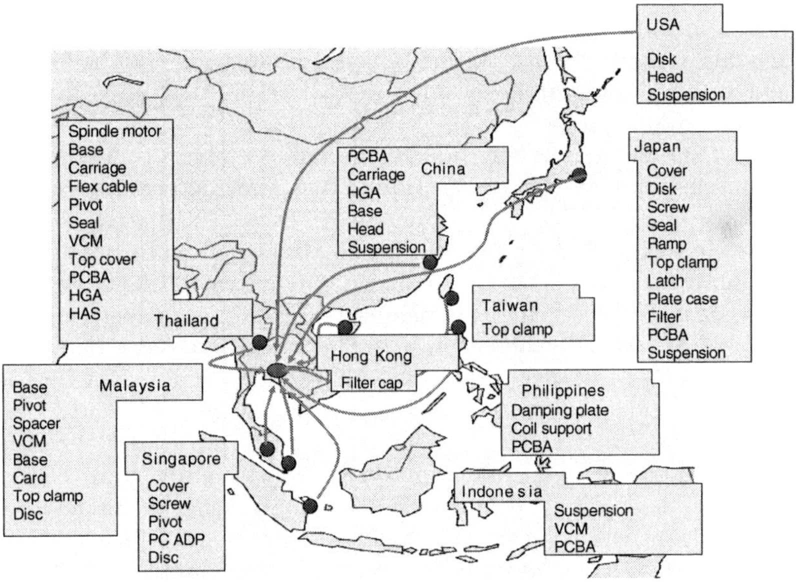

Source: Compiled by author, based on the interview at Hitachi Global Storage Technology (Thailand), August 2005.

parts from the host country of Thailand more than any other country except Japan. HGST Thailand has procured the same components and parts from multiple suppliers located in different countries; e.g. printed circuit boards (PCBA) from Indonesia (Solectron), China (Global Brands Manufacture, and Sanmina-SCI), Japan (Bridgestone), the Philippines (Ionix), and Thailand (Sanmina-SCI); bases from China (Brother Precision), Malaysia (Kenseisha), and Thailand (Wearns, an affiliate of Singapore-based); and head gimbal assembly (HGA) from China and Thailand. HGST procures disk media from China, Malaysia (Komag), Singapore (Hoya), Japan (Hoya) and the USA (HGST in San José). Malaysia (Komag) and Thailand (Hoya) export substraits to media factories in China and the United Sates. It should be noted that the assembler procures the same components and parts not only from suppliers within a country but also from overseas suppliers, and procures inter-firm rather than within the firm.

This multiple supplier procurement system has contributed not only to the diversification of production risk to a stable procurement system, but also to the promotion of global competition between suppliers.[18] The mixture of procurement from intra-firms and inter-firms makes it possible to expand production responding to an increase of demands, and benefits the innovation of technology.[19]

The fragmentation across countries assumes that there is a large diversity in locational advantages in human resources, infrastructure of supporting industry, and investment facilitation measures provided by government. Industrial clusters thereby become located in different countries and for different products reflecting differing locational advantages and product characteristics. But, in reality, against the assumption, apart from a few components such as disk media, HDD assemblers procure the same components and parts from multiple suppliers located in different countries.

What implication does the multiple supplier procurement system have? The multiple supplier procurement system implies that the difference in locational advantage across clusters is not as large for the assembler as initially assumed. The multiple supplier procurement system might be realized under low transportation costs. To put it differently, for small components and parts, transportation costs are low enough to offset the disadvantage of procuring from overseas suppliers, which have formed vertical intra-regional production networks in East Asia. Due to well-developed logistic service and low transportation costs, country industrial clusters have been integrated systematically, which has led to an expansion of intra-industry trade within the region.

6 Summary and conclusion

This chapter has introduced the argument that as multinational corporations have moved to cheap labor countries in East Asia, core firms have catalyzed their suppliers to move there. This is the core and supplier effect. American MNCs have outsourced some manufacturing processes to local firms since their suppliers have not followed. Consequently, various kinds of industrial clusters have been formed in East Asia. Manufacturing production sites that located in different countries have been systematically integrated, and manufacturing production processes have fragmented, especially in home and digital appliances and electronics industries, according to the oligopolistic production structure that prevails under global competition.

The hard disc drive industry (HDD) gives a good example demonstrating the fragmentation of manufacturing process. The HDD industry is dominated by the American assemblers Seagate, Maxtor and Western Digital, and the Japanese assemblers Hitachi/IBM, Fujitsu and Toshiba. The assemblers have acted as core firms, and have catalyzed HDD suppliers to form clusters in Singapore initially, and then in Thailand, the Philippines, and recently in Malaysia and China. Due to the core and supplier effect, almost the same make-ups of components and parts have clustered in these countries.

Generally, the fragmentation of the manufacturing process assumes that split manufacturing processes are located in different countries, reflecting each country's different locational advantages. But, in actuality, this study finds that the assembler procures the same components and parts from multiple suppliers located in different countries, and not only from suppliers within the country but also from overseas suppliers. Furthermore, the assembler procures the key parts not only from within its firm but also from other firms. The multiple supplier procurement system has diversified country risk and promoted competition between suppliers, and the mixture of procurements from intra-firms and inter-firms has enabled assemblers to increase production and quickly respond to demand.

What implications does the multiple supplier procurement system have? The system implies that the locational advantages between countries in East Asia are negligible for firms operating in East Asia, and correspondingly has helped to form vertical intra-regional production networks, leading to an expansion of intra-industry within the region. The multiple supplier procurement system is realized for small components and parts with low transportation costs. In other words, transportation costs across countries in East Asia have been low enough to offset the disadvantage of procuring the same parts and components not only from suppliers within country but also from overseas suppliers for tiny components and parts. This means that, as transportation costs are lower, multiple countries can prevail in order to diversify production risk. In this regard, the East Asia-wide FTA that incorporates the reduction of tariff and trade barriers, and the development of logistic services to lower transportation costs, will provide much more opportunity for firms to explore East Asia's vertical intra-regional production networks.

Notes

1. The original core–periphery model (Krugman 1979) was expounded by Krugman and Venables (1995).
2. Kuchiki uses the term "anchor" instead of core.
3. Recently, some head offices have allowed outsourcing to indigenous firms.
4. Transportation costs of Fujitsu Thailand, a hard disc drive producer, account for more than 1 percent of total sales, which is about half of labor cost of 2 percent of total sales (interview on August 25, 2005). Transportation cost of Soode Nagano, an HDD parts supplier, amounts to more than 1 percent of total sales, another 1 percent for packaging (interview, August 31, 2005). Canon Hightech Thailand, which produces inkjet printers, pays 2–5 percent of transportation cost for parts. Generally, purchasers pay transportation costs, in addition to parts costs (interview on August 25, 2005).
5. Communication costs are included in the broader definition of transportation costs which contains geographical transportation costs and other indirect costs from procurement to shipment. But here, communication costs are distinguished from transportation costs because of the importance in the anchor-subcontractor suppliers argument.
6. Interview with Engtek in Penang, August 30, 2005.
7. Interview with Soode in Johhor, August 31, 2005.
8. Nidec has a corporate strategy "made in market" that produces goods to nearby customers, which enables them to respond speedily and correctly to the needs of the customers. Nidec established the first overseas factory in 1989 in Singapore where the American final assemblers Seagate, Maxtor, Western Digital and IBM were clustered. In 1990, Nidec established Nidec Electronics Thailand, which started operations in Ayutthaya in 1991, and expanded facilities to Bankadi in 1993, and to Ro-jana, a district of Ayutthaya, in 1995, responding to the growing market. In 1995, Nidec set up a factory at the Laguna Industrial Estate in Manila to follow the Japanese HDD assemblers (Fujitsu, Hitachi and Toshiba). In 2002, Nidec established Nidec Zhe Jian in Pinghu city in China, where Seagate had started operations (see Nidec's home page at http://www.nidec.co.jp/OfficialHP/corporate/ network).
9. Interview with Soode in Johhor, August 31, 2005. Krugman (1991c) argues that the interaction of transportation costs, fixed costs and market size determines location.

10. Intervew with Venture Corporation, September 2, 2005.
11. The Board of Investment of Thailand classified the whole Kingdom of Thailand into three zones. Zone 1 was located in the Greater Bangkok area; Zone 2 and Zone 3 were the remote areas from Bangkok.
12. Fujitsu Thailand started the production of printers in 1988, and switched to 3.5 inch hard disc drives for desktop PCs in 1994. Interview at Fujitsu Thailand, August 25, 2005.
13. Interview at Hitachi Global Storage Technology, August 26, 2005.
14. See Komag home page (http://www.komag.com/company/company.html) September 26, 2005.
15. Interview LKT (Penang, Malaysia), August 30, 2005.
16. LKT was established in 1948. Seizing the opportunity when Intel outsourced its engineering business in 1972, LKT had diversified from construction business to engineering service to the electronics industry. Interview LKT (Penang, Malaysia), August 30, 2005.
17. See Belton Group (http://www.belton.com.hk/background.html: September 27, 2005).
18. Interview with Daisho Electronics Thailand, a subsidiary of Funai Electoronics, September 9, 2003.
19. Interview at Hitachi Global Storage Technology, August 26, 2005.

References

Deardorff, Alan V. (2001) "Fragmentation in Simple Trade Model," *North American Journal of Economics and Finance*, 13: 121–37.

Eng Teknologi Holding (2000) *SMI Globalization: 25 Years of Engtek Growth*, Eng Teknologi Holding.

Ernst, Dieter (1997) "From Partial to Systematic Globalization: International Production Networks in the Electronics Industry," paper prepared for the Sloan Foundation project on the Globalization in the Data Storage Industry, the Data Storage Industry Globalization Project Report 97–02, Graduate School of International Relations and Pacific Studies, University of California at San Diego (http://brie.berkeley.edu/pubs/pubs/wp/wp98.html, February 16, 2005).

Ernst, Dieter (1999) "How Globalization Reshapes the Geography of Innovation Systems: Reflection on Global Production Networks in Information Industries," paper prepared for DRUID 1999 Summer Conference on Innovation Systems, June 9–12 (http://www.ide.go.jp/Japanese/Inter/Sympo/pdf/krug_summary.pdf., January 12, 2005).

Fujita Masahisa (2004) "Future of East Asian Regional Economies," International Symposium on Globalization and Regional Integration from the Viewpoint of Spatial Economics, December 2, organized by the Institue of Developing Economies, IDE-JETRO (http://www.ide.go.jp/Japanese/Inter/Sympo/pdf/fujita_hand.pdf., January 12, 2005).

Hiratsuka, Daisuke (2004) "Structural Changes of Japanese Economy and its Implications for Malaysia: the Space of Industry in East Asia," paper presented at MIER National Economic Outlook 2005 Conference: Re-investing the Economy, December 7–8, Sheraton Imperial Hotel Kuala Lumpur, Malaysia.

Kuchiki, Akifumi (2005) "A Flowchart Approach to Asia's Industrial Cluster Policy," in Kuchiki and Tsuji, eds, *Industrial Clusters in Asia*, Basingstoke: Palgrave Macmillan.

Krugman, Paul (1979) "A Model of Innovation, Technology Transfer, and the World Distribution of Income," *Journal of Political Economy*, 187, 2 (April): 253–66.

Krugman, Paul (1991a) "History and Industry Location: the Case of the Manufacturing Belt," *American Economic Review*, 81, 2 (May): 80–3.

Krugman, Paul (1991b) "Increasing Returns and Economic Geography," *Journal of Political Economy*, 99, 3 (June): 483–99.

Krugman, Paul (1991c) *Geography and Trade*, Cambridge, Mass.: MIT Press.

Krugman, Paul (2004) "The New Economic Geography: Where Are We?" International Symposium on Globalization and Regional Integration from the Viewpoint of Spatial Economics, December 2, organized by the Institute of Developing Economies, IDE-JETRO (http://www.ide.go.jp/Japanese/Inter/Sympo/pdf/krug_summary.pdf., January 12, 2005).

Krugman, P. and Venables, A. (1995) "Globalization and the Inequity of Nations," *Quarterly Journal of Economics*, 110, 4 (November): 857–80.

Lobo, Sylvester (2000) "Stability Through Technology," July 15, http://www.dqindia.com/content/special/100071501.asp (February, 16 2005).

McKendrick, David G., Doner, Richard F. and Haggard, Stephan (2000) *From Silicon Valley to Singapore: Location and Competitive Advantage in the Hard Disc Drive Industry*, California: Stanford University Press.

Ryu, Shinkei (1989) "Taiwan no denshi sangyou to nihon kigyou no shinsyutu," in Takao Sasaki (ed.), *Nihon denshi sangyou no kaigai shinsyutu* (Japanese), Tokyo: Hosei University Press.

Touyou, Keizai (2004) *Kaigai Shinsyutu kigyou ichiran* (Japanese), Tokyo: Touyoukeizai Shinpousya.

UNCTAC (1984) *Transnational Corporations in the International Semiconductor Industry*, New York: United Nations.

UNCTAC (1987) *Transnational Corporations and the Electronics Industries of ASEAN Economies*, New York: United Nations.

Venables, Anthony J. (1999) "Fragmentation and Multinational Production," *European Economic Review*, 43: 935–45.

Venables, Anthony J. (2004) "European Integration: a View from Spatial Economics," paper presenred at "Globalization and Regional Integration from the Viewpoint of Spatial Economics," IDE-JETRO, Tokyo, December 12, 2004.

Western Digital (2002) *Annual Report* (http://www.wdc.com/en/library/company/annual02. pdf: February 26, 2005).

Western Digital (2003) *Annual Report* (http://www.wdc.com/en/library/company/annual03._pdf: February 26, 2005).

Wong, Poh-Kam (1999) "The Dynamics of HDD Industry Development in Singapore," Report 99–03. San Diego: University of California, Information Storage Industry Center.

7

A Comparison of De Jure Economic Integration in East Asia: Is East Asia Discriminating Against Itself?

Michael Freudenberg and Thierry Paulmier

1 Introduction

Thanks to the successive rounds of multilateral trade negotiations under the GATT/WTO, barriers to international trade as measured by multilateral tariffs have strongly decreased over the last decades, and tariff rates applied to trading partners have converged due to the application of the Most Favored Nation (MFN) regime. At the same time, however, understanding trade policy and market access issues has become very complex and the policies of countries often appear to be discriminatory, because of special conditions granted to developing countries (Generalized Systems of Preferences, GSP) and the least developed countries (LDC), and because of the proliferation of often overlapping regional and bilateral trade arrangements (Cernat and Laird 2003; Pangestu and Gooptu 2004).

This is also the case in East Asia. The latest major event for integrating East Asia occurred in November 2004 in Vientiane (Laos), where ASEAN and China agreed to create a free trade zone by 2010 for the original ASEAN 6 member states and by 2015 for the newer ASEAN member states, an area encompassing 1.8 billion consumers and a trading volume of more than US$100 billion. Before that, intra-ASEAN tariffs will be abolished in eleven significant sectors (with the exception of the automotive industry) by 2007.[1] Moreover, after an agreement signed with Singapore in 2002, Japan has recently decided to launch free trade agreement negotiations with Korea. Other arrangements are aimed at broader cooperation, including ASEAN+3 (China, Japan and Korea) and ASEAN+CER (Australia, New Zealand). Thus, regional integration in East Asia is underway but remains largely unfinished.

The objective of this chapter is to map current tariff levels within East Asian countries and accordingly to highlight the major features of protection and discrimination in this region, and the issues which arise from this analysis. As there is a trade-off between the breadth and the depth of a study, it was decided to favor breadth and provide the broad picture of market access in East Asia. From that perspective, this chapter addresses five main sets of questions at the overall and industry levels: (1) Is East Asia as a whole a protected region compared to NAFTA and the European Union? Does East Asia discriminate against itself vis-à-vis these two major regions and/or is it discriminated against by these two regions? (2) Which countries protect their domestic markets most within East Asia? (3) What are the major motivations underlying the tariff structure in Asia? (4) Which countries are facing the highest levels of protection in East Asia? (5) Are there asymmetries in the level of protection between tariffs faced and applied?

Section 2 presents the countries and sectors that are examined in this study, and describes the methodology that is used to calculate and compare tariff rates across countries based on a snapshot as of 2002. The following sections address the questions mentioned above. To do so, section 3 compares the levels of protection within and between East Asia, NAFTA and EU. Section 4 examines the tariffs that are applied by the importing countries to their partners. Section 5 sheds some light on the relationship between tariffs applied and revealed comparative advantages. Section 6 analyses the tariff barriers that the exporting countries face in their partners' markets. Section 7 compares the tariff barriers that are applied and faced by the East Asian countries within East Asia. Section 8 concludes.

2 Methodology

This section briefly presents countries and sectors included in the analysis, and describes the methodology used to render tariff barriers comparable. Due to the incompleteness of the data, non-tariff barriers are not mentioned in the analysis and show up only once in the annexes in a table comparing notifications across the region.

2.1 Country coverage and sector classification

In order to map the protection in East Asia, tariff barriers (and, where available, non-tariff barriers) are examined in a systematic manner for 15 countries in East Asia. The countries and three regional groupings in East Asia are China, Japan, NIEs 3 (Hong Kong, Korea and Taiwan),

ASEAN 6 (Brunei, Indonesia, Malaysia, the Philippines, Singapore and Thailand), and CLMV (Cambodia, Laos, Myanmar and Vietnam).

The results are also compared to two main regions: NAFTA (North American Free Trade Association: Canada, Mexico and USA); and the 25 members of the European Union (EU 25), which comprises both the former EU 15 countries and the 10 countries that have been members since 2004.

The study examines 15 industries that are defined in terms of the 2-digit chapters of the Harmonized System (HS, see Annex Table A–1): agriculture (HS 1–15), food and beverages (HS 16–24), mining products (HS 25–27), chemicals (HS 28–40), light industry (HS 41–43, 64–67, 94–96), wood and paper (HS 44–49), textile and clothing (HS 50–63), pottery products (HS 68–70), basic metals (HS 72–83), general machinery (HS 84), electrical machinery (HS 85), precision apparatus (HS 90–92), transportation machinery (HS 86–89), and other industries (HS 71, 93, 97–99). Together these 15 industry groupings cover all chapters of the HS.

The methodology used was developed by Bouët et al. (2001, 2002). Calculations used throughout this chapter are based on the *Market Access Map*, a database on tariffs and market access measures.[2] The reference year is 2002. For more information, the reader is also referred to the Market Access Map Internet site (www.macmap.org). The following will highlight the main features of the methodology.

A systematic comparison of trade barriers in East Asia necessarily needs to reduce the complexity of reality and use summary measures of market protection. To do so, it is important to take stock of the various trade regimes and the various instruments of protection, to quantify and to render them comparable, and finally, to aggregate the instruments of protection up to the desired level of analysis.

Thus, there are at least four main issues involved in comparing trade barriers across sectors and countries:

Multitude of trade regimes. There is an array of regional and bilateral trade arrangements, e.g. MFN (Most Favoured Nation) system, free trade areas, customs unions, as well as GSP for developing countries. It is important to identify and map these different trade regimes.

Multitude of instruments of protection. Although tariffs have been decreasing throughout the world for 40 years, they remain high in some countries and/or some sectors. Furthermore, tariffs are diverse; they can be notably ad valorem, specific, combined, mixed, variable, anti-dumping and two-tiered with a quota. It is essential to take into account all these instruments.

Comparability of instruments of protection. Even once the different instruments of protection are identified, they have to be "normalized" in order to be comparable across products and countries. One partial solution is to convert specific duties to ad valorem equivalents. It is thus possible to take into account and even to sum ad valorem and specific tariffs and accordingly combined tariffs, mixed tariffs and tariff quotas.

Aggregation into groups of products or groups of countries. For those trade barriers that can be rendered comparable, a decision has to be made concerning their aggregation. Often, the instruments of protection are applied for particular products (generally at the so-called "tariff-line level") and can differ across countries. In order to measure the overall level of protection of a sector, a country or a group of countries, the ad valorem equivalents have to be aggregated. There are different possible methods of weighting. The choice made for calculations in the analysis of this chapter is discussed below.

The remainder of this section takes a closer look at these four issues for tariff barriers. Unfortunately, the information on non-tariff barriers[3] is not available for all countries, which renders systematic comparisons with tariff barriers impossible. This is why the study focuses on tariff barriers, and only mentions information from non-tariff barriers where available or appropriate.

2.2 Country coverage and sector classification

Recent years have seen a proliferation of regional and bilateral trade arrangements in addition to existing multilateral trade agreements. Arrangements such as the Most Favoured Nation (MFN)[4] system, free trade areas, customs unions, or GSP[5] for developing countries coexist and often overlap with each other as well as with bilateral arrangements.

As a result, the policies of countries often appear to discriminate. A given importing country may apply a number of different tariff regimes to different groups of exporting countries, and certain instruments may only be enforced vis-à-vis specific partners (e.g. anti-dumping duties, prohibitions). It is thus important to identify and map these different trade regimes, and to take into account their bilateral dimension at the product level. A particular product item in the HS may be characterized by a unique tariff for all WTO members, or by a WTO tariff and a GSP tariff, or by several different trade regimes.

The rule applied in the Market Access Map, and used in this chapter, is as follows: if the exporting country is party to several trade regimes with the importing country, then the tariff used for analysis or displayed is the lowest one. However, it must be noted that the country does not necessarily benefit in reality from the best preferential treatment. Because of non-tariff barriers such as restrictive rules of origin, an individual exporter may still choose a tariff regime that has a slightly higher tariff but involves less paperwork and thus transaction costs.

The Market Access Map records information on trade barriers along four dimensions: products, importing countries, exporting countries, and instruments of protection. It includes several instruments of protection, of which three are taken into account in the evaluation of the level of protection: ad valorem duties, specific duties, and tariff quotas.

Ad valorem tariffs: a tariff calculated as a percentage of the value of goods cleared through customs. For example, 15 percent ad valorem tariff means 15 percent of the value of the entered merchandise.

Specific duties: a specific duty is a tariff expressed as a specific charge on the particular item to be imported. A hypothetical example of a specific tariff would be a rate of two dollars per pair of shoes regardless of their value.

Tariff quotas: quotas are explicit limits on the quantity of a good that can be imported or exported during a specified time period. Such limits are usually measured by physical quantity but sometimes by value. A quota may be applied on a selective basis, with varying limits set according to the country of origin or destination, or on a global basis that specifies only the total limit and thus tends to benefit more efficient suppliers. Quotas are frequently administered through a system of licensing. A tariff quota is defined as an annual import volume quota and two taxes. The smaller tariff, referred to as the inside quota tariff rate (IQTR), is applied to imports within the limits of the tariff quota. It is possible to import products in excess of the tariff quota, but these are usually charged at a much higher rate called the outside quota tariff rate (OQTR). This rate is meant to discourage imports above the quota limit.

The study does not take into account information on other instruments of protection, such as anti-dumping duties, preferential margins, prohibitions, and so-called "additional duties." This is mainly because these latter instruments cannot be rendered comparable, an important issue which is discussed next.

2.3 Comparability of instruments of protection: calculation of an ad valorem tariff equivalent

In the Market Access Map, and in this chapter, heterogeneous tariffs (ad valorem tariffs, specific tariffs and tariff quotas) are made comparable across products and partner countries, through the calculation of so-called "ad valorem" equivalents, or AVEs. An ad valorem equivalent is a specific tariff measure applied on unit quantities such as weight, number or volume, converted into a percentage of the value of goods cleared through customs through the use of a unit value. Only variable tariffs[6] and anti-dumping duties are not included in the calculations.

There are several methodologies for calculating AVEs. The method chosen depends on the intended application of the data. Most important to the process of calculating an AVE is the choice of the appropriate unit value, because it is the basis for the conversion of the specific tariff. The unit value is obtained by dividing the value of a transaction by the corresponding quantity. However, for each product there are different possible unit values for the analyst to choose from, including those based on bilateral trade flows, on world imports or on a country's imports of that product from a reference group of countries. In addition to being sensitive to the choice of methodology, ad valorem equivalent tariffs will also vary when the price of a product varies.[7]

To achieve comparability, the Market Access Map and this chapter first harmonize units to those to which specific tariffs are referring (e.g. kg, tons, litres, etc.) for a specific product and then convert the tariff expressed from the national currency to US dollars. Finally, using these numbers, AVEs are calculated for every specific tariff in the database. Unit values are calculated based on bilateral trade at the 6-digit level of the Harmonized System (HS). This means all tariff line products within an HS-6 group are assumed to have the same unit value. While this loss of detail may be seen as a limitation, this methodology makes it possible to compare unit values in different countries and eliminate very high and low values. The next two paragraphs describe the method of selection for the unit value applied for specific tariffs and tariff quotas:

Specific tariff: an ad valorem equivalent is calculated by dividing the specific tariff by the appropriate unit value of imports. The general principle is to prioritize a bilateral perspective; to the extent possible, bilateral unit values are used to calculate the ad valorem equivalent. For more details, see Bouët et al. (2002).

Tariff quotas: the Market Access Map has an ad valorem equivalent for each tariff quota, either by using a weighted average or by using the inside rate according to the mode of administration, as notified by the reporting country. For more details, see Bouët et al. (2002).

2.4 Aggregation of results over groups of products or countries

Once the various instruments of protection are converted into comparable units (ad valorem tariff equivalents), they have to be aggregated to measure the level of protection of a sector or an economy. However, there is no perfect aggregation method, and the various possible methods each have drawbacks.

In theory, tariffs should be aggregated on the basis of imports occurring under a hypothetical situation of free trade. However, the structure of potential imports in this situation is unknown.

Probably the most intuitive solution is to use the *country's imports* as weights. However, this creates a so-called endogeneity bias, as the value of imports of a particular product depends on the level of applied tariffs; high (low) tariffs tend to reduce (increase) imports. As a result, the aggregate level of protection is underestimated, since the contribution to the aggregate level of protection is underestimated for products with high tariffs and overestimated for products with low tariffs. This endogeneity bias arises whether the aggregation procedure is applied to products (to measure the importing country's level of protection for a particular sector and partner), to exporters (to measure the importing country's level of protection for a particular product and the world), or both to products and exporters (to measure the importing country's overall level of protection).

Another possibility is to weight tariffs with the structure of *world imports*, rather than domestic imports. However, this average has little chance of being representative of potential imports for many countries, especially when it is used as a benchmark to compare very different countries, such as developed with developing countries or small, highly specialized with large, relatively autonomous countries.

The solution adopted here is to weight the importing country's tariffs by the *import value of a reference group*[8] of similar countries to which the country belongs, which minimizes the above-mentioned difficulties. Bouët et al. (2002) define five reference groups on the basis of a hierarchical clustering analysis based on three indicators: GDP per capita (in terms of purchasing power parity), exports per capita and imports per capita. A sixth reference group was created for all those countries with missing data for which the cluster analysis could not be calculated (Annex Table A-2): Japan, Hong Kong, Singapore and Brunei are in the same cluster as the United States, the European Union, Canada, Australia and Switzerland; Indonesia and Vietnam are in the same cluster as India, Pakistan and Nigeria; China, the Philippines and Thailand are in the same group as Brazil, Russia, Turkey and Egypt; South Korea and Malaysia are in the same cluster as Mexico, Saudi Arabia, Poland, Hungary, Argentina and Chile; Taiwan is in the same cluster as New Zealand, Israel and the Czech Republic; Cambodia, Laos and Myanmar are in the residual group, together with countries as different as Bulgaria, Eritrea, Kuwait, Norway, South Africa, Tajikistan and Yemen.

At its most detailed level, the Market Access Map has information on tariffs for 169 importers, 238 exporters, and roughly 10 000 products.[9] Each of the most detailed levels of the three dimensions (product, importer, exporter) can be aggregated to any level (Table 7.1); for example, Korea is part of "NIE3," which in turn is part of "East Asia," which is part of the "World" total. It is possible to calculate the level of protection for any level of aggregation of the three dimensions; for example, the average tariff for chemicals applied by Japan to EU exporters, the average tariff for chemicals applied by Japan (to the world), or the overall tariff applied by Japan (i.e. to the world and for all products). The following methods are used when aggregating Table 7.1:

Tariff aggregation of products: the average bilateral tariff for a particular sector is obtained by weighting the importing country's tariff applied to each of the underlying products from the exporting country by the import value of the importing country's reference group for the same products and from the same exporter. For example, to calculate Japan's aggregate tariff rate for the automotive industry applied to China, the Japanese tariff of each automotive product is weighted by the average import value for that same Chinese product in Japan's reference group of countries. Japan's reference group of countries predictably includes the US and the EU, among others. Considering the relative importance of Japan, EU and US in the group, the effect of using the reference group will be to produce an average import value (and corresponding structure) close to an ideal country mixing the import structures of Japan, the EU and the US.

Table 7.1: Levels and method of aggregation for the three dimensions

		Product	*Exporter*	*Importer*
Levels of aggregation	Most detailed level	Color television receivers (HS 852812) Soya beans (HS 120100) Bodies for passenger carrying vehicles (870710)	Brunei, Cambodia, China, Hong Kong, Indonesia, Japan, Korea, Laos, Malaysia, Myanmar, Philippines, Singapore, Taiwan, Thailand, Vietnam	
	Intermediate level(s)	Agriculture, Food and beverages, Chemicals, etc.	ASEAN 6, CLMV, NIE 3, EU, NAFTA, East Asia, Rest of the world	
	Most aggregated level	All products	World	
Aggregation method		Relative importance of the product (within the sector) in the imports of the reference group (for the same importer and exporter)	Relative importance of the exporter (within the exporter's group) in the imports of the reference group (for the same importer and product/ sector)	Relative importance of the importer's total imports (within the importer's group)

Source: author.

Aggregation of exporting countries, i.e. the suppliers of a particular country: the importing country's tariff for a product/sector applied to each of the exporting countries is weighted by the import value of the country's reference group for the same product/sector and from the same exporting country. This allows the calculation of, for example, the average tariff for chemicals applied by Japan (to the world).

Tariff aggregation of importing countries: the procedure to obtain the average tariff levied by a group of importing countries on a particular product (or sector) originating from an exporting country (or region or world) is different from the two previous procedures. Here, the weight is not the import value of the reference group, but the *total* value of imports of the importing country. This is because the respective economic size of each of the importing countries has to be taken into account, which is assessed by the relative importance of national imports in the imports of the group. The tariff levied by each of the importing countries on the imports of the product/sector applied to the exporting country (region/world) is weighted by the total value of imports of the importing country. For example, to calculate the average tariff of the group NIEs 3 (Hong Kong, Korea and Taiwan) on chemicals exported by Japan, the Taiwanese tariff on chemicals imported from Japan is weighted by total Taiwanese imports, the Hong Kong tariff by total Hong Kong imports, and the Korean tariff by total Korean imports.

It has to be mentioned here that although the use of reference groups minimizes the endogeneity bias, the results of aggregate tariffs are strictly speaking not completely comparable. For example, even if two countries with two different reference groups applied exactly the same tariff for each product and each partner, they would have different aggregate tariffs because these tariffs would be weighted differently.

Likewise, the tariffs applied by a country and the tariffs its exporters face abroad, even if identical at the product level, may appear different for a particular sector because of the aggregation method, which is always from the point of view of the *importing* country. Thus, the tariffs a country *applies* are weighted by the imports from the partner of its *own* reference group, while the tariffs it *faces* are weighted by the imports from the country of its *partner's* reference group.

In the example of Table 7.2, despite identical tariffs applied and faced for each of the products in Japan's trade with China (respectively, 5 percent, 20 percent and 50 percent), Japan appears to apply

Table 7.2: Example of the structural effect on aggregate tariff levels: comparing tariffs applied and tariffs faced in bilateral trade between Japan and China

	Tariffs applied by Japan			*Tariffs faced by Japan*		
	Tariffs applied by Japan to China in %	*Weight of imports of product x from China in Japan's reference group*	*Contribution of weighted tariff to aggregate tariff*	*Tariffs faced by Japan applied by China in %*	*Weight of imports of product x from Japan in China's reference group*	*Contribution of weighted tariff to aggregate tariff*
Product 1	5	0.1	0.5	5	0.4	2.0
Product 2	20	0.5	10.0	20	0.5	10.0
Product 3	50	0.4	20.0	50	0.1	5.0
Sector (weighted)		1.0	30.5		1.0	17.0
Sector (non-weighted)	25			25		

Source: author.

much higher aggregate tariffs than it faces in China: 30.5 percent compared to 17.0 percent. This is because Japan's reference group imports from China relatively more of the high-tariff product 3 than of low-tariff product 1. In comparison, the simple average of the tariffs (the pure tariff effect) equals 25 percent in both cases: (5% + 20% + 50%)/3 = 25%. In other words, the difference in level of protection is only explained by the structural effect. Though not done in this study, it would have been useful to decompose the aggregate results and distinguish between structural effects and the pure tariff effect. As a result, the only tariffs that are fully comparable are the tariffs applied by two importing countries having the same reference group in their trade with a third country.

3 Is East Asia discriminating against itself?

A comparison of tariff barriers in East Asia with the EU and NAFTA shows that the state of protection in East Asia has the following features (Table 7.3).

Average tariffs within East Asia tend to be low in most sectors, but significant tariffs can be found for three sectors: agriculture, light industry, and food and beverages. Within East Asia the weighted average tariff for all products is 7 percent. While average tariffs are below 5 percent in most sectors, three sectors are characterized by a significant level of protection: the most protected sector in intra-East Asian trade is agriculture (with an average tariff of 41 percent), followed by light industry (27 percent), and food and beverages (22 percent). Agriculture and food and beverages are also the most protected industries within the EU and NAFTA. In general there is little protection within the EU and NAFTA in other sectors.

However, tariffs in trade among East Asian countries tend to be higher than those in intra-EU and intra-NAFTA trade. In every sector, East Asian importers apply higher tariffs to their East Asian partners than EU and NAFTA importers do to their respective regional counterparts. For *all products* the East Asian average tariff is 7 percent, whereas the average is 1 percent for NAFTA and 2 percent for the EU.[10]

In some sectors, East Asian exporters face higher tariffs in East Asian markets than they do in the EU and NAFTA, especially in agriculture, light industry, and food and beverages. The relatively higher tariffs in East Asia can also be found in general machinery, mining products, transportation machinery, and wood and paper, though to a much lesser extent.

Table 7.3: Tariff barriers in East Asia, EU and NAFTA, by sector, 2002 (*ad valorem tariff equivalents (%)*)

Importer	*East Asia*			*EU 25*			*NAFTA*		
Exporter	*East Asia*	*NAFTA*	*EU 25*	*East Asia*	*EU 25*	*NAFTA*	*East Asia*	*EU 25*	*NAFTA*
Agriculture	41.0	29.7	30.9	25.2	6.8	21.4	20.2	15.6	3.9
Light industry	26.8	8.3	12.8	4.9	0.0	2.2	8.7	9.6	0.1
Food and beverages	21.8	26.4	25.8	10.1	5.3	18.1	16.0	15.7	9.4
Textiles and clothing	7.3	7.6	7.8	6.2	0.0	4.9	10.9	9.7	0.1
Transportation machinery	4.6	2.8	8.6	3.4	0.0	6.8	3.3	2.9	0.0
Pottery products	2.9	3.6	4.4	1.4	0.1	2.9	5.7	5.6	0.5
Chemicals	2.4	3.0	2.7	0.8	0.0	4.9	4.1	4.2	0.2
Basic metals	1.8	2.6	2.3	1.5	0.5	4.0	3.0	2.7	0.3
Mining products	1.7	2.6	1.7	0.4	0.0	0.3	1.4	1.8	0.1
General machinery	1.5	1.9	2.5	0.3	0.0	1.3	1.1	1.7	0.0
Electrical machinery	1.4	1.5	2.2	1.0	0.0	1.3	2.5	3.2	0.1
Others	1.4	1.7	2.6	0.6	0.1	0.8	3.2	1.3	0.0
Wood and paper	1.4	1.3	1.5	0.4	0.0	1.0	1.0	1.0	0.0
Precision apparatus	1.2	1.3	2.0	0.3	0.0	1.1	1.3	2.1	0.1
All products	7.4	5.5	7.2	7.6	1.9	7.7	5.7	5.3	0.7

Source: Market Access Map, calculations by ITC.

Moreover, although East Asian importers tend to apply lower import tariffs to exporters from East Asian countries than to those from the EU and NAFTA, they apply significantly higher tariffs to their Asian partners in agriculture and light industry. In agriculture, East Asian importers apply an average tariff of 41 percent for East Asian exporters, but only of 25 percent for EU 25 exporters and 20 percent for exporters from NAFTA. The respective figures for light industry are 27 percent for East Asian, 5 percent for European and 9 percent for North American exporters. Because of structural differences – East Asia imports relatively more of the most protected products from East Asian countries than from EU and NAFTA – the overall average is higher for East Asian competitors (7.4 percent) compared to the EU (7.2 percent) and NAFTA (5.5 percent).[11]

In conclusion, East Asia as a whole is much less integrated than the EU or NAFTA. More surprisingly and paradoXically, East Asia discriminates against itself, firstly by applying to its countries tariffs relatively higher than those applied to them by NAFTA and EU (especially in agriculture, light industry and food and beverages), and secondly by applying to its countries tariffs relatively higher than those applied to the EU and NAFTA (especially in agriculture and light industry). To understand this discrimination paradox we will discuss the analysis at the country level to highlight the situation within East Asia when Asian countries export to or import from one another.

4 Which East Asian countries protect their domestic markets most from East Asian neighbors?

In order to identify which East Asian countries are discriminating the most against their partner countries, this section examines the tariffs that are *applied* by the importing countries.

Overall, that is for all products taken together, Malaysia, Cambodia, Thailand and Vietnam appear to be the countries with the highest level of protection in East Asia, while Hong Kong and Singapore offer virtually free access to their markets (Table 7.4). The average ad valorem tariff for all products applied by Malaysia to its East Asian partners is almost 23 percent, as compared to 0 percent applied by Hong Kong and Singapore. The strong diversity of East Asian countries in terms of economic development seems to be paralleled by a strong diversity in terms of tariffs applied. This, however, does not mean that there is a systematic, positive relationship between market openness and economic development: for example, Myanmar and the

Table 7.4: Tariff barriers applied by countries importing from East Asia, by importer and sector (*ad valorem tariff equivalents (%)*)

Importer	Agriculture	Light industry	Food and beverages	Textiles and clothing	Transportation machinery	Pottery products	Chemicals	Basic metals	Mining products	General machinery	Electrical machinery	Wood and paper	Others	Precision apparatus	**All products**
Malaysia	4.6	7.6	16.2	12.0	76.5	18.5	7.3	10.6	0.9	6.3	7.0	0.9	7.2	0.9	**22.9**
Cambodia	15.5	22.9	23.0	18.0	28.1	14.9	10.5	9.3	19.2	12.9	16.6	14.2	4.1	13.6	**18.8**
Thailand	41.6	12.2	42.5	19.8	39.9	16.8	11.7	11.9	1.4	7.4	8.0	8.6	10.8	6.1	**16.5**
Vietnam	17.2	25.4	39.5	25.7	33.2	21.0	5.6	8.4	12.0	7.8	12.0	12.5	4.2	2.2	**13.7**
Laos	11.6	16.9	22.6	8.6	15.5	5.3	8.6	6.5	8.4	6.7	7.7	11.1	13.7	5.7	**10.6**
Brunei	0.1	2.9	29.5	0.4	40.2	..	0.7	0.0	0.0	3.3	5.6	5.4	0.0	5.6	**10.3**
Japan	54.3	36.9	27.7	8.3	0.0	0.9	1.7	1.0	1.1	0.0	0.0	1.4	1.2	0.1	**10.2**
Korea	79.5	6.8	21.5	8.9	7.3	7.8	8.1	5.4	5.1	4.5	3.5	4.6	2.4	5.7	**9.3**
China	7.0	10.5	16.7	14.8	22.6	13.3	7.6	6.5	4.0	5.3	6.1	5.7	4.5	6.7	**8.8**
Taiwan	24.7	4.8	25.3	9.3	25.3	8.1	4.6	6.1	4.3	3.2	3.2	3.8	0.0	2.6	**7.7**
Indonesia	3.9	6.3	19.1	5.5	12.9	5.0	5.0	6.5	2.7	1.7	4.3	2.0	4.6	3.2	**5.5**
Philippines	15.3	4.1	15.0	4.8	8.0	4.3	3.6	3.2	2.9	1.5	1.5	3.1	4.6	2.3	**4.7**
Myanmar	4.9	6.5	15.5	9.8	5.7	3.0	2.5	2.0	1.6	1.5	3.5	5.2	13.2	3.2	**4.3**
Singapore	0.0	0.0	0.3	0.0	0.0	0.0	0.0	0.0	0.0	0.0	0.0	0.0	0.0	0.0	**0.0**
Hong Kong	0.0	0.0	0.0	0.0	0.0	0.0	0.0	0.0	0.0	0.0	0.0	0.0	0.0	0.0	**0.0**
East Asia	**41.0**	**26.8**	**21.8**	**7.3**	**4.6**	**2.9**	**2.4**	**1.8**	**1.7**	**1.5**	**1.4**	**1.4**	**1.4**	**1.2**	**7.4**
EU	25.2	4.9	10.1	6.2	3.4	1.4	0.8	1.5	0.4	0.3	1.0	0.4	0.6	0.3	7.6
NAFTA	20.2	8.7	16.0	10.9	3.3	5.7	4.1	3.0	1.4	1.1	2.5	1.0	3.2	1.3	5.7
Rest of world	50.3	6.6	36.8	10.6	8.0	7.6	5.5	6.8	10.6	4.8	5.6	5.5	5.8	3.8	13.1

Source: Market Access Map, calculations by ITC.

Philippines have below-average tariffs, whereas the opposite is true for Japan and Korea.

The highest overall bilateral trade barriers in intra-East Asian trade for all products are substantial for some country couples, with a maximum of 60 percent applied by Malaysia to Singapore (Annex, Table A-5). Malaysia also applies high tariffs to Japan (30 percent), Brunei and Hong Kong (about 25 percent each); Brunei applies high tariffs to Japan (33 percent); Japan does so to China and Hong Kong (32 percent and 21 percent, respectively), Cambodia to Hong Kong, Japan, Thailand and Taiwan (between 20 percent and 22 percent), Thailand to China, Singapore and Vietnam (21 percent each), and Korea to Hong Kong (20 percent). Besides Hong Kong's and Singapore's bilateral tariffs with East Asian countries (which are zero or close to zero), several countries apply overall bilateral tariffs of less than 3 percent: Malaysia with Vietnam; Brunei with the Philippines, Indonesia and Thailand; Japan with Cambodia, Laos, Malaysia and Myanmar; and Indonesia with Malaysia.

A closer examination reveals that the situation differs strongly across industries. In fact, substantially higher tariff barriers can be found in some sectors, especially at the bilateral level (see Annex, Tables A-6 and A-7).

In agriculture, which is the most protected industry in intra-East Asian trade (ad valorem tariff equivalents of 41 percent), Korea applies the highest tariff (80 percent), followed by Japan (54 percent) and Thailand (42 percent), while imports of agricultural goods into Singapore, Hong Kong and Brunei are virtually duty free and are lower than 5 percent for Indonesia, Malaysia and Myanmar. In terms of bilateral trade, Korea applies the highest tariffs for agricultural products from Japan (112 percent), Hong Kong (103 percent), Brunei (85 percent), Taiwan (73 percent) and Singapore (62 percent), Thailand discriminates mostly against Laos (84 percent), Myanmar (84 percent), Taiwan (79 percent) and Cambodia (63 percent), and Japan applies the highest tariffs to Hong Kong (73 percent) and Singapore (63 percent).

Light industry, the second most protected industry in East Asia (with average tariff equivalents of almost 27 percent), is particularly protected by Japan (almost 37 percent), followed by Vietnam and Cambodia. In contrast, Hong Kong and Singapore grant free access, and Brunei, the Philippines and Taiwan grant almost free access to their markets. Japanese tariffs for light industries are particularly high for imports from China, Indonesia and Thailand, with tariff equivalents ranging from 70 percent to 33 percent. Vietnam applies high tariffs for imports from the Philippines, China and Japan.

In food and beverages, the third most protected industry in East Asia in terms of ad valorem tariff equivalents (almost 22 percent), there are several countries with an above-average degree of protection: Thailand and Vietnam (around 40 percent each), followed by Brunei, Japan, Taiwan, Cambodia and Laos. In contrast, Hong Kong and Singapore grant free access. Brunei applies the highest rates to Singapore and Vietnam; Taiwan does so to the Philippines and Thailand; Thailand does so to Malaysia, Cambodia and Laos; and Vietnam does so to Singapore and Myanmar.

Tariffs for textiles and clothing are moderate with a regional average of 7.3 percent. While Brunei, Hong Kong and Singapore grant free access to their markets, Vietnam (about 25 percent), Thailand (20 percent) and Cambodia (18 percent) impose the highest tariffs, followed by China and Malaysia. Vietnam applies the highest tariffs to China, Korea, the Philippines, Malaysia, Taiwan and Singapore.

In the transportation machinery sector only Japan, Hong Kong and Singapore grant free access to their markets. Malaysia is an outlier in the sense that it applies a very high tariff of 77 percent. This is almost twice as high as the rates applied by the second and third most protected countries (Brunei and Thailand with about 40 percent) and more than 15 times the regional average rate (4.6 percent). Malaysia applies particularly high tariffs for transportation machinery from Singapore (113 percent), Korea and Japan (more than 80 percent each). This notably reflects Malaysia's protectionism in the field of automobile production.

In pottery products, chemicals, basic metals, mining products, general machinery, electrical machinery, wood and paper, precision apparatus and others, average regional tariffs are low (lower than 5 percent). This is due to the free or almost-free access granted by major markets such as Singapore, Hong Kong and Japan. In most cases, the remaining Asian countries impose moderate tariffs (lower than 15 percent) or low tariffs (lower than 5 percent), with the exceptions of Vietnam, Malaysia and Thailand in pottery products, and of Cambodia in mining products and electrical machinery.

5 What are the major motivations underlying the tariff structure in East Asia?

The previous section highlighted two main findings: aggregate tariff rates differ strongly across countries, and the rates applied by each country differ strongly across sectors (with the exceptions of Hong

Kong and Singapore which offer virtually free access for all sectors). In order to explore possible motivations for the countries' tariff structure, in this section we examine whether a country's tariff rates depend on whether it is a net exporter or a net importer for the sector. Table 7.5 shows some possible motivations for a country's tariff rates depending on its sectoral trade balance.

To apply this framework to intra-East Asian trade, we compare above-average tariff rates with a trade specialization index that divides net trade (X-M) in total trade (X+M) and ranges between –1 (only imports) and +1 (only exports). Negative values indicate that the country is a net importer for the sector, and positive values indicate that it is a net exporter. Figure 7.1 shows three typical cases of the relationship between trade specialization and tariffs applied in East-Asian trade. Table 7.6 shows the results for the most protected sectors for each country but Hong Kong and Singapore, and full results are

Table 7.5: Possible motivations for a country's tariff rates depending on its sectoral trade specialization

	Net importer	*Net exporter*
High tariffs	**"Defensive protectionism"** to protect domestic industry from international competition ("Infant industry" argument). **"Rent seeking activity"** (e.g. generation of tax revenues), if there is no domestic production. **Other reasons:** Political, environmental, heath-related, etc.	**"Offensive or unfair protectionism"** to protect exporting industries from international competition ("Economies of scale" argument). **Non-adapted tariff structure** that corresponds to past rather than current situation (possibly as a result of "defensive protectionism" in the past).
Low tariffs	**Stimulate competition** in domestic industry. **"Cost-reducing openness"** to keep costs of imports down, especially for "productive" imports (primary, intermediate and capital goods) used in other sectors.	**"Painless openness,"** as efficient export industries can stand foreign competition (and do not need to be protected). **Stimulate competition** in domestic industry. **"Cost-reducing openness"** to keep costs of imports down.

Source: author.

Figure 7.1: The relationship between trade specialization and tariffs applied in East Asian trade: three typical cases

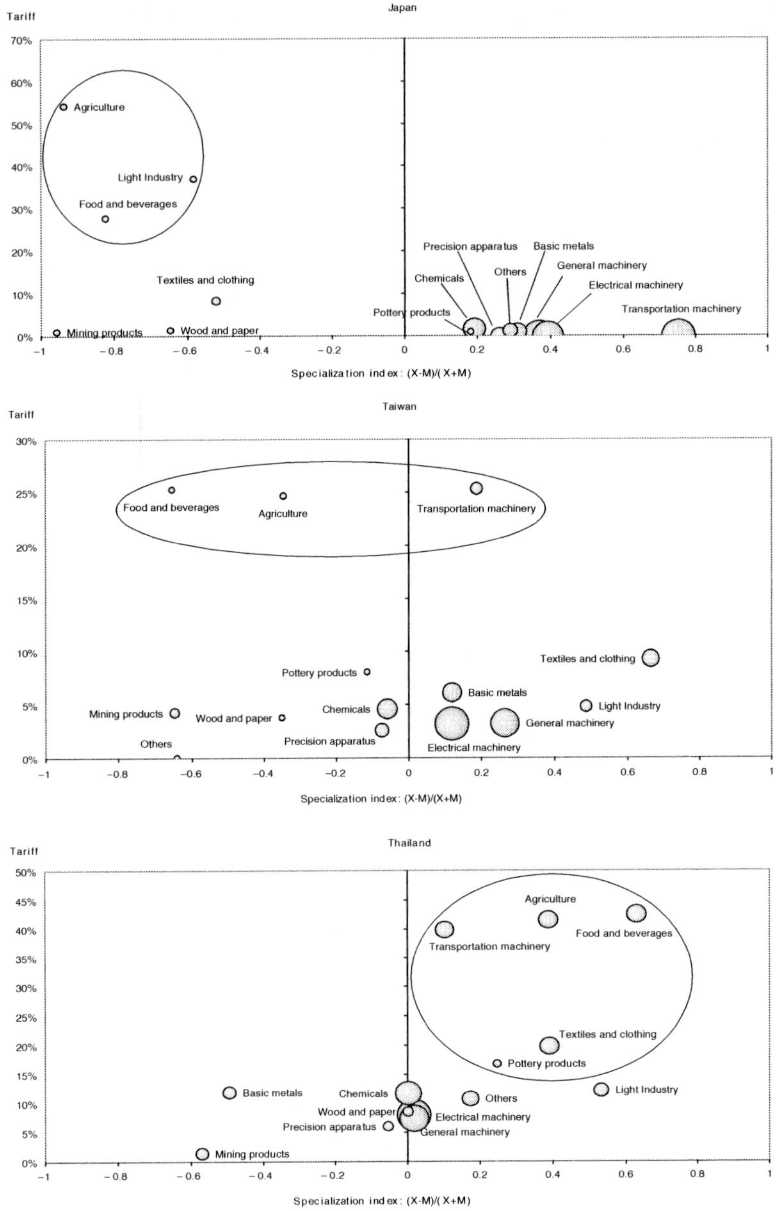

Note: The size of the bubbles is proportional to the share of the sectors in each country's total exports.
Source: Market Access Map and Trade Map, calculations by ITC.

Table 7.6: Nature of protection for most protected sectors in each country, 2002

Country	*Sector*	*Tariff applied*	*Index tariff applied (All products =100)*	*Share of industry in national exports*	*Share of industry in national imports*	*Index specialization (Net exports/ total trade)*	*Possible nature of protection*
Mainly defensive (or rent-seeking)							
Japan	Agriculture	54.3%	531	0%	9%	–0.94	Defensive
Japan	Light industry	36.9%	361	1%	4%	–0.58	Defensive
Japan	Food and beverages	27.7%	271	0%	4%	–0.82	Defensive
Korea	Agriculture	79.5%	854	1%	4%	–0.69	Defensive
Korea	Food and beverages	21.5%	231	1%	2%	–0.32	Defensive
Malaysia	Transportation machinery	76.5%	335	1%	3%	–0.53	Defensive
Brunei	Transportation machinery	40.2%	392	0%	16%	–1.00	Defensive
Brunei	Food and beverages	29.5%	288	0%	9%	–1.00	Defensive
Cambodia	Transportation machinery	28.1%	149	0%	12%	–0.97	Defensive
Cambodia	Food and beverages	23.0%	122	0%	8%	–0.99	Defensive
Cambodia	Light industry	22.9%	122	8%	3%	0.38	Offensive
Cambodia	Mining products	19.2%	102	0%	10%	–1.00	Defensive
Philippines	Agriculture	15.3%	327	4%	4%	–0.05	Defensive
Philippines	Food and beverages	15.0%	320	2%	3%	–0.23	Defensive
Philippines	Transportation machinery	8.0%	171	4%	4%	–0.05	Defensive
Philippines	Textiles and clothing	4.8%	101	7%	3%	0.33	Offensive

Table 7.6: Nature of protection for most protected sectors in each country, 2002 – *continued*

Country	*Sector*	*Tariff applied*	*Index tariff applied (All products =100)*	*Share of industry in national exports*	*Share of industry in national imports*	*Index specialization (Net exports/ total trade)*	*Possible nature of protection*
Both defensive (rent-seeking) and offensive (not adapted)							
Vietnam	Food and beverages	39.5%	287	3%	3%	–0.10	Defensive
Vietnam	Transportation machinery	33.2%	242	1%	9%	–0.79	Defensive
Vietnam	Textiles and clothing	25.7%	187	20%	13%	0.22	Offensive
Vietnam	Light industry	25.4%	185	25%	4%	0.69	Offensive
Vietnam	Pottery products	21.0%	153	1%	1%	0.26	Offensive
Vietnam	Agriculture	17.2%	125	15%	3%	0.61	Offensive
Mainly offensive (or not adapted)							
China	Transportation machinery	22.6%	256	4%	4%	–0.06	Defensive
China	Food and beverages	16.7%	188	2%	1%	0.57	Offensive
China	Textiles and clothing	14.8%	168	17%	5%	0.58	Offensive
China	Pottery products	13.3%	150	2%	1%	0.45	Offensive
China	Light industry	10.5%	118	13%	2%	0.80	Offensive
Thailand	Food and beverages	42.5%	258	8%	2%	0.63	Offensive
Thailand	Agriculture	41.6%	252	7%	3%	0.39	Offensive
Thailand	Transportation machinery	39.9%	242	7%	6%	0.10	Offensive
Thailand	Textiles and clothing	19.8%	120	7%	3%	0.39	Offensive
Thailand	Pottery products	16.8%	102	1%	1%	0.25	Offensive

Note: Only sectors with tariff rates above the national average are shown.

Source: Market Access Map and Trade Map, calculations by ITC.

reported in Annex, Table A-8. In total, four typical trade policy profiles can be distinguished.

1. Countries *playing by free trade rules*: Hong Kong and Singapore. Both city-states have a trade policy that is not sector-specific, as they grant duty free access to their domestic market for all sectors (Table 7.4). They are structurally dependent on imports for a wide range of products, and heavily taxing imports might penalize their economy. It seems that both countries have low tariffs in place to stimulate competition in domestic industry and to favor "productive" inputs (primary, intermediate and capital goods) at low cost.
2. Countries with mainly *defensive protectionism*: Japan, Korea, Malaysia, Brunei, Cambodia and the Philippines. These countries apply the highest tariffs in the sectors in which they suffer from comparative disadvantages. Figure 7.1, for example, shows that Japan is a net importer in the three sectors where it applies the highest tariffs: agriculture, light industry and food and beverages. It is impossible to infer from these figures the underlying rationale, but this constellation typically corresponds to either "defensive protectionism," where countries protect their domestic industry from international competition (e.g. the "infant industry" argument seems to apply to Malaysia in the case of transport machinery), or "rent seeking activity" to generate tax revenues (especially if there is no or no significant domestic production). Other reasons include political, environmental, and heath-related issues or the social impact of a sector in terms of employment.
3. Countries with mainly *offensive protectionism*: Thailand, China and Vietnam. These countries apply the highest tariffs for the sectors in which they enjoy a comparative advantage. For example, Thailand is a net exporter in the five sectors where it applies the highest tariffs: food and beverages, agriculture, transport machinery, textiles and clothing and pottery products (Figure 7.1). This situation suggests an "offensive or unfair protectionism," where countries protect their domestic export-oriented industries from international competition in order to strengthen their competitiveness in international markets, possibly through economies of scale. Another possible reason for this constellation is that the tariff structure corresponds to past rather than current industry situation, and is thus outdated.
4. Countries playing *wide-ranging protectionism*: Myanmar, Laos, Taiwan and Indonesia. These countries apply high tariffs in sectors with both comparative advantages and with disadvantages. For example, Taiwan protects domestic industries that are not competitive (food

and beverages, and agriculture) and others where it performs well (transport machinery) (Figure 7.1).

6 Which countries are facing the highest levels of protection in East Asia?

In order to identify which East Asian countries are the most discriminated against within East Asia this section examines the tariffs that exporting countries face in their partners' markets.

Overall (that is for all products taken together), it turns out that Hong Kong, China and Singapore are facing the highest levels of protection in East Asia, whereas the most favored countries are Myanmar, Malaysia, Cambodia, Laos and Taiwan (Table 7.7). The average ad valorem tariff equivalent for all products faced by Hong Kong in East Asian markets is 18 percent, as compared to as little as 2.5 percent for Myanmar.

On average, East Asian exporters appear not to receive preferential treatment in East Asia. On the contrary, the average intra-East Asian tariff rate for all products of 7.4 percent is slightly higher than the rate for the EU (7.2 percent) and markedly higher than the rate for NAFTA (5.5 percent).

As already mentioned in the previous section, bilateral trade barriers to intra-East Asian trade are found to be substantial for some country couples. Singapore faces the highest tariff rates in Malaysia (60 percent) and Thailand; Japan does so in Brunei, Malaysia and Cambodia; Brunei in Malaysia; Hong Kong faces high tariffs in Malaysia, Cambodia, Japan and Korea; Vietnam in Thailand; China in Japan and Thailand; and Thailand and Taiwan in Cambodia.

A closer examination reveals that the situation differs strongly across industries. In fact, as discussed in the previous section, substantially higher tariff barriers can be found in some sectors, especially at the bilateral level.

In agriculture, the most protected industry in intra-East Asian trade (ad valorem tariff equivalents of 41 percent), the highest tariffs faced are by exporters from Hong Kong (63 percent), Singapore (48 percent) and Brunei (42 percent), whereas those from Vietnam (10 percent), Indonesia, Laos, Myanmar and Malaysia enjoy the lowest tariff barriers (all lower than 15 percent). In terms of bilateral trade, exporters from Japan, Hong Kong and Brunei face the highest tariffs in Korea (112 percent, 103 percent, and 85 percent, respectively), and those from Laos, Myanmar and Taiwan in Thailand (all about 85 percent).

Table 7.7: Tariff barriers faced by countries exporting to East Asia, by exporter and sector, 2002 (*ad valorem tariff equivalents* (%))

Exporter	Agriculture	Light industry	Food and beverages	Textiles and clothing	Transportation machinery	Pottery products	Chemicals	Basic metals	Mining products	General machinery	Electrical machinery	Wood and paper	Others	Precision apparatus	**All products**
Kong Kong	62.7	14.9	25.6	8.4	7.0	3.4	2.3	1.7	0.4	2.7	2.4	5.1	1.9	1.7	**17.5**
China	18.0	55.2	21.8	7.6	1.9	1.3	1.4	0.8	2.3	0.2	0.8	3.8	1.3	0.5	**16.2**
Singapore	48.0	8.2	25.8	6.6	15.6	2.6	2.5	1.5	1.5	1.1	0.8	3.1	1.2	1.3	**12.0**
Indonesia	11.6	43.4	16.4	7.4	15.4	4.4	2.9	1.1	2.4	0.7	2.2	0.6	2.5	1.1	**6.5**
Brunei	42.0	10.5	21.4	6.5	3.6	2.5	2.2	1.9	1.2	1.6	1.6	0.9	1.2	0.9	**6.1**
Thailand	23.0	24.0	20.4	6.9	2.9	3.6	2.3	1.2	2.5	0.7	1.0	3.5	1.3	1.2	**6.6**
Philippines	23.3	11.4	15.1	11.9	12.3	6.7	2.5	1.4	3.2	1.6	0.4	1.6	1.0	1.6	**6.1**
Taiwan	22.0	7.7	25.5	8.3	5.4	4.5	5.0	2.8	0.9	0.9	0.5	2.1	4.2	3.8	**3.5**
Korea	15.3	13.9	28.8	8.3	4.4	4.0	4.1	2.1	1.9	1.2	0.9	0.6	1.2	2.5	**5.0**
Japan	22.4	3.6	11.6	8.6	4.0	6.4	4.7	5.0	2.0	3.3	3.5	3.5	1.4	3.1	**5.0**
Vietnam	9.8	20.6	7.3	5.4	10.4	4.4	3.5	1.3	2.8	2.1	3.8	0.1	1.1	1.4	**5.6**
Cambodia	17.0	2.1	26.6	2.5	4.4	4.4	2.5	1.3	1.6	1.4	7.4	0.5	1.1	3.1	**3.2**
Malaysia	14.2	7.5	28.1	7.0	1.7	2.7	2.1	1.7	2.9	0.4	0.4	1.8	3.0	0.9	**2.8**
Laos	13.3	2.1	26.8	3.4	4.2	4.1	2.3	1.3	1.7	1.3	5.4	0.2	1.3	3.1	**3.2**
Myanmar	13.5	3.6	21.3	3.4	3.0	4.1	2.5	1.3	1.4	1.7	2.7	0.2	1.1	3.3	**2.5**
East Asia	**41.0**	**26.8**	**21.8**	**7.3**	**4.6**	**2.9**	**2.4**	**1.8**	**1.7**	**1.5**	**1.4**	**1.4**	**1.4**	**1.2**	7.4
EU	30.9	12.8	25.8	7.8	8.6	4.4	2.7	2.3	1.7	2.5	2.2	2.6	1.5	2.0	7.2
NAFTA	29.7	8.3	26.4	7.6	2.8	3.6	3.0	2.6	2.6	1.9	1.5	1.7	1.3	1.3	5.5
Rest of world	20.7	22.5	23.1	5.9	7.2	3.4	2.9	1.5	2.0	1.3	1.9	0.6	1.5	1.4	6.3

Source: Market Access Map, calculations by ITC.

Regarding light industry, the second most protected industry in East Asia (with an effective average tariff of almost 27 percent), China (55 percent) and Indonesia (43 percent) are particularly penalized, while Laos (2 percent), Cambodia, Japan and Myanmar face very favorable tariff barriers (lower than 5 percent). Exporters from China, Indonesia and Thailand face tariffs particularly in Japan, as is the case for exporters from the Philippines, China and Japan in the Vietnamese market.

As for food and beverages, the third most protected industry in East Asia in terms of ad valorem tariff equivalents (almost 22 percent), Korea, Malaysia, Laos, Cambodia, Singapore, Hong Kong and Taiwan face the highest tariff barriers in East Asia (between 25 percent and 29 percent). Tariffs are lowest for Vietnam (7 percent) and Japan (12 percent).

In textiles and clothing, the level of tariff barriers is relatively moderate in East Asia (7.3 percent). At the country level, tariffs range from 2.5 percent (Cambodia) to 12 percent (Philippines). Japan, Hong Kong, Korea, Taiwan, China and Indonesia face tariffs higher than the regional average albeit similar to those of EU and NAFTA (between 7.4 percent and 8.6 percent).

The average tariff rate in East Asia is low in transportation machinery at 4.6 percent. However, some Asian exporting countries suffer from significant discriminatory treatment in the region. That is the case notably for Singapore (16 percent), Indonesia (15 percent) and to a lesser extent the Philippines (12 percent) and Vietnam (10 percent). Even NAFTA and the EU benefit from significantly preferential access with an average tariff rate of 2.8 percent and 8.6 percent respectively.

In pottery products, chemicals, basic metals, mining products, general machinery, electrical machinery, wood and paper, precision apparatus and others, all Asian countries enjoy relatively low tariffs (lower than 8 percent). The EU and NAFTA display tariffs that are higher than the regional average, except NAFTA in wood and paper. In each of these sectors, the EU and NAFTA benefit from a better tariff than some Asian countries (between two and nine countries according to the sector). However, the tariff gap is never higher than 5 percent except vis-à-vis Cambodia in electrical machinery.

7 Are there asymmetries in the level of protection between tariffs faced and applied?

The previous sections have shown that bilateral trade barriers can be substantial for some industries and country pairs, and that tariffs applied can be very different from tariffs faced. However, as mentioned before, the results of aggregate tariffs are generally speaking not fully comparable, because the weights are based on the reference group of the *importing* country; that is, the tariffs a country applies are weighted by the imports from the partner in its own reference group, while the tariffs it faces are weighted by the imports from the country of its partner's reference group. A strong difference between aggregate tariffs applied and tariffs faced thus does not necessarily mean an asymmetric treatment of a country's imports and exports.

Though it goes beyond the scope of this research to decompose the aggregate results and distinguish between structural effects and the pure tariff effect, it may nevertheless be useful to compare tariffs applied and tariffs faced. It has to be kept in mind, however, that the more the results are aggregated, the more structural differences may come into effect.

Overall (that is for all products and partners taken together), two groups of countries can be distinguished in East Asian trade depending on the difference between tariffs applied and tariffs faced (Figure 7.2).

Aggregate tariffs applied are substantially higher than tariffs faced for Malaysia and Cambodia, followed by Thailand, Vietnam, Laos, Japan, Korea, Brunei, Taiwan and Myanmar. For Malaysia, applied tariffs

Figure 7.2: Tariffs applied and tariffs faced in intra-Asian trade: all products, 2002

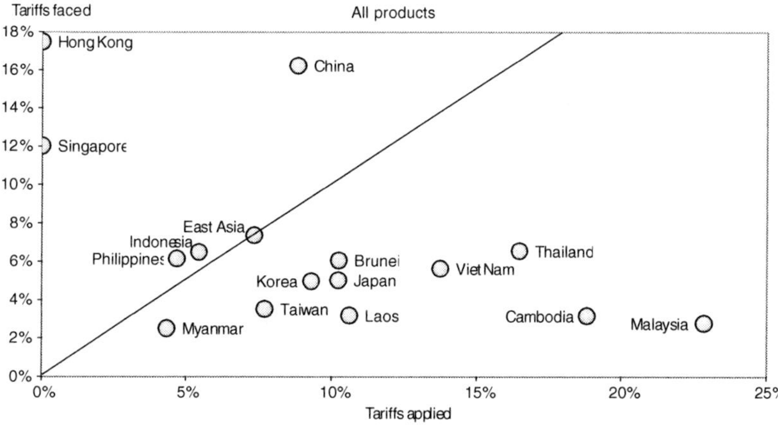

Note: Tariff barriers are expressed in ad valorem tariff equivalents (%).
Source: Market Access Map, calculations by ITC.

(22.9 percent) are more than seven times or 20 percentage points higher than tariffs faced (2.8 percent).

In contrast, aggregate tariffs applied are substantially lower than tariffs faced for Hong Kong, Singapore and China. Hong Kong and Singapore, the most liberal countries in East Asia, grant free access to their market to their Asian partners, but their partners impose on them on average among the highest tariffs in the region (17 percent and 12 percent respectively). China faces an average tariff almost double to the one it applies, 16 percent against 9 percent.

Examining the differences between tariffs applied and tariffs faced by industry, the main results are as follows.

In agriculture, Korea's aggregate applied tariffs (80 percent) are more than five times or 65 percentage points higher than the tariffs its exporters face in East Asia (15 percent). Strong positive differences can also be found for Japan (+32 percentage points) and Thailand (+19 percentage points). In contrast, Hong Kong, Singapore and Brunei grant free access to their East Asian partners, but face the highest tariffs in the region (mainly due to the tariffs applied to them by Korea and Japan); the difference between the two tariffs is as much as –63 percentage points for Hong Kong, –48 for Singapore and –41 for Brunei.

In food and beverages, Vietnam, Japan and Thailand register the highest positive differences. Vietnam applies an average tariff (39 percent) of more than five times or 32 percentage points higher than the one it faces (7 percent). In contrast, Singapore and Hong Kong grant free access to their markets, but face amongst the highest average tariff in the region (notably due to the tariffs imposed by Japan, Vietnam and Thailand); the difference is about –25 percentage points for both countries.

In light industry, tariffs applied are much higher than tariffs faced in Japan (+33 percentage points), Cambodia (+21) and Laos (+15), and much lower in China (–45) and Indonesia (–37).

In textiles and clothing, several countries have much higher applied tariffs than faced tariffs, led by Malaysia (+20 percentage points), Cambodia (+16), and Thailand (+13), whereas the opposite is true for Hong Kong (–8), the Philippines and Singapore (–7 each).

In transportation machinery, Malaysia (+75 percentage points), Thailand and Brunei (+37 each), Cambodia and Vietnam (both about +23), China and Taiwan (about +20 each) and Laos (+11 points) have much higher applied tariffs than faced tariffs, whereas the opposite is true for Singapore (–16 points).

A bilateral analysis by sector to identify the most asymmetric bilateral tariff treatment in East Asia reveals different characteristics (Annex, Table A-9).

The differences between bilateral tariffs applied and tariffs faced can be substantial, and are higher than 100 percentage points in the case of Malaysian tariffs applied to Singapore for transportation machinery (+114 points) and Korean tariffs applied to Hong Kong for agriculture (+103 points).

A particularly strong asymmetric tariff treatment seems to exist for the following importing markets: transportation machinery in Malaysia (penalizing Singapore, Japan and Korea), agriculture in Korea (penalizing Hong Kong, Japan, Brunei and Singapore), agriculture in Thailand (penalizing Myanmar and Laos) and agriculture in Japan (Hong Kong and Singapore).

Hong Kong and Singapore suffer from asymmetric bilateral treatment in virtually the same industries and from the same partners. Their exporters face substantially higher rates for agriculture in Japan, Korea and Thailand; for food and beverages in Brunei, Cambodia, Japan and Laos, Thailand and Vietnam; and for transportation machinery in Malaysia and Thailand.

Even the apparently most protected country, Malaysia, seems to suffer from asymmetric bilateral treatment in several industries. For example, the rates Malaysia applies are much lower than those it faces for food and beverages with Thailand, Vietnam and Taiwan; for agriculture with Japan, Korea, Taiwan, Thailand and Vietnam; and for both mining products and for light industry with Cambodia and Vietnam.

8 Conclusion

This chapter examined in a systematic manner the state of protection within East Asian countries in 2002. The analysis is mainly based on tariff measures (through the use of ad valorem equivalents), which reduces the level of complexity and provides a broad, albeit simplified, picture of reality that can be used to draw the attention of policy-makers. Unfortunately, the information on non-tariff barriers is not available for all countries, which renders systematic comparisons with tariff barriers impossible. Furthermore, the study does not take into account the role of duty drawback systems and other trade/FDI facilitation measures that may override import tariffs.

Though average tariffs within East Asia tend to be low in most sectors, significant barriers can be found for agriculture, light industry, and food and beverages. This result is partially corroborated using non-tariff barriers; agriculture and food and beverages, two of the industries with high tariff barriers not only in East Asia but also in the EU and

NAFTA, are also among the industries with the highest non-tariff barriers in all three regions.

Tariffs among East Asian countries tend to be higher than those in intra-EU and intra-NAFTA trade. This result is not surprising, given the lesser extent of economic integration in East Asia than in Europe and North America. However, in some sectors, East Asian exporters face higher average tariffs in East Asian markets than they do in EU and NAFTA markets, especially in agriculture, light industry, and food and beverages. In other words, EU and NAFTA grant better market access conditions to East Asia than East Asia does to itself in some sectors. More paradoxically, although East Asian importers tend to apply lower import tariffs to exporters from East Asia than to those from EU and NAFTA, they apply significantly higher tariffs in agriculture and light industry. This situation argues in favor of a strengthening of the economic integration in East Asia.

Whereas Hong Kong and Singapore *play by free trade rules*, the remaining Asian countries continue to use trade policy for strategic objectives. The findings suggest that Thailand, China and Vietnam practice an "offensive protectionism" instrument of export promotion. On the other hand, Japan, Korea, Philippines, Brunei and Malaysia practice a "defensive protectionism" instrument either for national security reasons (e.g. agriculture in Japan and Korea) or to protect infant or inefficient domestic industries (e.g. transportation machinery in Malaysia). Myanmar, Laos, Taiwan, Indonesia and Cambodia apply "wide-ranging protectionism" combining the defense of competitive and uncompetitive industries.

Aggregating over the various importing countries allows one to calculate the average tariff faced by a particular country. This is useful to examine which are the most discriminated countries in East Asia. The chapter suggests that Hong Kong, China and Singapore face the highest levels of protection in East Asia, whereas the most favored countries are Myanmar, Malaysia, Cambodia, Laos and Taiwan.

The difference between tariffs applied and tariffs faced suggests some asymmetries in bilateral tariff treatment. For Hong Kong, Singapore and China, aggregate applied tariffs are substantially lower than faced tariffs, while they are substantially higher for Malaysia and Cambodia, followed by Thailand, Vietnam, Laos, Japan, Korea, Brunei, Taiwan and Myanmar. At the industry level, the differences between bilateral tariffs applied and tariffs faced can be substantial. This also suggests substantial scope for future market access negotiations and economic integration in East Asia.

Annex Table A-1: Classification of the 15 sectors in terms of the harmonized system (HS)

Sector and 2-digit chapter of the HS	*Sector and 2-digit chapter of the HS*
Agriculture (HS 1–15)	**Wood and paper (44–49)**
01 Live animals	44 Wood and articles of wood, wood charcoal
02 Meat and edible meat offal	45 Cork and articles of cork
03 Fish, crustaceans, molluscs, aquatic invertebrates nes	46 Manufactures of plaiting material, basketwork, etc.
04 Dairy products, eggs, honey, edible animal product nes	47 Pulp of wood, fibrous cellulosic material, waste etc.
05 Products of animal origin, nes	48 Paper & paperboard, articles of pulp, paper and board
06 Live trees, plants, bulbs, roots, cut flowers etc.	49 Printed books, newspapers, pictures etc.
07 Edible vegetables and certain roots and tubers	
08 Edible fruit, nuts, peel of citrus fruit, melons	**Textile and clothing (50–63)**
09 Coffee, tea, mate and spices	50 Silk
10 Cereals	51 Wool, animal hair, horsehair yarn and fabric thereof
11 Milling products, malt, starches, inulin, wheat gluten	52 Cotton
12 Oil seed, oleagic fruits, grain, seed, fruit, etc., nes	53 Vegetable textile fibres nes, paper yarn, woven fabric
13 Lac, gums, resins, vegetable saps and extracts nes	54 Manmade filaments
14 Vegetable plaiting materials, vegetable products nes	55 Manmade staple fibers
15 Animal, vegetable fats and oils, cleavage products, etc.	56 Wadding, felt, non-wovens, yarns, twine, cordage, etc.
	57 Carpets and other textile floor coverings
Food and beverages (16–24)	58 Special woven or tufted fabric, lace, tapestry etc.
16 Meat, fish and seafood food preparations nes	59 Impregnated, coated or laminated textile fabric
17 Sugars and sugar confectionery	60 Knitted or crocheted fabric
18 Cocoa and cocoa preparations	61 Articles of apparel, accessories, knitted or crocheted
19 Cereal, flour, starch, milk preparations and products	62 Articles of apparel, accessories, not knitted or crocheted
20 Vegetable, fruit, nut, etc. food preparations	63 Other made textile articles, sets, worn clothing etc.
21 Miscellaneous edible preparations	
22 Beverages, spirits and vinegar	**Pottery products (68–70)**
23 Residues, wastes of food industry, animal fodder	68 Stone, plaster, cement, asbestos, mica, etc. articles
24 Tobacco and manufactured tobacco substitutes	69 Ceramic products
	70 Glass and glassware

Annex Table A-1: Classification of the 15 sectors in terms of the harmonized system (HS) – *continued*

Sector and 2-digit chapter of the HS	*Sector and 2-digit chapter of the HS*
Mining products (25–27)	**Basic metals (72–83)**
25 Salt, sulphur, earth, stone, plaster, lime and cement	72 Iron and steel
26 Ores, slag and ash	73 Articles of iron or steel
27 Mineral fuels, oils, distillation products, etc.	74 Copper and articles thereof
Chemicals (28–40)	76 Aluminium and articles thereof
28 Inorganic chemicals, precious metal compound, isotopes	78 Lead and articles thereof
29 Organic chemicals	79 Zinc and articles thereof
30 Pharmaceutical products	80 Tin and articles thereof
31 Fertilizers	81 Other base metals, cermets, articles thereof
32 Tanning, dyeing extracts, tannins, derivs, pigments etc.	82 Tools, implements, cutlery, etc. of base metal
33 Essential oils, perfumes, cosmetics, toiletries	83 Miscellaneous articles of base metal
34 Soaps, lubricants, waxes, candles, modeling pastes	**General machinery (84)**
35 Albuminoids, modified starches, glues, enzymes	84 Nuclear reactors, boilers, machinery, etc.
36 Explosives, pyrotechnics, matches, pyrophorics, etc.	**Electrical machinery (85)**
37 Photographic or cinematographic goods	85 Electrical, electronic equipment
38 Miscellaneous chemical products	**Transportation machinery (86–89)**
39 Plastics and articles thereof	86 Railway, tramway locomotives, rolling stock, equipment
40 Rubber and articles thereof	87 Vehicles other than railway, tramway
Light industry (41–43, 64–67, 94–96)	88 Aircraft, spacecraft, and parts thereof
41 Raw hides and skins (other than furskins) and leather	89 Ships, boats and other floating structures
42 Articles of leather, animal gut, harness, travel goods	**Precision apparatus (90–92)**
43 Furskins and artificial fur, manufactures thereof	90 Optical, photo, technical, medical, etc. apparatus
64 Footwear, gaiters and the like, parts thereof	91 Clocks and watches and parts thereof
65 Headgear and parts thereof	92 Musical instruments, parts and accessories
66 Umbrellas, walking-sticks, seat-sticks, whips, etc.	**Others (71, 93, 97–99)**
67 Bird skin, feathers, artificial flowers, human hair	71 Pearls, precious stones, metals, coins, etc.
94 Furniture, lighting, signs, prefabricated buildings	93 Arms and ammunition, parts and accessories thereof
95 Toys, games, sports requisites	97 Works of art, collectors pieces and antiques
96 Miscellaneous manufactured articles	98 Commodities specified at chapter level only
	99 Commodities not elsewhere specified

Annex Table A-2: The reference groups

Group 1	*Group 2*	*Group 3*	*Group 4*	*Group 5*	*Residue group*
Indonesia Vietnam	China Philippines Thailand	South Korea Malaysia	Brunei Hong Kong Japan Singapore	Taiwan	Cambodia Lao P.D.R. Myanmar
Armenia Bangladesh Benin Bhutan Bolivia Burkina Faso Cameroon Central African Rep. Chad Congo Congo, D.R. Côte d'Ivoire Ecuador Ethiopia Georgia Ghana Guinea Guinea-Bissau Honduras India Kenya Kyrgyzstan Lesotho Madagascar Malawi Mali Mauritania Moldova, Rep. Mozambique Nepal Nicaragua Niger Nigeria Pakistan Papua New Guinea Rwanda Senegal Solomon Islands Sudan Tanzania Togo Uganda Uzbekistan Zambia Zimbabwe	Albania Algeria Belarus Belize Bosnia and Herz. Botswana Brazil Colombia Cuba Dominica Dominican Rep. Egypt El Salvador Equat. Guinea Gabon Grenada Guatemala Guyana Iran Jamaica Jordan Kazakhstan Latvia Lebanon Lithuania Macedonia, Rep. Maldives Morocco Namibia Panama Paraguay Peru Romania Russian Fed. Serbia & Montenegro Sri Lanka Suriname Tunisia Turkey Turkmenistan Ukraine Venezuela	Antigua and Bar Argentina Bahrain Chile Costa Rica Croatia Estonia Hungary Mauritius Mexico Oman Poland Saudi Arabia Seychelles Slovenia Trinidad and Tobago Uruguay	Australia Canada European Union Iceland Switzerland United States	Bahamas Barbados Czech Republic Israel Malta New Zealand United Arab Emirates	Azerbaijan Bermuda Bulgaria Cyprus Eritrea Kuwait Libyan Arab Jamahiriya Mayotte Montserrat Norway Qatar St Kitts and Nevis St Lucia St Vincent & Grenadines Slovak Republic South Africa Swaziland Syrian Arab Republic Tajikistan Vanuatu Yemen Yugoslavia

Annex Table A-3: Number of notified products by importing country and sector

Exporter	Agriculture	Chemical	Food and beverages	Textiles and clothing	Light industry	Wood products	Transportation machinery	Precision apparatus	Electrical machinery	General machinery	Basic metals	Mining products	Pottery products	Ohters	**All products**
Japan	480	621	163	..	58	45	9	40	..	13	23	22	15	12	1,502
Thailand	278	520	50	..	2	..	5	..	27	10	10	5	6	..	913
Singapore	208	462	15	9	15	..	20	5	5	7	..	..	..	1	747
Indonesia	420	63	20	..	..	..	..	..	..	..	..	3	..	..	506
Malaysia	229	30	12	29	5	5	1	..	35	11	12	13	..	1	383
Vietnam	62	32	89	..	..	..	45	3	..	..	..	..	..	..	231
Philippines	..	39	..	3	1	..	31	..	..	..	..	..	..	..	74
China	13	..	..	..	..	..	..	..	..	..	..	..	..	..	13
Brunei	3	3	..	..	..	..	..	..	..	..	..	..	..	..	6
Sum East Asia	*1,693*	*1,770*	*349*	*41*	*81*	*50*	*111*	*48*	*67*	*41*	*45*	*43*	*21*	*14*	*4,375*
Mexico	413	480	152	13	65	44	1	38	1		5	5	1	1	1,219
United States	362	93	105	350	60	59	68	13	40	40	5	2	2	2	1,201
Canada	467	42	..	3	66	34	23	..	7	12	4	..	..	3	661
Sum NAFTA	*1,242*	*615*	*257*	*366*	*191*	*137*	*92*	*51*	*48*	*52*	*14*	*7*	*3*	*6*	*3,081*
EU 15	97	33	23	2	92	25	..	17	..	..	..	..	..	3	292

Note: The numbers for East Asia are obtained by aggregating the information from 9 of the 15 countries under examination: Brunei, China, Indonesia, Japan, Malaysia, Philippines, Singapore, Thailand and Vietnam. Likewise for NAFTA, the information was aggregated from the three member countries. This is done for illustrative purposes, as there may be double-counting, when several countries notify the same product.

Source: Market Access Map, calculations by ITC.

Annex Table A-4: Share of notified products in importing countries' sector imports

Exporter	Agriculture	Chemical	Food and beverages	Textiles and clothing	Light industry	Wood products	Transportation machinery	Precision apparatus	Electrical machinery	General machinery	Basic metals	Mining products	Pottery products	Ohters	**All products**
Japan	99.7	69.8	79.1	..	11.9	29.6	43.6	38.9	..	2.5	4.3	30.9	13.3	1.7	31.7
Thailand	66.1	40.8	52.7	..	0.0	..	3.1	..	5.2	4.5	0.7	29.9	1.2	..	12.0
Indonesia	98.2	2.7	0.3	..	..	..	..	..	..	..	..	0.6	..	..	8.0
Vietnam	33.6	2.7	39.3	..	..	..	53.0	1.1	..	..	..	..	..	..	7.5
Malaysia	66.0	4.0	14.1	2.6	2.9	2.5	0.1	..	5.0	2.5	1.3	1.4	..	0.0	5.7
Singapore	41.7	24.7	6.8	0.8	3.2	..	27.3	1.3	0.6	0.4	..	..	..	0.0	4.6
Philippines	..	4.0	..	2.2	3.9	..	55.6	..	..	..	..	..	..	..	2.6
Brunei	16.3	0.3	..	..	..	..	..	..	..	..	..	..	..	..	0.7
China	0.4	..	..	..	..	..	..	..	..	..	..	..	..	..	0.0
United States	84.8	41.4	41.7	84.6	15.8	35.4	88.8	9.0	13.4	3.1	0.6	9.8	3.6	0.1	32.7
Canada	95.6	6.2	..	0.0	11.1	16.5	46.0	..	1.8	2.6	1.7	..	..	0.4	16.0
Mexico	96.2	26.1	91.4	4.9	23.5	13.0	1.7	21.5	0.0	..	0.7	45.5	2.9	0.0	13.5
EU 15	21.0	1.7	11.6	0.4	39.0	22.4	..	3.7	..	..	..	..	..	0.8	4.4

Source: Market Access Map, calculations by ITC.

Annex Table A-5: Tariff barriers in bilateral trade: all products (*ad valorem tariff equivalents (%)*)

	Japan	China	ASEAN 6	Brunei	Indonesia	Malaysia	Philippines	Singapore	Thailand	CLMV	Cambodia	Laos	Myanmar	Vietnam	NIEs 3	Hong Kong	Korea	Taiwan	East Asia	EU 25	NAFTA	ROW
Japan	..	23	9	8	9	3	7	13	9	3	3	3	2	8	15	21	6	3	10	8	7	8
China	9	..	9	9	8	6	7	12	7	9	9	9	9	9	9	9	9	8	9	8	7	8
ASEAN 6	3	3	4	3	3	2	5	44	1	2	2	2	2	2	4	5	4	3		7	3	3
Brunei	33	3	6	..	2	4	2	8	3	5	4	5	5	4	7	4	19	2	10	9	29	5
Indonesia	9	7	5	5	..	3	6	3	5	5	6	6	6	4	6	6	7	7	5	6	6	7
Malaysia	30	7	26	26	3	..	8	60	4	4	5	5	5	1	19	25	12	11	23	23	16	9
Philippines	6	12	4	4	5	4	..	4	4	4	4	3	4	5	5	6	6	4	5	5	6	6
Singapore	0	0	0	0	0	0	0	..	0	0	0	0	0	0	0	0	0	0	0	0	0	0
Thailand	17	21	17	16	18	15	16	21	..	15	14	14	14	21	16	19	16	11	16	15	14	16
CLMV	15	15	13	13	16	15	16	11	14	15	15	15	15	10	13	12	16	16		12	12	15
Cambodia	21	15	19	19	15	18	18	18	20	13	..	13	13	14	21	22	19	20	19	18	16	17
Laos	13	11	10	11	12	10	9	9	10	9	9	..	9	12	12	12	10	13	11	10	10	10
Myanmar	5	5	4	5	6	3	4	3	3	5	4	4	..	6	4	4	4	7	4	4	3	5
Vietnam	16	16	13	13	16	16	17	11	14	16	16	16	16	..	13	12	17	17	14	12	12	16
NIEs 3	6	3	3	3	4	2	4	4	4	3	3	3	2	4	8	17	1	2		6	5	4
Hong Kong	0	0	0	0	0	0	0	0	0	0	0	0	0	0	0	..	0	0	0	0	0	0
Korea	14	9	8	9	6	6	7	10	6	6	6	6	6	7	17	20	..	6	9	12	10	8
Taiwan	7	8	8	7	8	6	12	8	12	12	13	13	9	12	7	8	6	..	8	8	5	10
East Asia	5	16		6	6	3	6	12	7		3	3	2	6		17	5	4	7	7	6	6
EU	11	6	6	5	4	4	7	15	9	2	0	0	6	5	17	22	8	7	8	2	8	4
NAFTA	5	6	5	5	4	3	4	8	4	8	2	22	4	7	10	14	3	5	6	5	1	5
ROW	14	9	12	12	14	11	13	18	13	13	12	12	14	14	17	20	13	9	13	10	12	13
World	9	7		5	5	4	7	13	7		2	5	6	6		20	7	6		4	6	5

Note: Importers are in rows, exporters in columns.
Source: Market Access Map, calculations by ITC.

Annex Table A-6: Tariff barriers applied by importing countries in intra-East Asian trade, by sector (*ad valorem tariff equivalents (%)*)

All products		*Agriculture*		*Light industry*		*Food and beverages*		*Textiles and clothing*	
Malaysia	(22.9)	Korea	(79.5)	Japan	(36.9)	Thailand	(42.5)	Vietnam	(25.7)
Cambodia	(18.8)	Japan	(54.3)	*East Asia*	*(26.8)*	Vietnam	(39.5)	Thailand	(19.8)
Thailand	(16.5)	Thailand	(41.6)	Vietnam	(25.4)	Brunei	(29.5)	Cambodia	(18.0)
Vietnam	(13.7)	*East Asia*	*(41.0)*	Cambodia	(22.9)	Japan	(27.7)	China	(14.8)
Laos	(10.6)	Taiwan	(24.7)	Laos	(16.9)	Taiwan	(25.3)	Malaysia	(12.0)
Brunei	(10.3)	Vietnam	(17.2)	Thailand	(12.2)	Cambodia	(23.0)	Myanmar	(9.8)
Japan	(10.2)	Cambodia	(15.5)	China	(10.5)	Laos	(22.6)	Taiwan	(9.3)
Korea	(9.3)	Philippines	(15.3)	Malaysia	(7.6)	*East Asia*	*(21.8)*	Korea	(8.9)
China	(8.8)	Laos	(11.6)	Korea	(6.8)	Korea	(21.5)	Laos	(8.6)
Taiwan	(7.7)	China	(7.0)	Myanmar	(6.5)	Indonesia	(19.1)	Japan	(8.3)
East Asia	*(7.4)*	Myanmar	(4.9)	Indonesia	(6.3)	China	(16.7)	*East Asia*	*(7.3)*
Indonesia	(5.5)	Malaysia	(4.6)	Taiwan	(4.8)	Malaysia	(16.2)	Indonesia	(5.5)
Philippines	(4.7)	Indonesia	(3.9)	Philippines	(4.1)	Myanmar	(15.5)	Philippines	(4.8)
Myanmar	(4.3)	Brunei	(0.1)	Brunei	(2.9)	Philippines	(15.0)	Brunei	(0.4)
Singapore	(0.0)	Hong Kong	(0.0)	Hong Kong	(0.0)	Singapore	(0.3)	Singapore	(0.0)
Hong Kong	(0.0)	Singapore	(0.0)	Singapore	(0.0)	Hong Kong	(0.0)	Hong Kong	(0.0)

Transportation machinery		*Pottery products*		*Chemicals*		*Basic metals*		*Mining products*	
Malaysia	(76.5)	Vietnam	(21.0)	Thailand	(11.7)	Thailand	(11.9)	Cambodia	(19.2)
Brunei	(40.2)	Malaysia	(18.5)	Cambodia	(10.5)	Malaysia	(10.6)	Vietnam	(12.0)
Thailand	(39.9)	Thailand	(16.8)	Laos	(8.6)	Cambodia	(9.3)	Laos	(8.4)
Vietnam	(33.2)	Cambodia	(14.9)	Korea	(8.1)	Vietnam	(8.4)	Korea	(5.1)
Cambodia	(28.1)	China	(13.3)	China	(7.6)	Indonesia	(6.5)	Taiwan	(4.3)
Taiwan	(25.3)	Taiwan	(8.1)	Malaysia	(7.3)	Laos	(6.5)	China	(4.0)
China	(22.6)	Korea	(7.8)	Vietnam	(5.6)	China	(6.5)	Philippines	(2.9)
Laos	(15.5)	Laos	(5.3)	Indonesia	(5.0)	Taiwan	(6.1)	Indonesia	(2.7)
Indonesia	(12.9)	Indonesia	(5.0)	Taiwan	(4.6)	Korea	(5.4)	*East Asia*	*(1.7)*
Philippines	(8.0)	Philippines	(4.3)	Philippines	(3.6)	Philippines	(3.2)	Myanmar	(1.6)
Korea	(7.3)	Myanmar	(3.0)	Myanmar	(2.5)	Myanmar	(2.0)	Thailand	(1.4)
Myanmar	(5.7)	*East Asia*	*(2.9)*	*East Asia*	*(2.4)*	*East Asia*	*(1.8)*	Japan	(1.1)
East Asia	*(4.6)*	Japan	(0.9)	Japan	(1.7)	Japan	(1.0)	Malaysia	(0.9)
Japan	(0.0)	Singapore	(0.0)	Brunei	(0.7)	Brunei	(0.0)	Singapore	(0.0)
Singapore	(0.0)	Hong Kong	(0.0)	Singapore	(0.0)	Singapore	(0.0)	Hong Kong	(0.0)
Hong Kong	(0.0)	Brunei	(0.0)	Hong Kong	(0.0)	Hong Kong	(0.0)	Brunei	(0.0)

General machinery		*Electrical machinery*		*Others*		*Wood and paper*		*Precision apparatus*	
Cambodia	(12.9)	Cambodia	(16.6)	Laos	(13.7)	Cambodia	(14.2)	Cambodia	(13.6)
Vietnam	(7.8)	Vietnam	(12.0)	Myanmar	(13.2)	Vietnam	(12.5)	China	(6.7)
Thailand	(7.4)	Thailand	(8.0)	Thailand	(10.8)	Laos	(11.1)	Thailand	(6.1)
Laos	(6.7)	Laos	(7.7)	Malaysia	(7.2)	Thailand	(8.6)	Korea	(5.7)
Malaysia	(6.3)	Malaysia	(7.0)	Philippines	(4.6)	China	(5.7)	Laos	(5.7)
China	(5.3)	China	(6.1)	Indonesia	(4.6)	Brunei	(5.4)	Brunei	(5.6)
Korea	(4.5)	Brunei	(5.6)	China	(4.5)	Myanmar	(5.2)	Myanmar	(3.2)
Brunei	(3.3)	Indonesia	(4.3)	Vietnam	(4.2)	Korea	(4.6)	Indonesia	(3.2)
Taiwan	(3.2)	Korea	(3.5)	Cambodia	(4.1)	Taiwan	(3.8)	Taiwan	(2.6)
Indonesia	(1.7)	Myanmar	(3.5)	Korea	(2.4)	Philippines	(3.1)	Philippines	(2.3)
Myanmar	(1.5)	Taiwan	(3.2)	*East Asia*	*(1.4)*	Indonesia	(2.0)	Vietnam	(2.2)
East Asia	*(1.5)*	Philippines	(1.5)	Japan	(1.2)	Japan	(1.4)	*East Asia*	*(1.2)*
Philippines	(1.5)	*East Asia*	*(1.4)*	Taiwan	(0.0)	*East Asia*	*(1.4)*	Malaysia	(0.9)
Singapore	(0.0)	Japan	(0.0)	Singapore	(0.0)	Malaysia	(0.9)	Japan	(0.1)
Japan	(0.0)	Singapore	(0.0)	Hong Kong	(0.0)	Hong Kong	(0.0)	Singapore	(0.0)
Hong Kong	(0.0)	Hong Kong	(0.0)	Brunei	(0.0)	Singapore	(0.0)	Hong Kong	(0.0)

Source: Market Access Map, calculations by ITC. The industries are ranked in decreasing order of ad valorem equivalents in intra-East Asian trade.

Annex Table A-7: 15 highest bilateral trade barriers in intra-East Asian trade (%), by sector

All products		*Agriculture*		*Light industry*		*Food and beverages*		*Textiles and clothing*	
MYS-SGP	(60.5)	KOR-JPN	(112.0)	JPN-CHN	(70.1)	BRN-SGP	(90.6)	VNM-CHN	(32.5)
BRN-JPN	(33.3)	KOR-HKG	(103.4)	JPN-IDN	(55.9)	TWN-PHL	(77.1)	VNM-KOR	(31.8)
MYS-JPN	(29.7)	KOR-BRN	(85.3)	JPN-THA	(33.2)	TWN-THA	(73.3)	VNM-PHL	(28.9)
MYS-BRN	(25.8)	THA-LAO	(84.2)	VNM-PHL	(30.7)	THA-MYS	(69.1)	VNM-MYS	(28.4)
MYS-HKG	(24.7)	THA-MMR	(83.7)	VNM-CHN	(30.1)	BRN-VNM	(68.9)	VNM-TWN	(27.6)
JPN-CHN	(22.6)	THA-TWN	(79.4)	VNM-JPN	(28.4)	THA-KHM	(61.7)	VNM-SGP	(26.0)
KHM-HKG	(21.7)	KOR-TWN	(72.6)	KHM-JPN	(28.0)	THA-LAO	(59.1)	THA-CHN	(25.8)
THA-CHN	(21.3)	JPN-HKG	(72.5)	*East Asia*	*(26.8)*	VNM-SGP	(55.9)	VNM-MMR	(24.9)
THA-SGP	(21.2)	THA-KHM	(63.3)	VNM-LAO	(26.6)	THA-MMR	(49.3)	VNM-KHM	(24.7)
JPN-HKG	(21.0)	KOR-MYS	(63.1)	VNM-MMR	(26.6)	THA-IDN	(48.8)	VNM-IDN	(23.1)
THA-VNM	(21.0)	JPN-SGP	(62.7)	VNM-KHM	(26.6)	VNM-MMR	(47.6)	VNM-JPN	(23.0)
KHM-JPN	(20.9)	KOR-SGP	(62.4)	KHM-HKG	(26.5)	PHL-CHN	(47.5)	VNM-BRN	(22.1)
KOR-HKG	(20.4)	MYS-IDN	(57.0)	JPN-VNM	(26.3)	VNM-LAO	(47.0)	KHM-JPN	(22.1)
KHM-THA	(20.1)	KOR-KHM	(55.7)	THA-CHN	(24.1)	VNM-KHM	(47.0)	THA-BRN	(22.0)
KHM-TWN	(19.9)	KOR-LAO	(55.5)	VNM-IDN	(23.9)	THA-HKG	(46.8)	KHM-LAO	(21.9)
	(...)		(...)	JPN-KOR	(23.4)		(...)		(...)
East Asia	*(7.4)*	*East Asia*	*(41.0)*		(...)	*East Asia*	*(21.8)*	*East Asia*	*(7.3)*

Transportation machinery		*Pottery products*		*Chemicals*		*Basic metals*		*Mining products*	
MYS-SGP	(113.7)	THA-IDN	(28.0)	KHM-KOR	(17.7)	VNM-IDN	(14.4)	KHM-MYS	(22.1)
MYS-KOR	(83.7)	VNM-JPN	(26.6)	KHM-MYS	(13.8)	THA-HKG	(13.0)	KHM-THA	(22.0)
MYS-JPN	(81.9)	VNM-IDN	(25.8)	LAO-IDN	(13.8)	THA-BRN	(12.9)	KHM-SGP	(22.0)
MYS-BRN	(72.6)	MYS-CHN	(24.6)	THA-TWN	(13.8)	MYS-HKG	(12.8)	KHM-BRN	(20.4)
BRN-JPN	(58.5)	THA-CHN	(24.6)	KHM-HKG	(13.3)	MYS-TWN	(12.7)	KHM-PHL	(19.9)
MYS-HKG	(57.2)	THA-VNM	(24.5)	LAO-KHM	(13.3)	THA-JPN	(12.7)	KHM-KOR	(19.6)
MYS-KHM	(56.7)	VNM-PHL	(24.0)	LAO-MMR	(13.3)	THA-KOR	(12.6)	VNM-KOR	(14.2)
MYS-MMR	(54.5)	VNM-CHN	(23.7)	THA-KHM	(13.0)	THA-CHN	(12.4)	VNM-MYS	(13.1)
MYS-LAO	(54.5)	MYS-TWN	(22.6)	THA-LAO	(12.9)	MYS-JPN	(12.4)	VNM-LAO	(13.0)
BRN-KOR	(52.9)	VNM-KHM	(21.8)	THA-MMR	(12.9)	THA-TWN	(12.4)	VNM-KHM	(13.0)
VNM-TWN	(52.1)	VNM-LAO	(21.8)	LAO-VNM	(12.8)	MYS-SGP	(12.1)	VNM-MMR	(13.0)
THA-IDN	(48.1)	VNM-MMR	(21.8)	KHM-CHN	(12.8)	THA-MYS	(12.1)	VNM-IDN	(12.8)
MYS-TWN	(48.1)	THA-PHL	(21.3)	THA-IDN	(12.7)	VNM-TWN	(11.3)	VNM-SGP	(12.2)
THA-KOR	(47.6)	VNM-BRN	(21.2)	THA-CHN	(12.6)	MYS-CHN	(11.1)	VNM-HKG	(12.1)
VNM-MMR	(47.0)	MYS-THA	(21.2)	THA-KOR	(12.3)	THA-SGP	(10.6)	KHM-VNM	(12.0)
	(...)		(...)		(...)		(...)		(...)
East Asia	*(4.6)*	*East Asia*	*(2.9)*	*East Asia*	*(2.4)*	*East Asia*	*(1.8)*	*East Asia*	*(1.7)*

General machinery		*Electrical machinery*		*Others*		*Wood and paper*		*Precision apparatus*	
KHM-KOR	(14.9)	KHM-CHN	(21.1)	KHM-PHL	(39.1)	KHM-KOR	(26.8)	KHM-HKG	(17.9)
KHM-TWN	(14.4)	KHM-HKG	(21.0)	KHM-THA	(39.1)	KHM-CHN	(25.7)	KHM-CHN	(15.8)
KHM-JPN	(14.3)	KHM-SGP	(19.1)	KHM-CHN	(38.9)	KHM-IDN	(20.5)	KHM-PHL	(15.7)
KHM-HKG	(14.2)	VNM-IDN	(18.5)	LAO-KHM	(29.8)	LAO-IDN	(19.8)	KHM-TWN	(15.5)
KHM-CHN	(13.9)	KHM-TWN	(18.0)	LAO-MMR	(29.8)	VNM-IDN	(19.7)	KHM-THA	(15.4)
KHM-IDN	(13.4)	KHM-LAO	(17.2)	LAO-MYS	(29.1)	LAO-VNM	(19.7)	KHM-JPN	(15.0)
TWN-VNM	(13.1)	KHM-MMR	(17.2)	LAO-KOR	(29.1)	KHM-VNM	(19.6)	KHM-SGP	(14.7)
KHM-BRN	(12.7)	KHM-THA	(16.9)	KHM-TWN	(27.5)	KHM-MYS	(17.3)	KHM-VNM	(14.5)
KHM-VNM	(12.4)	KHM-IDN	(16.8)	THA-JPN	(27.4)	KHM-THA	(17.1)	KHM-IDN	(14.4)
VNM-CHN	(12.4)	VNM-SGP	(16.8)	THA-HKG	(26.8)	LAO-CHN	(16.8)	KHM-KOR	(14.1)
VNM-MYS	(12.4)	KHM-KOR	(16.7)	THA-SGP	(26.2)	VNM-MMR	(16.0)	KHM-MYS	(13.2)
VNM-THA	(12.3)	VNM-PHL	(16.4)	LAO-PHL	(26.1)	LAO-KOR	(16.0)	KHM-LAO	(11.7)
KHM-THA	(12.2)	KHM-VNM	(16.2)	LAO-THA	(26.1)	VNM-KHM	(15.9)	KHM-MMR	(11.7)
KHM-LAO	(12.2)	KHM-MYS	(15.8)	LAO-CHN	(26.0)	VNM-LAO	(15.9)	KHM-BRN	(11.3)
KHM-MMR	(12.2)	KHM-BRN	(15.7)	LAO-TWN	(25.5)	THA-TWN	(15.8)	CHN-TWN	(9.6)
	(...)		(...)		(...)		(...)		(...)
East Asia	*(1.5)*	*East Asia*	*(1.4)*	*East Asia*	*(1.4)*	*East Asia*	*(1.4)*	*East Asia*	*(1.2)*

Note: The first country is the importer, the second one the exporter (ad valorem equivalent tariff in %).

BRN: Brunei	CHN: China	HKG: Hong Kong	IDN: Indonesia	JPN: Japan
KHM: Cambodia	KOR: Korea	LAO: Laos	MMR: Myanmar	MYS: Malaysia
PHL: Philippines	SGP: Singapore	THA: Thailand	TWN: Taiwan	VNM: Vietnam

Source: Market Access Map, calculations by ITC.

Annex Table A-8: Importance of industries in national imports and exports and their revealed comparative advantage

	Agriculture	Basic metals	Chemicals	Electrical machinery	Food and beverages	General machinery	Light industry	Mining products	Others	Pottery products	Precision apparatus	Textiles and clothing	Transportation machinery	Wood and paper
Share of industry in country's total exports														
Brunei	0.0	0.0	0.0	0.0	0.0	0.0	0.0	94.4	0.0	0.0	0.0	5.6	0.0	0.0
Cambodia	0.7	0.2	0.9	0.1	0.1	0.1	8.1	0.0	1.6	0.0	0.0	87.2	0.2	0.7
China	3.0	5.7	7.1	20.7	1.8	18.6	12.7	2.9	1.0	1.6	3.0	16.7	3.6	1.7
Hong Kong	0.8	3.6	6.9	33.5	0.5	14.5	14.2	0.2	3.3	0.4	6.9	12.5	1.1	1.6
Indonesia	9.0	4.0	9.8	10.0	2.4	4.6	5.6	29.2	0.7	1.1	0.9	11.5	1.4	9.9
Japan	0.2	6.5	10.9	22.2	0.3	20.0	0.9	0.4	4.6	1.0	6.2	1.6	24.6	0.7
Korea	0.7	7.0	10.6	28.4	0.8	16.4	1.7	3.6	1.8	0.5	1.8	7.7	17.9	1.1
Laos	7.5	1.4	1.1	1.2	0.4	0.1	3.0	1.5	1.9	0.0	0.0	49.7	0.1	32.0
Malaysia	6.6	2.9	8.7	37.8	1.6	18.8	2.2	10.2	1.9	0.7	2.4	2.1	0.8	3.5
Myanmar	20.3	1.9	0.7	0.3	0.6	0.1	1.9	27.2	1.3	0.0	0.1	26.1	0.1	19.5
Philippines	4.1	1.7	1.9	50.7	2.0	20.4	2.0	2.0	0.6	0.5	2.4	6.9	3.6	1.0
Singapore	0.8	2.2	13.4	38.0	1.2	22.5	0.5	8.5	4.7	0.2	3.3	1.7	1.9	0.9
Taiwan	1.1	9.5	10.4	29.2	0.3	20.8	3.5	2.3	0.4	0.6	4.9	7.9	3.8	0.9
Thailand	7.0	3.6	13.0	21.3	7.5	16.0	4.2	3.2	5.4	1.2	2.0	6.9	6.5	2.0
Vietnam	15.0	1.3	3.6	5.5	2.6	2.0	24.6	19.6	0.8	1.3	0.6	20.5	1.1	1.6
East Asia	2.3	5.4	9.3	26.1	1.3	18.0	6.0	4.1	2.6	0.9	4.1	8.4	9.7	1.6

Annex Table A-8: Importance of industries in national imports and exports and their revealed comparative advantage – *continued*

	Agriculture	Basic metals	Chemicals	Electrical machinery	Food and beverages	General machinery	Light industry	Mining products	Others	Pottery products	Precision apparatus	Textiles and clothing	Transportation machinery	Wood and paper
Share of industry in country's total imports														
Brunei	7.2	11.1	10.3	8.0	9.2	10.8	3.3	2.2	0.9	1.8	2.0	11.6	16.4	3.8
Cambodia	1.9	4.0	9.7	3.6	8.1	5.9	3.4	9.9	1.8	1.2	0.7	35.1	12.5	2.2
China	3.2	9.5	13.7	25.2	0.5	17.3	1.5	9.1	0.8	0.6	6.3	4.7	4.2	3.2
Hong Kong	2.6	3.8	7.7	32.1	1.2	14.2	10.2	2.1	4.7	0.7	5.0	12.1	1.8	1.7
Indonesia	7.3	8.4	18.1	5.4	4.3	13.2	1.2	24.5	0.1	0.7	1.0	4.6	7.6	3.4
Japan	8.9	4.2	9.1	12.6	3.9	10.7	4.4	23.4	3.1	0.9	4.5	6.3	4.3	3.8
Korea	4.0	8.8	10.6	21.6	1.7	11.2	2.1	23.3	2.3	1.3	4.7	3.5	2.5	2.4
Laos	2.6	7.0	9.2	13.4	11.1	8.4	1.3	16.0	3.0	2.9	1.0	9.8	13.0	1.3
Malaysia	3.2	7.0	9.0	43.3	2.0	14.8	0.9	6.0	3.6	0.7	3.2	1.4	3.4	1.7
Myanmar	7.0	9.5	13.9	7.2	4.0	15.5	2.1	10.6	2.1	0.9	1.1	13.9	10.8	1.6
Philippines	4.2	5.1	9.2	38.8	2.9	15.6	0.9	11.3	0.2	0.5	2.4	3.2	3.7	2.1
Singapore	1.9	3.8	8.1	35.3	1.6	18.6	1.3	13.7	2.5	0.6	3.7	2.3	5.6	1.1
Taiwan	2.8	8.9	13.8	27.3	1.8	14.3	1.4	12.8	1.9	1.0	6.8	1.9	3.1	2.3
Thailand	3.3	11.1	13.7	21.8	1.8	16.4	1.4	12.3	4.0	0.8	2.4	3.2	5.6	2.1
Vietnam	3.5	10.2	15.3	8.2	3.0	15.4	4.4	10.6	2.4	0.8	1.8	12.7	8.7	2.8
East Asia	4.5	6.8	10.9	24.2	2.0	14.3	3.4	13.8	2.5	0.8	4.8	5.4	3.9	2.7

Annex Table A-8: Importance of industries in national imports and exports and their revealed comparative advantage – *continued*

	Agriculture	Basic metals	Chemicals	Electrical machinery	Food and beverages	General machinery	Light industry	Mining products	Others	Pottery products	Precision apparatus	Textiles and clothing	Transportation machinery	Wood and paper
Indicator of specialization: (X-M) / (X+M) in %														
Brunei	–98.7	–99.6	–100.0	–100.0	–99.7	–100.0	–99.2	98.5	–100.0	–98.7	–100.0	19.7	–100.0	–100.0
Cambodia	–48.3	–89.4	–84.5	–95.2	–98.8	–96.6	38.2	–99.9	–7.3	–97.8	–98.9	40.4	–96.9	–52.2
China	–1.6	–22.1	–29.1	–6.7	56.9	6.5	80.0	–49.5	15.8	45.0	–33.3	58.3	–5.8	–28.6
Hong Kong	–54.6	–8.9	–10.6	–3.3	–47.8	–4.4	10.7	–85.2	–22.3	–31.0	9.8	–4.0	–28.3	–8.0
Indonesia	39.4	–5.3	0.6	55.2	2.0	–21.3	79.7	38.2	79.0	51.3	22.4	64.7	–49.3	68.9
Japan	–93.7	31.1	19.1	36.9	–82.4	39.2	–58.4	–95.7	29.0	18.1	26.0	–52.2	75.2	–64.8
Korea	–69.0	–7.7	3.9	17.6	–31.6	22.5	–8.0	–71.1	–6.4	–42.2	–41.5	41.0	77.5	–32.5
Laos	14.7	–83.6	–89.8	–92.2	–96.6	–99.2	3.7	–92.0	–55.1	–100.0	–95.6	39.8	–99.4	83.5
Malaysia	44.4	–30.2	10.1	5.1	0.4	23.5	51.5	36.5	–20.4	11.9	–2.9	30.8	–53.4	43.8
Myanmar	47.2	–67.7	–91.0	–91.7	–74.9	–99.3	–5.8	42.2	–26.1	–96.7	–89.2	28.7	–98.9	84.4
Philippines	–5.0	–52.1	–68.8	9.0	–22.5	9.1	35.4	–71.8	43.4	–4.6	–4.5	33.0	–5.5	–36.9
Singapore	–36.5	–20.3	30.0	9.7	–8.4	15.4	–36.8	–17.5	35.0	–33.2	1.3	–7.7	–43.9	–4.9
Taiwan	–34.7	11.9	–5.9	11.9	–65.5	26.4	48.5	–64.8	–64.1	–11.5	–7.5	66.4	18.7	–35.1
Thailand	38.7	–49.5	0.2	1.8	62.9	1.9	53.2	–57.1	17.4	24.7	–5.3	39.0	10.3	0.1
Vietnam	61.2	–77.9	–63.4	–21.7	–9.7	–77.4	68.8	28.1	–53.0	26.5	–53.2	21.6	–79.0	–29.4
East Asia	–27.9	–6.6	–2.3	9.2	–16.3	16.5	32.7	–50.5	8.9	12.7	–3.1	26.4	46.8	–19.1

Note: The indicator of specialization (X-M) / (X+M) in % varies between –100% (net importer) and +100% (net exporter).

Annex Table A-9: Most asymmetric bilateral tariff barriers in intra-East Asian trade (*ad valorem tariff equivalents (%)*)

Difference	*High tariff importer – Low tariff importer – Sector*	*Difference*	*High tariff importer – Low tariff importer – Sector*
113.7	**Malaysia** (113.7)–Singapore (0)–Transport. mach.	35.8	**Cambodia** (39.1)–Philippines (3.3)–Others
103.4	**Korea** (103.4)–Hong Kong (0)–Agriculture	35.8	**Thailand** (48.8)–Indonesia (13)–Food & bev.
90.6	**Brunei** (90.6)–Singapore (0)–Food & bev.	35.5	**Thailand** (35.5)–Japan (0)–Transport. mach.
89.4	**Korea** (112.0)–Japan (22.6)–Agriculture	35.3	**Thailand** (48.9)–China (13.6)–Agriculture
85.3	**Korea** (85.3)–Brunei (0)–Agriculture	35.1	**Cambodia** (35.1)–Japan (0)–Transport. mach.
81.9	**Malaysia** (81.9)–Japan (0)–Transport. mach.	34.9	**Taiwan** (41.6)–Philippines (6.7)–Agriculture
77.5	**Thailand** (83.7)–Myanmar (6.2)–Agriculture	34.9	**Thailand** (39.7)–Myanmar (4.8)–Transport. mach.
77.3	**Malaysia** (83.7)–Korea (6.5)–Transport. mach.	34.7	**Thailand** (47.5)–Philippines (12.8)–Agriculture
72.5	**Japan** (72.5)–Hong Kong (0)–Agriculture	33.7	**Vietnam** (40.7)–Japan (7)–Food & bev.
68.0	**Thailand** (84.2)–Laos (16.1)–Agriculture	33.5	**Thailand** (36.4)–Brunei (2.9)–Food & bev.
62.7	**Japan** (62.7)–Singapore (0)–Agriculture	32.1	**Taiwan** (32.1)–Japan (0)–Transport. mach.
62.4	**Korea** (62.4)–Singapore (0)–Agriculture	32.0	**Taiwan** (37)–Indonesia (5.0)–Agriculture
60.0	**Thailand** (69.1)–Malaysia (9.0)–Food & bev.	31.9	**Vietnam** (31.9)–Japan (0)–Transport. mach.
60.0	**Taiwan** (77.1)–Philippines (17.1)–Food & bev.	31.9	**Vietnam** (47)–Cambodia (15.1)–Food & bev.
58.5	**Brunei** (58.5)–Japan (0)–Transport. mach.	31.7	**Taiwan** (73.3)–Thailand (41.6)–Food & bev.
58.4	**Korea** (63.1)–Malaysia (4.7)–Agriculture	31.7	**Thailand** (31.7)–Hong Kong (0)–Transport. mach.
57.8	**Japan** (70.1)–China (12.3)–Light industry	31.5	**Japan** (31.9)–Singapore (0.4)–Food & bev.
57.2	**Malaysia** (57.2)–Hong Kong (0)–Transport. mach.	31.3	**Thailand** (31.3)–Hong Kong (0)–Agriculture
55.9	**Vietnam** (55.9)–Singapore (0)–Food & bev.	31.2	**Cambodia** (31.2)–Hong Kong (0)–Transport. mach.
55.8	**Malaysia** (57.0)–Indonesia (1.1)–Agriculture	31.1	**Thailand** (46.2)–China (15.1)–Food & bev.
55.3	**Japan** (55.3)–Brunei (0)–Agriculture	31.1	**Korea** (32.5)–Indonesia (1.4)–Agriculture
53.3	**Thailand** (63.3)–Cambodia (10.0)–Agriculture	30.8	**Thailand** (42.1)–Philippines (11.2)–Food & bev.
52.7	**Malaysia** (54.5)–Myanmar (1.8)–Transport. mach.	30.8	**Vietnam** (38.1)–Malaysia (7.3)–Food & bev.
50.0	**Korea** (72.6)–Taiwan (22.6)–Agriculture	30.8	**Japan** (30.8)–Hong Kong (0)–Food & bev.
48.3	**Japan** (55.9)–Indonesia (7.5)–Light industry	30.4	**Thailand** (42.6)–Indonesia (12.2)–Agriculture
46.8	**Thailand** (46.8)–Hong Kong (0)–Food & bev.	30.2	**Vietnam** (47.6)–Myanmar (17.4)–Food & bev.
46.7	**Thailand** (79.4)–Taiwan (32.7)–Agriculture	30.0	**Brunei** (68.9)–Vietnam (38.9)–Food & bev.
46.6	**Malaysia** (72.6)–Brunei (26.0)–Transport. mach.	29.5	**Brunei** (46.7)–Laos (17.3)–Transport. mach.

Annex Table A-9: Most asymmetric bilateral tariff barriers in intra-East Asian trade (*ad valorem tariff equivalents (%)*) – *continued*

Difference	*High tariff importer – Low tariff importer – Sector*	*Difference*	*High tariff importer – Low tariff importer – Sector*
46.0	**Korea** (50.4)–China (4.4)–Agriculture	29.4	**Vietnam** (47)–Laos (17.5)–Food & bev.
45.4	**Brunei** (52.9)–Korea (7.5)–Transport. mach.	29.3	**Thailand** (34.3)–Malaysia (5.1)–Agriculture
45.1	**Korea** (49.1)–Myanmar (4.0)–Agriculture	29.2	**Brunei** (29.2)–Hong Kong (0)–Food & bev.
44.8	**Malaysia** (54.5)–Laos (9.6)–Transport. mach.	29.2	**Laos** (29.8)–Cambodia (0.6)–Others
42.4	**Thailand** (47.6)–Korea (5.2)–Transport. mach.	29.1	**Laos** (29.1)–Korea (0)–Others
42.2	**Philippines** (47.5)–China (5.3)–Food & bev.	29.0	**Thailand** (33)–Philippines (3.9)–Transport. mach.
41.7	**Korea** (55.5)–Laos (13.8)–Agriculture	28.9	**Thailand** (44.7)–Laos (15.8)–Transport. mach.
41.5	**Korea** (55.7)–Cambodia (14.2)–Agriculture	28.8	**Malaysia** (28.8)–Singapore (0)–Food & bev.
41.2	**Thailand** (48.1)–Indonesia (6.9)–Transport. mach.	28.5	**Laos** (29.1)–Malaysia (0.6)–Others
40.9	**Malaysia** (56.7)–Cambodia (15.9)–Transport. mach.	27.5	**Cambodia** (28.0)–Japan (0.5)–Light industry
40.7	**Thailand** (40.7)–Singapore (0)–Transport. mach.	27.4	**Thailand** (27.4)–Japan (0)–Others
39.8	**Cambodia** (39.8)–Hong Kong (0)–Food & bev.	27.0	**Vietnam** (30.7)–Philippines (3.7)–Light industry
39.2	**Thailand** (61.7)–Cambodia (22.5)–Food & bev.	26.8	**Taiwan** (43.8)–China (16.9)–Food & bev.
39.2	**Malaysia** (44.3)–Philippines (5.2)–Transport. mach.	26.8	**Thailand** (26.8)–Hong Kong (0)–Others
39.1	**Brunei** (46.7)–Myanmar (7.6)–Transport. mach.	26.6	**Vietnam** (26.6)–Japan (0)–Pottery products
39.0	**Thailand** (39.0)–Singapore (0)–Food & bev.	26.5	**Laos** (26.5)–Hong Kong (0)–Food & bev.
38.8	**Vietnam** (47.0)–Myanmar (8.2)–Transport. mach.	26.5	**Cambodia** (26.5)–Hong Kong (0)–Light industry
38.6	**Vietnam** (38.6)–Hong Kong (0)–Food & bev.	26.4	**Vietnam** (47.0)–Laos (20.6)–Transport. mach.
38.4	**Malaysia** (48.1)–Taiwan (9.7)–Transport. mach.	26.2	**Korea** (43.6)–Taiwan (17.3)–Food & bev.
38.0	**Thailand** (59.1)–Laos (21.1)–Food & bev.	26.2	**Thailand** (26.2)–Singapore (0)–Others
37.9	**Vietnam** (44.1)–Korea (6.2)–Transport. mach.	26.1	**Thailand** (51.0)–Vietnam (24.9)–Agriculture
36.9	**Cambodia** (39.1)–Thailand (2.2)–Others	26.0	**Vietnam** (26.0)–Singapore (0)–Textiles & clothing
36.7	**Thailand** (49.3)–Myanmar (12.5)–Food & bev.	26.0	**Vietnam** (28.9)–Philippines (2.9)–Textiles & clothing
36.5	**Vietnam** (47.0)–Philippines (10.5)–Transport. mach.	25.9	**Cambodia** (25.9)–Singapore (0)–Food & bev.
36.2	**Cambodia** (38.9)–China (2.6)–Others	25.5	**Cambodia** (27.5)–Taiwan (2.0)–Others
36.1	**Thailand** (36.1)–Brunei (0)–Agriculture	25.5	**Vietnam** (52.1)–Taiwan (26.6)–Transport. mach.
35.9	**Thailand** (35.9)–Singapore (0)–Agriculture		(…)

Note: The difference is calculated as the higher tariff minus the lower one.

Source: Market Access Map, calculations by ITC.

Notes

1. This concerns only the initial member countries (Brunei, Indonesia, Malaysia, the Philippines, Singapore and Thailand). The new members benefit from an additional delay of five years.
2. The Market Access Map integrates information on the major instruments of protection (ad valorem and specific duties, prohibitions, tariff quotas, anti-dumping duties) and tariff regimes (e.g. MFN, GSP). Information is available for 169 importing countries, 238 exporting countries and territories, and products at the national "tariff line" level (which for some countries exceeds 10 000 product items). It is based on different data sources: *Tariff data* come from national sources and the UN Tariff and Market Access Database (UN TARMAC) of ITC and UNCTAD. *Preferential tariff data* come directly from regional and bilateral trade agreements. *Tariff quota data* come from the Agricultural Market Access Database (AMAD, www.amad.org); the WTO (agricultural notification of tariff quotas); and national sources for bilateral and regional tariff quota agreements. *Anti-dumping duty data* come from notifications from member countries of the WTO regarding anti-dumping duties and ITC collection directly from some countries. *Trade data* come from: national sources; IDB (integrated database) of the WTO; and the COMTRADE database of the United Nations Statistics Division (UNSD). UNSD holds the copyright to the COMTRADE database. The basic information on *tariff quotas* and related imports is based on country notifications to the WTO (http://docsonline.wto.org/gen_search.asp). At the same site, the method for administrating tariff quotas is documented too, and this information (see document G/AG/NG/S/8/Rev.1) is used to calculate the tariff equivalents.
3. Non-tariff barriers, especially technical barriers to trade (TBT) and sanitary and phytosanitary measures (SPS), have become more and more important for several reasons: the growing concern of consumers (especially in developed countries) regarding environmental and sanitary risks; the argument of environmental risks is sometimes a convenient justification to protectionism; and the growing relative importance of residual obstacles when tariffs are very low. The Market Access Map distinguishes among different kinds of measures: authorizations; prohibitions; prior surveillance; quota; financial measures; monopolistic measures; and technical measures. At stake is that these "measures" do not become "barriers" to trade. We aim to identify importing countries with the most restrictive practices in terms of products notified on the basis of environmental considerations by the importers. An environmental measure is taken into account in the analysis only if the importer notifies it regularly, i.e. every year from 1998–2002. The relative importance of notified products is expressed in two ways: the number of products concerned; and their share in imports, i.e. the value of imports of products concerned divided by the value of total imports.
4. The *Most Favored Nation (MFN) tariff* is the tariff applied by WTO members to goods from other WTO members with which they have concluded a preferential trade arrangement. In the case of WTO non-members, the application of these rates may be a requirement of a bilateral trade agreement.

5. The *Generalized System of Preferences (GSP)*, in force since 1971, gives developing countries a margin of preference in the tariff rates their goods face in the markets of developed countries and in this way increases their competitiveness. To meet its GSP commitment, each developed country determined its own system of preferences, specifying the goods, the margins of preference, and in some cases, the value or volume of goods that would benefit from preferential treatment. Twenty-seven developed countries have GSP programmes. The tariff reductions since 1971 as a result of multilateral trade negotiations and unilateral actions have reduced the importance of the GSP to many developing country exporters, but it remains important in the trade policies of many developing countries.
6. Variable tariffs are levied on the basis of the composition of the products for which the information is missing. Example of tariff: USD 0.88/kg on magnesium content *plus* 20 percent of the value.
7. See von Kirchbach and Mimouni (2003) who found that specific tariffs tend to discriminate against exports from low-income countries, whose producers often specialize in the lower price-quality segment of export markets. In addition, the price decrease for many commodities in recent years has further penalized many of the least developed countries, as the ad valorem equivalent of specific duties for these commodities increased correspondingly. Protection is equal for a US$20-per-ton specific tariff and a 20 percent ad valorem tariff, when the price equals US$100 per ton. If the price falls to US$50 per ton, however, the same specific tariff is equivalent to a 40 percent protection level.
8. Reference groups are also used in some cases to convert specific tariffs to ad valorem equivalent tariffs. The reference group's unit values are used when unit values in the bilateral trade of a country reporting a specific duty are missing or when they diverge significantly (by a factor of 5) from the reference group's average unit value.
9. The number of products at the so-called "tariff-line level" differs across countries. It is, for example, about 16 000 items for the United States. In this study, the simple average of tariff-line level data is used to aggre-gate them to the 6-digit level of the Harmonized System which has about 5000 product items.
10. It must be noted that calculations for the EU 25 were made with 2002 tariffs, meaning before the entry of the new ten EU members in 2004. This is why tariffs within the EU are not all zero (which they have been since 2004).
11. It must be noted that available evidence suggests that agriculture and food and beverages – two industries with high tariff barriers in all three regions – are also among the industries with the highest non-tariff barriers. Results appear consistent whether measured in terms of the number of notified products (Annex, Annex Table A-3) or their share in imports (Annex Table A-4). The differences between tariff and non-tariff barriers appear most striking for chemicals, which have relatively low tariff barriers but high non-tariff barriers.

References

Bouët, Antoine, Fontagné, Lionel, Mimouni, Mondher and Pichot, Xavier (2001) "Market Access Maps: a Bilateral and Disaggregated Measure of Market Access," International Trade Center UNCTAD/WTO (ITC), Research Papers, Geneva, April.

Bouët, Antoine, Fontagné, Lionel, Mimouni, Mondher and von Kirchbach, Friedrich (2002) "Market Access Map for GTAP: an Assessment of Bilateral Protection in Merchandise Trade," Paper prepared for the GTAP conference, Taipei, June.

Cernat, Lucian and Laird, Sam (2003) "North, South, East, West: What's Best? Modern RTA's and Their Implications for the Stability of Trade Policy," Centre for Research in Economic Development and International Trade (CREDIT) Research Paper no. 03/11, University of Nottingham.

Fontagné, Lionel, Mimouni, Mondher and von Kirchbach, Friedrich (2001) "A First Assessment of Environment-Related Trade Barriers," Mimeo, November.

Pangestu, Mari and Gooptu, Shan (2004) "New Regionalism: Options for East Asia," Chapter 3 in *East Asia Integrates: A Trade Policy Agenda for Shared Growth,* ed. Kathie Krumm and Homi Kharas, World Bank.

Von Kirchbach, Friedrich and Mimouni, Mondher (2003) "Market Access Barriers: a Growing Issue for Developing Country Exporters?" *International Trade Forum*, Issue 2.

8

Regionalization in East Asia: Simulations Using a CGE Model MIRAGE

Michel Fouquin

1 Introduction

East Asian[1] trade diplomacy is very active these days negotiating all sorts of trade agreements within the East Asia Zone as well as with non-East Asian partners such as the USA, Australia or New Zealand. Difficulties in multilateral trade negotiations tend to favor regional agreements; it even seems plausible to see regional agreements proliferate while no progress is made at WTO.

What are the economic benefits for East Asia to build a regional bloc in a world of growing regionalization? This is the subject of this chapter. In order to obtain these impacts it is now usual to rely on the CGE model. Here we use the MIRAGE model developed by CEPP.

For our analytical purpose, we simulate a scenario where major regions are creating regional trade blocs: one in East Asia, one in America corresponding to the FTAA project, one in Europe including Mediterranean countries, and one between Mercosur and EU. In our simulation exercise we consider only these projects and suppose that the remaining barriers to trade will last with no changes. Another possibility would have been to simulate bilateral based regionalization, but for two reasons we made a different choice: first there is an infinity of possible bilateral agreements; second, the complexity of the scenario, given the differing content of each bilateral agreement, makes it difficult to take it into account in a world model.

We also decided that the agricultural sector will be excluded more or less from these negotiations. Agriculture is at the heart of most conflicts while barriers to trade remain often sky-high. In the case of East Asia it is clear that some very sensitive products will be excluded from any agreement. This is the case for rice products. So liberalization is limited to industrial products in the following exercise.

In the following sections, first we look briefly at the trade barriers of East Asia. Then, we introduce the outline of the MIRAGE model, and show the simulation impacts on region and country. In the last section, based on the simulated results, we discuss the prospect of regionalization.

2 Barriers to trade

If we want to evaluate the impact of such agreements we need first to measure the heights of barriers to trade on a bilateral basis. This is done with MAcMap-HS6 (Bouët et al. 2004), a database providing a consistent ad valorem equivalent measure of tariff duties and tariff rate quotas for 163 countries and 208 partners, at the 6-digit level of the Harmonized System (5111 products). It is based on a joint effort by ITC (UNCTAD-WTO joint venture, Geneva) and CEPII (Paris) to systematically collect and harmonize the relevant information, to compute and aggregate an ad valorem equivalent of applied protection, well suited for analytical purposes (in particular Computable General Equilibrium Analysis). Special emphasis is put on minimizing the endogeneity bias in the aggregation procedure, by making use of a weighting scheme based on groups of countries ("reference groups"). Structural differences in export specialization, as reflected in unit values, are also acknowledged when computing ad valorem equivalents and tariff rate quotas rents are estimated. The resulting quantitative assessment is illustrated in Table 8.1 for the automotive industries taken as an example. This is only a synthesis of the detailed tariffs available.

China has high tariffs and discriminates more against Korea (35.1 percent) and Japan (28.4 percent) than against the United States (24.2 percent). Thailand has very high tariffs against Japan and Korea and slightly lower tariffs towards the rest of the world. Mexico has no tariff vis-à-vis NAFTA but keeps tariffs of nearly 20 percent for the rest of the world. EU keeps some tariffs in the range of 9 percent while Japan has almost no tariff protection and the United States tariffs are only 3 percent on average.

Another characteristic of tariffs is that they tend to be higher on final products than on intermediate goods. This is true for automotive products where on average finished products have tariffs twice as high as tariffs on parts and components. This naturally tends to favor a vertical division of labor within industries.

Table 8.1: Automotive tariffs before regional liberalization (ad valorem equivalent in %) (2001)

Automotive products	*China*	*Japan*	*Korea*	*India*	*USA*	*Mexico*	*Argentina*	*Brazil*	*EU 25*
Australia	5.1	16.8	20.9	14.0	10.4	12.3	7.2	12.0	8.9
Rest of the world	0.1	1.6	1.3	0.2	2.8	2.6	1.1	0.1	0.2
China	–	28.4	35.1	27.5	24.2	29.9	34.8	29.9	27.5
Rest of Asia	9.2	20.8	24.3	18.6	21.9	13.5	31.3	36.3	15.5
Japan	–	–	–	–	–	–	–	–	–
Korea	5.9	8.1	–	8.1	8.2	8.4	8.3	8.1	8.1
Thailand	24.3	40.4	48.8	41.4	36.8	42.3	49.7	43.3	40.5
India	36.9	62.4	44.1	–	53.4	50.1	36.9	49.2	54.8
Canada	2.7	5.4	5.5	3.5	0.0	0.0	3.5	3.8	5.1
USA	1.1	3.0	2.8	1.6	–	0.0	5.9	3.0	3.5
Mexico	17.0	19.2	21.8	17.1	0.5	–	19.1	18.8	19.3
Rest of America	9.6	15.1	16.6	12.5	11.8	30.9	15.9	10.9	18.2
Argentina	16.0	19.3	20.4	17.6	17.3	21.0	–	13.4	18.9
Brazil	19.3	24.9	29.4	26.3	23.0	26.9	21.1	–	24.9
EU 25	0.7	9.4	10.4	3.0	7.1	3.4	8.2	3.4	–
Other Europe	3.6	4.5	5.3	7.1	6.0	0.8	6.5	8.7	2.3
Russia (Fed)	7.0	13.3	16.4	7.6	9.5	16.1	14.4	13.9	13.2
Turkey	4.3	9.1	12.2	10.1	7.4	9.9	13.0	10.6	0.2
Middle East	7.4	9.2	11.4	12.0	8.9	5.1	18.9	12.5	6.0
Rest of Africa	16.1	26.2	25.6	18.4	31.4	30.1	30.0	25.4	24.1
South Africa	11.9	22.4	26.7	17.4	17.9	26.8	23.4	23.2	22.6

Note: Importing countries are put in rows, exporting partners are in columns, only the main exporting zones are shown here due to limited space.

Source: MAcMap.

What seems clear (and this hypothesis is confirmed by other data on other industrial products) is that East Asian developing countries tend to discriminate against East Asian countries. This shows that all the discussions about the creation of an FTA will have to go a long way.

3 Regionalization simulation with MIRAGE

Using the CEPII general equilibrium model MIRAGE, which we will present shortly, we will then simulate the impact of a scenario of world regionalization limited to industrial products with a special focus on the automotive sector. Agriculture products were excluded from the simulation.

After Marrakech's agreements in 1994 and Doha's Ministerial Conference decision to launch in 2001 a new round of multilateral negotiations for development, the stakes of trade policies appear poorer than ever at the center of the globalization process. In this context, delivering a rigorous and detailed quantitative analysis of a large scope of trade agreements is most useful (Hertel 1997), for policy-makers as well as for the public debate. This is the reason why the CEPII has decided to build a multi-sector, multi-region computable general equilibrium (CGE) model, nicknamed MIRAGE (for *Modeling International Relationships in Applied General Equilibrium*), devoted to trade policy analysis.

MIRAGE describes imperfect competition in an oligopolistic framework *à la* Cournot. It accounts for horizontal product differentiation linked to varieties, but also to geographical origin (nested Armington-Dixit-Stiglitz utility function). A new calibration procedure allows the available information on these aspects to be used efficiently. The modeling is done in a sequential dynamic set-up, where the number of firms by sector adjusts progressively, and where installed capital is assumed to be immobile, even across sectors. Capital reallocation therefore only results from the combined effect of depreciation and investment. This makes it possible to describe the adjustment lags of capital stock, and the associated costs.

Compared to previously applied CGE trade models, MIRAGE has in addition three main distinctive features, aimed at improving the description of trade policies' main transmission channels:

- FDIs are explicitly described, with a modeling theoretically consistent with agents' behavior, and with a domestic investment setting. We choose a rather conservative modeling strategy which gives a neutral role to FDI on productivity and to export.
- A notion of vertical product differentiation is introduced, by distinguishing two quality ranges, according to the country of origin of the product.
- Trade barriers are estimated by the MAcMaps describe above. As a result, MIRAGE is based on a description of trade barriers that, besides its precision, preserves the bilateral dimension of the information, in contrast to what is commonly done in applied modeling.

Except for data on trade barriers, the model uses the GTAP (Global Trade Analysis Project) 6 database (see Dimaranan and McDougall 2002). This allows a wide flexibility in choosing the sectoral and geographical aggregations of MIRAGE, that may be changed for each application.

Regionalization is supposed to be developing simultaneously in America (FTAA), East Asia (ASEAN+3) and Europe. Tariffs within region are supposed to tend towards zero (see Table 8.2 for automotive pro-

Table 8.2: Tariff equivalent for automotive products after regional liberalization

Automotive products	*China*	*Japan*	*Korea*	*India*	*USA*	*Mexico*	*Argentina*	*Brazil*	*EU 25*
Australia	5.1	16.8	20.9	14.0	10.4	12.3	7.2	12.0	8.9
Rest of the world	0.1	1.6	1.3	0.2	2.8	2.6	1.1	0.1	0.2
China	–	–	–	27.5	24.2	29.9	34.8	29.9	27.5
Rest of Asia	4.4	10.8	11.4	18.6	21.9	13.5	31.3	36.3	15.5
Japan	–	–	–	–	–	–	–	–	–
Korea	–	–	–	8.1	8.2	8.4	8.3	8.1	8.1
Thailand	–	–	–	41.4	36.8	42.3	49.7	43.3	40.5
India	36.9	62.4	44.1	–	53.4	50.1	36.9	49.2	54.8
Canada	2.7	5.4	5.5	3.5	0.0	–	–	–	5.1
USA	1.1	3.0	2.8	1.6	–	–	–	–	3.5
Mexico	17.0	19.2	21.8	17.1	0.0	–	–	–	19.3
Rest of America	9.6	15.1	16.6	12.5	1.0	11.1	0.5	0.4	18.2
Argentina	16.0	19.3	20.4	17.6	0.0	–	–	–	0.0
Brazil	19.3	24.9	29.4	26.3	0.0	–	–	–	0.1
EU 25	0.7	9.4	10.4	3.0	7.1	3.4	6.5	0.4	–
Other Europe	3.6	4.5	5.3	7.1	6.0	0.8	6.5	8.7	2.3
Russia (Fed)	7.0	13.3	16.4	7.6	9.5	16.1	14.4	13.9	13.2
Turkey	4.3	9.1	12.2	10.1	7.4	9.9	13.0	10.6	0.2
Middle East	7.4	9.2	11.4	12.0	8.9	5.1	18.9	12.5	6.0
Rest of Africa	16.1	26.2	25.6	18.4	31.4	30.1	30.0	25.4	24.1
South Africa	11.9	22.4	26.7	17.4	17.9	26.8	23.4	23.2	22.6

Note: Importing countries are put in rows, exporting partners are in columns, only the main exporting zones are shown here due to limited space.

Source: MAcMap.

ducts) in five years' time for developed nations and in ten years' time for developing countries. The simulation exercise was done on a fifteen-year period. Among other major hypotheses is the phasing out of the AMF (see Fouquin 2002 for an application to the textile industry).

4 Regional impacts: trade creation is driving regionalization in East Asia

Global bilateral trade impacts are shown in Figure 8.1. In East Asia as well as in America, the intra-regional trade is increasing very fast while extra-regional trade is decreasing only marginally, which implies that trade creation resulting from the abolition of trade barriers between East Asian and American partners is the dominant effect. East Asia manufacturing intra-regional trade increases by more than US$160 billion and decreases by less than US$23 billion vis-à-vis the rest of the world. The figures of FTAA are, respectively, US$70 billion and US$10 billion. For the EU 25, the results are somewhat different.

Figure 8.1: Trade creation versus trade diversion in manufacturing products (US$ billion)

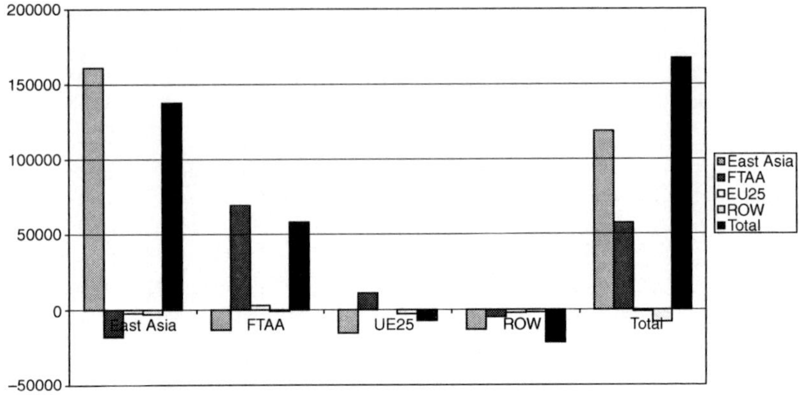

Source: MIRAGE-CEPII.

The figures are small because regional integration has already been achieved. Small gains (US$3 billion) are registered with FTAA due to the EU–Mercosur agreement and small losses with East Asia (US$2 billion). The rest of the world loses small market to all regions. If we consider the product by product impact we found that diversion is very strong in the automotive case (see Table 8.3).

In terms of trade balances (see Figure 8.2) the EU 25 improves its position like the rest of the world, while FTAA and East Asia are losing. The main reason for East Asia and FTAA losing is that the increase in intra-regional trade diminishes their resources for the other markets so that their decline in export outside their regions is higher than the decline in their extra-regional imports (see Table 8.3).

5 Detailed results by country or by zone

The biggest export winner is, first of all, Japan (Figure 8.3); the other big winners are China and Latin American countries. For the automotive sector, Japan is in fact the main benefactor from the reduction in tariffs on a regional basis in terms of export. It gains US$11 billion in the last year of the simulation, which is equivalent to roughly 700 000 cars; it also increases its exports by US$18 billion in mechanical industries, and US$15 billion for other industries (mainly consumption products). Brazil, Mexico and Argentina are the other winners in the automotive industry, with exports gains of US$6 billion, US$4 billion

Table 8.3: Bilateral regional variations in trade

Total

	East Asia	*FTAA*	*EU 25*	*ROW*	*Total*
East Asia	160801.2	-13320.6	-15438.8	-13180.1	118861.7
FTAA	-17974	69235.2	11121.2	-4963.4	57419
EU25	-2207.2	3127	0	-1970.3	-1050.5
ROW	-2817.6	-893.4	-2782.6	-1543.7	-8037.3
Total	137802.4	58148.2	-7100.2	-21657.5	167192.9

Automotive industry

	East Asia	*FTAA*	*EU 25*	*ROW*	*Total*
East Asia	19654.1	-787.4	-3872.4	-415.2	14579.1
FTAA	-4913.2	17898	2519.6	-384.3	15120.1
EU25	-610.5	751.2	0	-303.8	-163.1
ROW	-660.7	140.2	-113.2	-71.6	-705.3
Total	13469.7	18002	-1466	-1174.9	28830.8

Mechanical

	East Asia	*FTAA*	*EU 25*	*ROW*	*Total*
East Asia	71722.6	-7479.1	-7639.1	-2945.7	53658.7
FTAA	-7152.1	25712.9	6098.8	-1683.1	22976.5
EU25	-454.4	140.4	0	-1011.6	-1325.6
ROW	-750	-550	-1216.4	-523	-3039.4
Total	63366.1	17824.2	-2756.7	-6163.4	72270.2

Other industries

	East Asia	*FTAA*	*EU 25*	*ROW*	*Total*
East Asia	69424.5	-5054.1	-3927.3	-9819.2	50623.9
FTAA	-5908.7	25624.3	2502.8	-2896	19322.4
EU25	-1142.3	2235.4	0	-654.9	438.2
ROW	-1406.9	-483.6	-1453	-949.1	-4292.6
Total	60966.6	22322	-2877.5	-14319.2	66091.9

and US$3 billion respectively. China increases its exports in other industries by US$28 billion but cannot increase its automotive exports. The same can be said for other East Asian countries.

Figure 8.2: Impact on bilateral trade balances of manufacturing products (US$ billion)

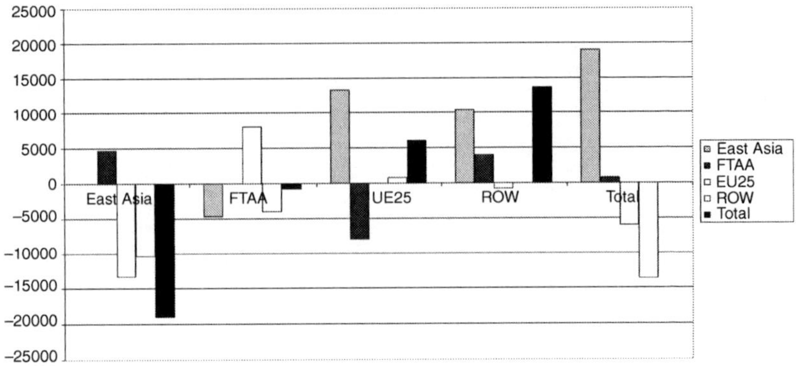

Source: MIRAGE-CEPII.

Japan increases its exports to East Asian countries which were still highly protected in 2004. China is the main driving force of Japanese exports by increasing its imports of mechanical products by US$26 billions (see Figure 8.4) and by US$5 billion for automotive products.

Korea loses on the American automotive market due to the competition of Canada, Mexico and Mercosur countries. Latin American countries benefit from a preferred access to the United States market.

European countries which are already wide open to international trends do not register gains; rather they suffer from a relative dis-

Figure 8.3: Regionalization's impact on exports (US$ million)

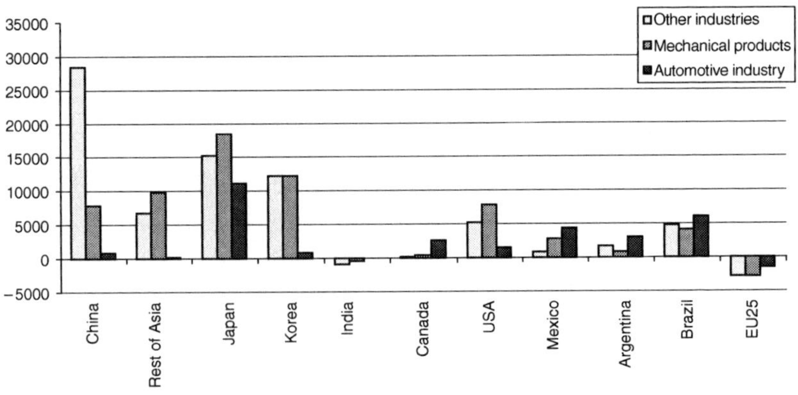

Source: MIRAGE-CEPII.

Figure 8.4: Regionalization's impact on imports (US$ thousands)

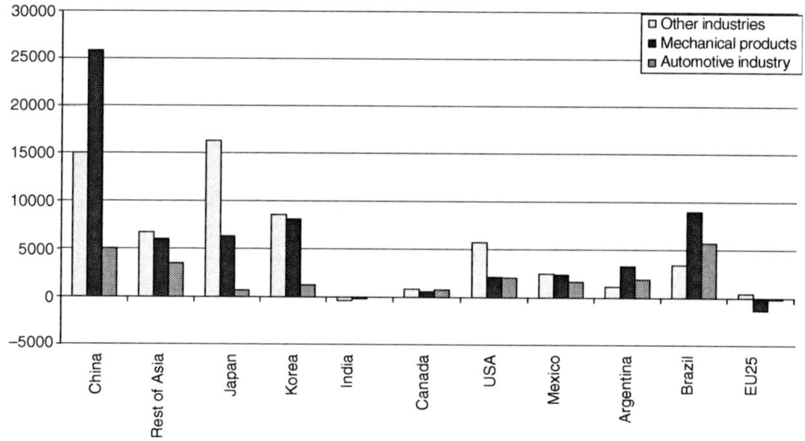

Source: MIRAGE-CEPII.

Figure 8.5: Regionalization's impact on net exports (US$ million)

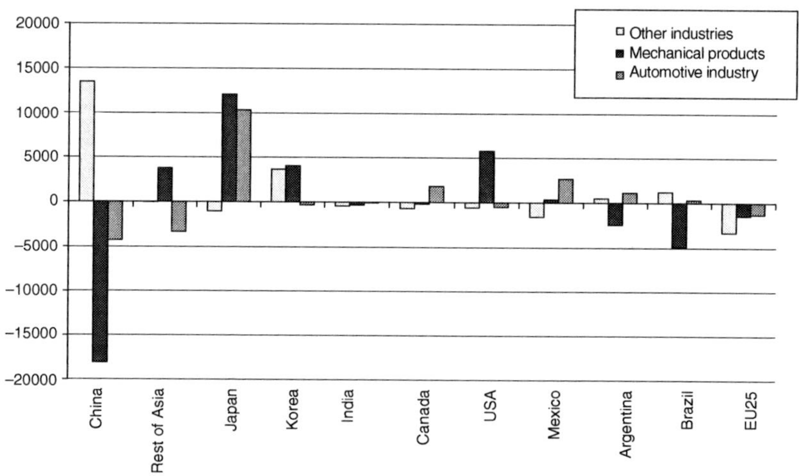

Source: MIRAGE-CEPII.

advantage in their exports to the outer regions, notably towards East Asia with a loss of US$1.8 billion vis-à-vis China to the profit of Japanese exporters. These losses are not balanced by gains towards Latin American countries.

The net results of these changes (see Figure 8.5) confirms that Japan is a net winner with US$10 billion in net export gains of automobile products and gains of US$12 billion in mechanical products. China wins US$13 billion in the net exports of other industrial products, but loses US$18 billion in mechanical products. East Asia loses exports of automotive products and does not gain on other industries nor on mechanical products. The United States is the second winner in the mechanical products exports with a US$6 billion gain.

Up to now we have shown the worldwide results of de jure regionalization on trade patterns but in order to get an idea of the regionalization's impact on each region and country we need to have another indicator: impact on each national production expressed as a percentage gain in production (see Figure 8.6).

Korea and Japan increase their automotive production by 25 percent, and Brazil's production increases by 14 percent. The decline is important for other Asian regions with a loss of 9 percent for China, 20 percent for the rest of East Asia, and 15 percent for India. Among American countries the US and Canada lose 5 percent and 10 percent respectively while Brazil gains +14 percent, and Argentina and Mexico gain 6 percent each. The EU is almost untouched by these evolutions. As a conclusion we find that Japan has a strong interest in Asian regional agreements with other East Asian countries, in particular if agreement included all the mechanical industries and notably automotive products. This is how a natural division of labor would evolve if

Figure 8.6: Regionalization's impact on output (%)

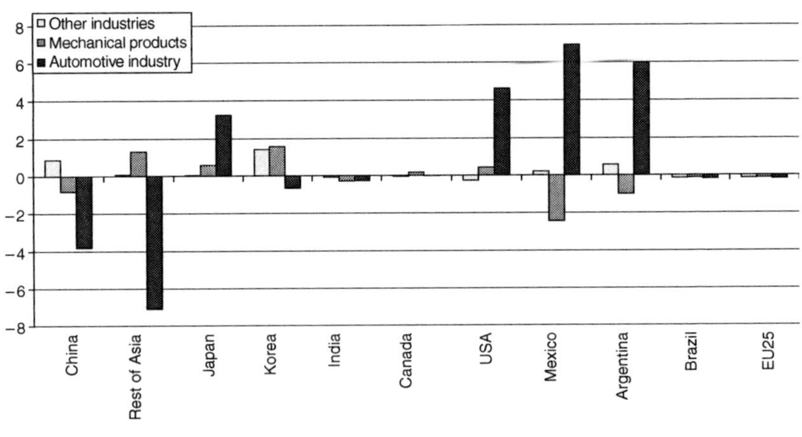

Source: MIRAGE-CEPII.

all obstacles to trade were eliminated between East Asian countries. But on the other hand, the other East Asian countries might have more interest in keeping their protectionist systems in order to develop new and more sophisticated industries such as the automotive industry. The Korean government and carmakers have been able to develop their national automotive industry through high walls of protection while supporting export expansion.

As a conclusion to the simulation exercises we find that the natural evolution of trade would increase the division of labor reinforcing Japan's industrial domination, maintaining China as an assembling zone of low technological products, while Korea and Taiwan would share some of the benefits with Japan. The rest of East Asia would return to its natural specialization in primary products. Needless to say, local governments would act against such spontaneous evolution through strong industrial policy. First of all the Chinese government has the ambition to build a fully integrated automobile industry following Japanese lessons and probably with some help of Japanese firms.

6 Prospects of regionalization in East Asia: some tentative wishful thinking

China is central to East Asia regionalization. Before China's accession to the WTO, regional cooperation was rather weak and limited for two main reasons: first, most East Asian countries fear US reaction to any attempt to create a fortress Asia; second, most Asian countries were also reluctant to engage in a global trade liberalization including agriculture and sensitive products, as was the APEC project of a Pacific agreement including Latin and North American countries as well as East Asian partners.

This has completely changed since China became a WTO member. First, in the accession negotiation China engaged in a far-reaching process of trade liberalization which made China the most open country among developing countries of the region. Second, China is trying to become an East Asia leader and to secure its sources of primary products. Third, given the size of the Chinese market, every partner wants to secure its access to that market. Finally, most East Asian countries have a trade surplus vis-à-vis China. Therefore China's strategy for development will have far-reaching consequences for the rest of Asia.

China faces many challenges. Three of the largest are: (1) macroeconomic challenges, including the risk of unsustainable high growth due to shortages of energy and other primary products; (2) the risk of a financial crisis; (3) the industrial policy challenge to build independent industries, as for the time being Chinese export successes are mostly based on FDI.

For the last twenty years the Chinese leadership has demonstrated an extraordinary capacity to master a transition from an almost wholly communist state (notably in the rural areas where the use of money had almost disappeared) to a kind of market economy open to the world. Chinese economic achievements compare well to South Korea and Taiwan in the 1960s and 1970s.

China's entry to WTO is probably the major factor that anchored China to the world economy and guaranteed the stability of that choice for the long run. Nevertheless there are some crucial questions which are not yet resolved.

Up to now China's specialization and industrialization process can be described as quite similar to the Mexican kind: it is following an assembly model with a decisive role played by FDI. Foreign firms in special zones make more than 50 percent of Chinese exports (see Chapter 5). These zones have only limited autonomous capabilities, as they have to import a lot of components from these foreign firms.

That kind of industrialization is very different from the choice made, for example, by Brazil or India which are more based on vertically domestic integrated industries with high local contents.

If China is to follow Japanese steps then it will try to develop a fully industrial integrated industry but probably with foreign participation. The automotive industry development will probably be at the core of China's industrial strategy.

Like the Koreans in the 1970s, China lacks engineering capabilities, as well as management techniques, not to mention marketing design and other advanced ideas. These are needed to produce the crucial components; therefore China needs to import foreign technology. It took twenty years for Korea to build an independent industry at the world standard. After the Asia crisis only one automotive company survived as an independent maker in Korea.

The Chinese automotive sector was opened to foreign investment in 2003. Large investments by major automakers were then announced by Nissan, Toyota, GM and others. Foreign companies are looking for a share of the domestic market, which is expected to grow rapidly. Given the potential size of the market and Chinese tariff structure, it is highly likely that the Chinese government will favor complete localization of the parts and components of the automotive industry in China as well as assembly units, contrary to what has been done in ASEAN countries where MNCs, given the small size of each market, have decided to organize an international division of labor within ASEAN countries.

In general, the size of the Chinese market will encourage a full vertical integration rather than an international division of labor, even if this will take time. Again making reference to Japanese and Korean historical experience, China will develop a forward kind of economic integration; this will at first tend to reduce trade flows within the region. Following the same line of reasoning China will need more primary goods coming from ASEAN, so that we may go back to a form of inter-industry kind of division of labor.

Another argument is that international expansion such as that of the past ten years is not sustainable. China's share of world trade was abnormally low before the 1990s with Japan exporting four times more than China. By 2004, China was exporting as much as Japan, and its surplus vis-à-vis the United States was as large as Japan's. This trend will have to come to an end and be replaced by a more inward strategy.

7 Summary and conclusions

The creation of an East Asian bloc including Japan, Korea, Taiwan, ASEAN 10 and China, Hong Kong and Singapore will have strong trade creating effects and rather weak diversion effects. Countries outside the bloc will essentially lose opportunities which may have lasting effects. Trade creation has positive effects on members but it tends to reinforce what may be called a natural specialization rather than an upscale movement. Regional integration favored high value-added industries in Japan and Korea while the other members tend to lose: this is the case in the automobile industry for example. The less developed countries tend to specialize in labor-intensive industries (China) and natural resources based industry (ASEAN 10).

These results do not include two important aspects of regional integration: variations in transportation costs and foreign direct investment impacts on productivity. In theory as exchanges increase, the international costs of transportation should decrease due to scale economies. And increasing the role of FDI should give an impulse to productivity growth, but this was not included in the simulations due to insufficient empirical proofs.

These simulations show that in the automotive case, for example, Chinese policy is very restrictive, first in terms of tariffs notably on parts and components. Secondly it forbids the establishment of fully foreign founded companies. As a consequence foreign firms may tend to try to establish joint ventures and vertically integrated firms in China. In future research we should try to address these questions.

Creating an East Asian trade bloc is a major challenge. It may necessitate progress made in other areas such as those implied by the creation of an Asian community. It is also facing the problems of deepening and enlargement (to India and/or to Australia and New Zealand). This is one reason explaining the success made in the signing of bilateral agreements which are an easier way to make progress in integrating the Asian zone, but it also has its limitations such as complexity.

The question of agriculture is still a big impediment to the development of that zone and should be included in the future. Pressure from WTO negotiation might help Japan and Korea to start reforming their highly protectionist policies.

Note

1. East Asia includes Japan, Korea, China, Taiwan, Hong Kong and Singapore; plus Southeast Asia including Indonesia, Thailand, Malaysia, Philippines, Vietnam, Laos, Cambodia and Myanmar.

References

Antoine Bouët, Decreux, Yvan, Fontagné, Lionel, Jean, Sébastien and Laborde, David (2004) "A Consistent, Ad-Valorem Equivalent Measure of Applied Protection Across the World: the MAcMap-HS6 Database," CEPII's Working Paper 2004–22.

Dimaranan, Beatrix and McDougall, R. A. (2002) *Global Trade Assistance and Production: the GTAP 5 Database*, Center for Global Trade Analysis, Purdue University.

Fouquin, Michel (2002) "Trade in Textiles and Clothing: Comparing Multilateral and Regional Trade Agreements," with R. Avisse, in *Integration and Trade Review*, 17, 6, July–December.

Hertel, Thomas (ed.) (1997) *Global Trade Analysis: Modeling and Applications*, Cambridge: Cambridge University Press.

Index

NB: Page numbers in bold refer to figures and diagrams